LIVING the FARM SANCTUARY LIFE

LIVING the FARM SANCTUARY LIFE

THE ULTIMATE GUIDE TO EATING MINDFULLY, LIVING LONGER, AND FEELING BETTER EVERY DAY

GENE BAUR with Gene Stone

RODALE

Rodale books may be purchased for business or promotional use or for special sales.
For information, please write to:
Special Markets Department, Rodale Inc., 733 Third Avenue, New York, NY 10017

Printed in the United States of America

Rodale Inc. makes every effort to use acid-free ♾, recycled paper ♻.

Back cover recipes: (top, left) Gardein Bolognese, page 241; (top, right) Berrylicious Fruit Tart, page 279; and (bottom, right) Hearts of Palm Cakes with Dill Mayo, page 188

Book design by Christina Gaugler

Recipes reprinted by permission:

Glazed Carrot Salad (page 152) from *Afro-Vegan: Farm-Fresh African, Caribbean, and Southern Flavors Remixed* by Bryant Terry, text copyright © 2014 by Bryant Terry. Used by permission of Ten Speed Press, an imprint of the Crown Publishing Group, a division of Penguin Random House LLC. All rights reserved.

Vegiterranean Tempeh Sandwich with White Bean Rosemary Spread (page 163)
Copyright © December 23, 2014 Julieanna Hever. Reprinted by permission of Da Capo Lifelong Books, a member of the Perseus Books Group.

Tal Ronnen's Agave-Lime Grilled Tofu with Asian Slaw and Mashed Sweet Potatoes (page 227)
from *The Conscious Cook* by Tal Ronnen. Copyright © 2009 by Tal Ronnen and Melcher Media.
Reprinted by permission of HarperCollins Publishers.

Pan-Seared Herb Seitan with Cauliflower Puree and Truffled White Wine Sauce (page 230) from *Candle 79 Cookbook: Modern Vegan Classics from New York's Premier Sustainable Restaurant* by Joy Pierson, copyright © 2011 by Candle Family Foods, LLC. Used by permission of Ten Speed Press, an imprint of the Crown Publishing Group, a division of Random House LLC. All rights reserved.

Ellen Red Beans and Rice (page 246) from *Vegan Cooking for Carnivores:
Over 125 Recipes So Tasty You Won't Miss the Meat* by Roberto Martin. Copyright © 1999 by Roberto Martin. Reprinted by permission of Grand Central Publishing.

Library of Congress Cataloging-in-Publication Data is on file with the publisher.

ISBN 978-1-62336-489-2

Distributed to the trade by Macmillan

4 6 8 10 9 7 5 3   hardcover

We inspire and enable people to improve their lives and the world around them.
rodalebooks.com

CONTENTS

INTRODUCTION

Close your eyes and imagine this: You step out of your daily life and into a favorite storybook. You're back with "The Farmer in the Dell," standing on a beautiful green pasture. All around you roam the wonderful farm animals you've loved since you were a child: the sheep, the cows, the chickens, and more, all living in harmony. You feel a sense of tranquility around you and even inside you.

Wherever you look, you see complete contentment. Nestled in a lovely green valley surrounded by rolling hills, sparkling lakes, and preserved forests are homey red barns that remind you of the one in *Charlotte's Web*. Cheerful animals wander in and out, jumping and skipping through open doors. Beyond the barns, you see more pastures abounding with more pigs, chickens, goats, turkeys, and cows, and in the background you hear a symphony of happy moos, clucks, grunts, and squawks.

You see and feel . . . *peace*. Here, chewing mouths and twitching ears and the sounds of play are the only distractions around. All seems to be right with the world from sunrise, when the roosters crow as the buttery sun warms up the dewy green grass, till sunset, when the animals start to become drowsy after a tough day of eating and ruminating and playing and sleeping. You wonder, is this real? Or is this a fairy tale?

Now open your eyes.

This is a real place, in the real world.

This is Farm Sanctuary, the world's premier refuge for farm animals. At our farms in New York and California, we provide comfortable homes for approximately 1,000 pigs, cows, chickens, ducks, geese, turkeys, sheep, and goats.

This is a place that gives back something most of us have lost, and returns people to a simpler, happier time and place where we lived more in harmony with nature, other species, and our core values.

We also do a great deal of serious educational work, such as keeping the public informed about the plight of factory-farmed animals. We host 100-plus events and appearances a year, many featuring celebrities such as Martha Stewart, Ellen DeGeneres, Alec Baldwin, Mary Tyler Moore, Emily Deschanel, Moby, Chevy Chase, Alicia Silverstone, Kevin Nealon, Steve-O, John Corbett, Allison Janney, Jesse Eisenberg, Jon Hamm, and others. And we lobby vigorously for laws and policies that support animal welfare.

Each year we also host thousands of guests from all over the country who come to enjoy these extraordinary farms where people and animals interact as friends, companions, and playmates. None of these creatures is ever eaten or used to produce milk or eggs; they live fully and freely for the rest of their existence. That's why our visitors call Farm Sanctuary "the Happiest Place on Earth."

This book is designed to help you share in some of that happiness.

What's it like to visit Farm Sanctuary?

Because Farm Sanctuary offers a view of the world so different from what we see in most of our everyday lives, visitors here seldom leave without having had some kind of transformative experience.

People are inspired by a variety of exchanges. Some are moved by touch, by feeling the wool on a sheep's back—which, by the way, is nothing like touching a sweater, but involves sinking your hands into a deep, soft-textured coat growing on a warm, living creature. And when a cow rambles over to you and asks with her big brown eyes to be petted, it's like no other experience in the world. Many of these gentle giants, who can weigh up to 3,000 pounds, are like huge puppies! The pigs, earthy animals who root around in the soil and roll in the mud, also love to be petted. Pigs

enjoy belly rubs so much that they'll roll over and let you scratch their tummies, grunting happily in appreciation.

Other visitors are moved by sights, like our goats, the farms' entertainers. Nearly everyone delights in discovering how playful and interactive they are—much like their dogs back home. The goats jump with joy, sometimes competing to see which of them can spring the highest.

And did you know that sheep adore attention? They will even paw you with their front hoof, similar to the way a dog or a cat uses its paw to tap your shoulder or knee to get noticed. Chickens are also affectionate and will come right up to you. Sometimes they will sit on your lap and let you stroke their feathers, and they'll coo just like a house cat might purr. Often, the animals who sur-

prise people the most are the turkeys, who are friendly, social, and curious about everything. A turkey may adopt you for the day and follow you around like a loyal dog.

All of the amazing animals you'll meet at Farm Sanctuary are rescues—like cats and dogs you would see at your local animal shelter. And when you learn the circumstances of their rescue, your own troubles seem to dissipate for a moment. Many people burst into tears after hearing their stories—it is such an emotional release, especially for animal lovers who are haunted by the realities of conventional factory farming. For others who know little about farm animals and factory farming, the experience is the start of a journey of learning and questioning.

Some of the many questions we get from visitors

to Farm Sanctuary include: Where do the animals come from? (All over the country.) How many animals do you have? (About 1,000.) Do any of the animals eat meat? (No. All of our animals eat a plant-based diet.)

But the most common question we get is: How can we be as happy back at home as we are when we're at Farm Sanctuary?

That's what this book will explain: how you can bring the happiness of Farm Sanctuary into your own life. And not just happiness—you can also benefit from reduced stress, a trimmer waistline, increased health and vitality, and improved longevity. On top of that, you'll be helping to make the world a better place!

Think about it. If you can live well and be happy without causing unnecessary harm, why wouldn't you? For many people, it's because

10 Small Steps

OF COURSE IT WOULD be wonderful if everyone who came to Farm Sanctuary, or everyone who read this book, immediately became a plant-based eater. I doubt that's going to happen. But many of Farm Sanctuary's visitors start on their vegan journey by making small changes in their diet. And small steps often lead to much larger ones.

For instance, just eating less meat is a great start. That's how my own journey began. When I was in high school, I learned about the cruelty that young calves endure in veal production, and I swore off veal for good.

Here are 10 suggestions to get you started on your own journey.

1. Participate in Meatless Monday, a program endorsed by the Johns Hopkins Bloomberg School of Public Health. It encourages people to forgo meat one day a week (meatlessmonday.com).

2. Try learning more about specific food industry practices and then avoid the cruelest animal products, like veal, caged eggs, chicken meat, and foie gras. This discourages inhumane practices and sends a market signal that such cruelty is outside the bounds of acceptable conduct in our society.

3. Use plant-based milks and creamers, like those made from soy, rice, almond, or coconut, in place of cows' milk on your cereal and in your coffee. There has been a huge increase in the flavors and varieties available in mainstream groceries in the past couple of years. I used soy milk for decades, and today I prefer vanilla-flavored almond milk.

4. Shop at your farmers' market for fresh seasonal produce—it is healthy and supports a more local, humane, and sustainable food system. My favorites are berries and greens during the summer, and squash and apples in the fall. Fruit is a sweet snack that can be enjoyed right away, and I sometimes snack

they have developed bad habits without truly considering them and because they don't realize how easy it is to make simple adjustments that have profound consequences. The Greek philosopher Socrates made an important point: "The unexamined life is not worth living." I believe this statement holds for our food choices as well: When we examine them, it's clear we can do a lot better.

This book will help you examine the way you eat. The Five Tenets you will soon be reading will guide you through a new philosophy of diet and life. The recipes that follow will provide you with almost 100 ways to prepare delicious meals that prove a plant-based diet isn't just good for your health, for the earth, and for the animals. It tastes great as well!

on the greens as well. When I travel, I love getting to know the local farming community and culture by visiting farmers' markets.

5. Replace meat in recipes with plant-based options. For example, instead of meatballs, try veggie meatballs or even just veggies in spaghetti sauce. In many recipes, you can leave the meat out entirely. Check out the recipes starting on page 111 for plenty of dishes without meat.

6. Eat ethnic! The animal-centered diet we consume in the United States is a modern development. Explore and rediscover traditional ethnic dishes, including Chinese, Middle Eastern, Mexican, Indian, Ethiopian, and many others, which tend to be plant based.

7. Consider the advice of food experts and authors such as *New York Times* columnist Mark Bittman, who suggests we go "vegan before 6:00," or bestselling food expert Michael Pollan, who says, "Eat food. Not too much. Mostly plants."

8. Enjoy fashion with compassion when shopping for clothes. For more information and tips, check out top fashion designer John Bartlett's suggestions on page 32.

9. Substitute! There's a whole range of meatless meat substitutes, including veggie burgers and hot dogs, cold cuts, nuggets, cutlets, sausages, fillets, and even roasts. Explore and enjoy the many possibilities. You don't have to give up your barbecues and picnics, but you can make them much healthier!

10. Get to know beans, the mainstay of the legume family. There are so many different kinds of beans, and there's so much you can do with them to add protein and flavor to your meals. I use white or garbanzo beans in salads to make them heartier, and I pack my chili with kidney and pinto beans. I like lentils and lima beans on their own with just a touch of seasoning. And I love beans with steamed greens, such as navy beans with kale, or black-eyed peas with collard greens.

PART 1
A HAPPIER, HEALTHIER,
MORE COMPASSIONATE LIFE

A BRIEF HISTORY of
FARM SANCTUARY

I don't think it would surprise anyone who knew me when I was a child that I'd someday devote my life to a cause like Farm Sanctuary. Thinking and caring about nature and animals has been important to me since I was a toddler.

I grew up in Southern California, in the Hollywood Hills near Griffith Park. Among my earliest memories is watching with total fascination the local coyotes, skunks, snakes, gophers, raccoons, and deer. I was concerned from a very young age about the harm people caused animals. I remember well the time a deer became stuck in a neighbor's chain-link fence and had to be killed; the event had a powerful impact on me.

The first time I fell in love, it was with Tiger, a tabby kitten I adopted when I was not even 10 years old. I slept on the upper bunk of my bunk bed, and Tiger used to jump all the way up to lie next to me as I was sleeping, impressing me with both his athleticism and his love. When he became sick and died a few years later, I was overcome with grief.

Despite my love for animals, it didn't occur to me not to eat them. Everyone did, including the rest of my large family (I'm the eldest of six kids). I grew up on the same basic diet eaten by most Americans, and although I did have occasional qualms about eating animals, for the most part I finished off whatever was placed in front of me. When I was a teenager, I even acted in commercials for McDonald's and Kentucky Fried Chicken to earn college money. (These ads haven't resurfaced—with luck, they're gone for good.)

Although I wasn't a vegan when I was young, I did develop an interest in all kinds of social causes. Perhaps this was an outgrowth of what I

some of the great activists of the 1960s and 1970s: Cesar Chavez, Gloria Steinem, Martin Luther King Jr., Ralph Nader.

My interest in activism led me to examine the relationship between humans and other animals, and I soon came to realize that animal agriculture was a cruel, inefficient, and wasteful system. Then I read Frances Moore Lappé's book *Diet for a Small Planet* and realized that eating animals was not necessary for our health. That was the clincher. The world was going hungry, and eating animals was both cruel and completely unnecessary. And so, in 1985, I became a vegan. I was just finishing my degree in sociology at California State University, Northridge and was motivated to make a difference. My background as an activist and a new commitment to the animal rights movement led me, along with my friend Lorri Houston, with whom I founded Farm Sanctuary, to become a full-time advocate—as I've been ever since.

> "ONE DAY THE ABSURDITY OF THE ALMOST UNIVERSAL HUMAN BELIEF IN THE SLAVERY OF OTHER ANIMALS WILL BE PALPABLE. WE SHALL THEN HAVE DISCOVERED OUR SOULS AND BECOME WORTHIER OF SHARING THIS PLANET WITH THEM."
>
> —MARTIN LUTHER KING JR.

learned at Catholic school—especially the church's basic moral teaching (central to most faiths) that the strong must protect the weak. I always wanted to make a positive difference, whether that meant volunteering with terminally ill children at Children's Hospital in Hollywood or working on campaigns with environmental groups such as Greenpeace. And I was profoundly influenced by folk musicians such as Pete Seeger and Peter, Paul and Mary, who often played at the Greek Theater in Griffith Park. Perched on the tree-covered hillside on summer nights, I would listen in on their concerts. I was also informed and inspired by

At the time, only a few books or articles had been written about the plight of farm animals, and there was not a lot of effort going into improving the situation. So, with the help of some friends, Lorri and I decided to tackle the issue. One of these friends owned a row house in Wilmington, Delaware; it was in bad shape, but he was willing to let us use it. So we fixed it up and, from 1986 to 1989, that house became our base of operations. Farm Sanctuary was born.

The name just occurred to us one day. Farm Sanctuary. It sounded good. We didn't have a big vision for what it would become, and we didn't have a concrete plan to start any actual farms.

We just wanted to start *something* that would combat what we felt was a brutal and indefensible industry, and to offer a new voice and a new model.

We began our work by visiting farms, stockyards, and slaughterhouses to document conditions—mostly surreptitiously—and immediately began rescuing and rehabilitating animals and letting them stay in our little backyard until we could find loving homes for them.

Our first animal was Hilda.

It was 1986, and we were spending a lot of time at the Lancaster stockyards in Lancaster, Pennsylvania. It was a massive place, with acres and acres of stalls, pens, and alleyways—it once handled as many as 300,000 animals per year. We'd walk around taking photos, documenting the intolerable conditions. Sometimes, if we could, we'd introduce ourselves to the workers and explain our mission. They didn't get it.

Most of all, they couldn't understand our diet. I remember one of the workers asking us, in all seriousness, "What in the world do you people eat?

Corn silage?" We'd also get questions like, "Vegetarian? Is that some kind of Eastern religion?"

Behind the stockyard's main facility was the "dead pile," where animals that died were left for the renderer, who would use their carcasses for animal feed, soap, and fertilizer. One day as we were taking photos, revolted by the clump of rotting pigs, sheep, and cows thick with buzzing maggots, one of the sheep lifted her head and looked right at us. She wasn't dead at all. Our jaws dropped, and our hearts melted.

Although we had no legal right to move her, we couldn't just leave her there, so we took her off the pile. Our assumption was that the poor creature would have to be euthanized, but after we smuggled her out, we found a veterinarian willing to examine her. As he did, Hilda—as we later named her—perked up and stood on her wobbly legs. She later recovered.

Hilda was shy and, not surprisingly, afraid of people. But within months she met Jelly Bean, a sheep we had just rescued. The two animals bonded, and for the next 10 years they were

inseparable, day and night, until Hilda finally died peacefully in her sleep. We buried her at our Watkins Glen, New York, sanctuary. Jelly Bean lived a while longer until she, too, died of old age. She is also buried at Watkins Glen, not far from her lifelong friend.

We found another of our wonderful animals, Hope the pig, at an unloading area of the stockyard. She couldn't walk, so the workers had abandoned her there. It turned out she had a broken hind leg that had been left untreated and was calcifying. So we scooped her up and brought her home.

Hope was gentle and shy. When we fed her, some of our other pigs would try to move in and take her food. One in particular, Raquel, was especially ravenous and used to push Hope aside in hopes of finishing off her meals. I would tell Raquel "no!" She knew she was in the wrong, and it turned into a game. Whenever I would feed Hope, I would position myself so I could see Raquel but she couldn't see me. Her eyes would widen, her ears would perk up, and it became clear she was thinking, "I don't see that feeder anywhere; I wonder if he is still watching or if I can get away with this." She just loved food too much.

Then one day we rescued Johnny, a much younger pig, who immediately bonded with Hope. Johnny became Hope's constant companion, and he always made sure that whenever she was fed, no one else could get at her food. Johnny and Hope loved each other and spent countless hours snuggling together in the straw bedding. But Hope was a lot older than Johnny, and when she died, Johnny was overcome with grief. Although he was still young, sadly, he died just a couple of weeks later. As far as we could tell, it was of a broken heart.

Back then (the late 1980s), we were rescuing many animals who, like Hilda and Hope, had been discarded and written off as dead, and we were spending a lot for the best veterinary care possible. At first, the vets told us point-blank that we were wasting our money and time. Why put all this effort into helping animals who were of no monetary value and who had been slated for death in the first place? It didn't make economic sense, they thought. But eventually they began to accept us. That was mostly because we always paid our bills on time and tried to be easy clients—even as we challenged the veterinarians' assumptions about farm animals.

They never quite understood our attachment to the creatures, however. Our different perspectives became especially evident the time we noticed that one of the rats on the farm wasn't looking too good. (Believe it or not, we had grown rather fond of him.) So we called the vet and told him that we thought the rodent needed to be euthanized. The vet hemmed and hawed, and pretty much told us we were crazy, but eventually he agreed to do it.

Then, a couple of weeks later, our sheep came down with parasitic worms, and we needed medicine to treat them. I took one of the worms from the sheep so I could show it to the vet to help him diagnose what type of disease the animals had.

"I have one of the worms here," I explained over the phone.

There was a long silence.

Finally, the veterinarian asked in a confused, stammering voice, "And what specifically do you want us to do for the worm?"

We never did attend to worms, but the veterinarian's reaction showed that we were pushing boundaries. (As the years have passed, I'm happy to say that an increasing number of vets are coming to appreciate farm animals as we do at Farm Sanctuary.)

As we rescued more and more animals, keeping them all in our Wilmington backyard, we noticed that the neighborhood kids were constantly peering through the fence or knocking on our door, asking if they could see and pet them. It became apparent that these creatures could play a powerful role as ambassadors. After all, Farm Sanctuary wasn't just a sanctuary—it was also an educational and transformational place. We realized we could turn Farm Sanctuary into a positive experience for visitors by sharing the rescued animals' stories. It was much easier to speak about the horrors of factory farming amid the hopeful stories of rescued animals.

To support our ongoing investigations of farms, stockyards, and slaughterhouses, and to pay for the care of our animals, we began raising money by going to zoos, ecofestivals, and animal rights conferences and handing out pamphlets we'd written about our animals. But in the early days, our most successful fund-raising tool turned out to be selling veggie hot dogs out of a Volkswagen van at Grateful Dead concerts. These concerts were basically traveling festivals, so they attracted thousands of people, most of whom were receptive to our message of love, compassion, and tofu on a bun. We were able to make several thousand dollars in a couple of days at each concert stop. It was also at a Grateful Dead concert that a so-called Deadhead gave us the idea for our first bumper sticker, which read:

If you love animals called pets,
Why do you eat animals called dinner?

We also did some vegan catering to raise funds, and sometimes that required a lot of tofu. So we searched out a source of bulk tofu, eventually finding a farmer near Avondale, Pennsylvania, who sold it. (He didn't actually grow soybeans—he bought the beans and then created the tofu.) The farmer liked us, and when he discovered our mission, he offered us the use of some of his extra acreage. His barns needed attention and improvements, but we gathered volunteers, pitched in, and created our first Farm Sanctuary on an actual farm.

Although we now had a small farm, we quickly realized that we needed a larger one. We soon found a property in Watkins Glen, in the Finger Lakes region of New York. The 175-acre plot included a seven-bedroom house, barns, trac-tors, and equipment—all for $100,000. We looked at it, liked it, and bought it in the fall of 1989. Like the land in Avondale, the farm needed a lot of work. For example, we found pig skulls and bones strewn around the grounds. But we got to work, and, by the summer of 1990, we were able to bring the animals up from Pennsylvania. They, and we, finally had a permanent home.

Since we opened the Watkins Glen site, we've had about 100,000 visitors. Some of them were already vegans when they showed up, and others—such as Biz Stone, the cofounder of Twitter, and Brian Greene, the theoretical physicist at Columbia University—became vegans as a result of their visits.

One of our most interesting visitors was the fur farmer whose operation was located across the street. At first our relationship was strained,

but we invited him to our events, and soon his young son started volunteering for us. Then one day the fur farmer told me, "I really don't like killing the animals the way I do." He asked us what kind of vegetables we liked, and then closed down the fur farm and started growing plant foods, which he sold at a stand across the street.

Three years later, one of our members donated around 100 acres of land to Farm Sanctuary. Located near Orland, California, the property is about 150 miles north of San Francisco. (Today we have 300 acres there.) More recently we obtained another farm, this time in Acton, California, about 45 minutes north of Los Angeles and spanning 26 acres. We now own a total of more than 500 acres of land.

For the past 25 years, Farm Sanctuary has continued doing the same work as when we began: rescue, education, and advocacy.

That last piece picked up in the early 1990s, when I started discussing these issues with politicians across the country. Most people, including our elected leaders, don't realize just how much factory farms dominate American food production and how abusive their practices are toward animals. (If you'd like to know more about this system, please read my book, *Farm Sanctuary: Changing Hearts and Minds about Animals and Food*, or go to farmsanctuary.org/learn/factory-farming.)

That began to change in 1991, when the House of Representatives' Agriculture Committee's Subcommittee on Livestock, Dairy, and Poultry invited me to testify at hearings on the handling of downed animals (those too sick or injured to stand) at stockyards. We at Farm Sanctuary also began to work on state legislation to outlaw the marketing of downed animals and to promote and pass initiatives to prohibit the confinement systems that are such an affront to animal welfare. For example, we were behind the 2002 Florida initiative to ban gestation crates—tiny metal enclosures barely 2 feet across that sows (female pigs used for breeding) can't even turn around in. We also helped sponsor a successful 2006 Arizona proposition that requires pigs and calves raised for veal to be kept in enclosures at least large enough to turn around in and to fully extend their limbs. And in 2008 we helped pass California's Proposition 2, which requires farmers to give more space to egg-laying hens, veal calves, and pregnant pigs.

Similarly, also in California, we

"FARM ANIMALS ARE FAR MORE AWARE AND INTELLIGENT THAN WE EVER IMAGINED AND, DESPITE HAVING BEEN BRED AS DOMESTIC SLAVES, THEY ARE INDIVIDUAL BEINGS IN THEIR OWN RIGHT. AS SUCH, THEY DESERVE OUR RESPECT. AND OUR HELP. WHO WILL PLEAD FOR THEM IF WE ARE SILENT? THOUSANDS OF PEOPLE WHO SAY THEY 'LOVE' ANIMALS SIT DOWN ONCE OR TWICE A DAY TO ENJOY THE FLESH OF CREATURES WHO HAVE BEEN TREATED SO WITH LITTLE RESPECT AND KINDNESS JUST TO MAKE MORE MEAT."

—JANE GOODALL, PRIMATOLOGIST AND UN MESSENGER FOR PEACE

helped achieve a ban on the force-feeding of ducks and geese for *foie gras*, along with a ban on its sale, which took effect in 2012. We have urged restaurants and food retailers to include options for vegetarians and were instrumental in getting Burger King to launch its veggie burger.

Whatever we do, our objective is always the same: to change how society views and treats farm animals. We encourage people to make informed choices that are aligned with compassionate values and that support our interest in being well and living on our planet in an ecologically sustainable way. We strive to live according to our better angels and to set a good example.

This means that we don't just preach to the choir. We spend as much time as possible talking to the people who actually work in factory farms or whose actions support them. These people are

not our enemies, and we are not theirs. We make every attempt to be as respectful as possible, and we find that most people share similar values and interests. Even people who publicly oppose our efforts will sometimes approach me after a meeting or lecture and tell me that their daughter is a vegetarian or their son is a vegan.

We don't aim to hurt anyone or to destroy anyone's livelihood. We simply encourage people to consider new possibilities. And we always try to identify opportunities that align with people's interests as well as the interests of other animals and the planet. For example, if we're meeting with people in the dairy industry, we talk to them about the benefits of producing nondairy milks in place of cows' milk. A vast array of plant-based milks is now available, and the market for them is growing. Some people have listened and made that switch—quite profitably. The point is we are not against farmers but against cruelty.

Often, farmers will tell me that all their money and resources are invested in a particular kind of farm. I know they can't change overnight, but I do encourage them to start exploring other options. With an open mind and a desire to move in a positive direction, anything can happen—and I have seen it happen. Farmers in the Midwest who had grown conventional soybeans for animal feed have been able to increase their income by producing organic soybeans for tofu and other human food products instead.

I believe that everyone *can* make a significant change in their lives. To that end, we encourage everyone who comes to Farm Sanctuary, and everyone who reads this book, to consider the Five Tenets explained in the next chapter, and to reflect on how following them might improve your life and the lives of those around you.

THE FIVE TENETS of
FARM SANCTUARY LIVING

At Farm Sanctuary, we hope that everyone has a chance to live a full and happy life, no matter what kind of being you are, who your mother was, or how many legs you have.

People want to be good, but the pressures of life can lead us adrift, causing us to stray from our best selves. Without realizing it, we can act in ways that are misaligned with our better angels. We forget to live a life of compassion, we fail to appreciate the importance of empathy in the world, and we overlook humane principles on a day-to-day basis.

Humans are complex. We have the capacity to express enormous cruelty or enormous kindness. Certainly the vast majority of us would prefer to live kindly rather than cruelly, to be healthy instead of sick, and to live in accordance with our values and interests. To achieve this vision, I encourage people to live according to a set of Five Tenets that can help us live more happily on this earth together.

1. *Live and Eat in Alignment with Your Values*

2. *Engage in a Mindful Connection with Animals*

3. *Engage in a Mindful Connection with Your Food*

4. *Eat Plants . . . for Your Health*

5. *Eat Plants . . . for the Health of the Earth*

I believe that if you follow these guidelines, you will help not only animals but also yourself. You will be the best person you can be physically, emotionally, and spiritually. You will sleep better at night, you will create less harm in the world, and you will feel healthier and more enlivened.

Kindness is contagious, and it is beautiful to see it spread. When you start living according to these tenets, you will inspire others to do the same, and you will become a model of the kind of compassionate living to which I think most people aspire.

Following these tenets will also make you happy. This is one reason why so many people think Farm Sanctuary is the Happiest Place on Earth.

TENET 1:
Live and Eat in Alignment with Your Values

Do you want to be a good person? Most of us do. To this end, each of us tries to live in a way that we believe is decent and compassionate. We want to harmonize our ideals with our actions, what we believe with how we behave. Most people believe that the torture of animals is wrong, so we aim not to torture animals and may even feel that our government shouldn't allow such torture. Many of us also believe that the environment should be protected, so we avoid polluting and support policies that help safeguard nature in sensible ways.

Most of us make sincere attempts to be consistent in our lives—at work and at home, about politics and religion, with regard to health and exercise. And yet, when it comes to the sources of our food, many of us experience a disconnect between what we believe and what we eat. We espouse kindness but don't make kind food choices. Instead of living in accordance with our natural empathy and compassion, we look the other way.

Looking the other way prevents us from taking responsibility for our food selections. It creates a dissonance between our principles and our actions. And when people ignore or try to rationalize a problem, the problem is perpetuated. Of course people who aren't vegan are not bad people. But they may have bad habits. Good people do bad things. No one is perfect. We all struggle and aspire to do the best we can.

The Farm Sanctuary way of living offers you a chance to do better: to match your heart with your food choices and, in so doing, help solve many of modern life's quandaries, ranging from the intolerable plight of animals in the factory farming sys-

tem to our nation's poor health (see Tenet 4) to environmental devastation (see Tenet 5).

Consumers generally understand that there is something wrong with our industrialized food system, but they are afraid to find out more. Too often, when the issue of factory farming comes up, people say, "Don't tell me. I don't want to know." But if every one of us made mindful choices about our food, we would be able to make a huge difference in our world.

So as a first step, we at Farm Sanctuary want you to open your eyes, your mind, and your heart. I know that this isn't always easy. It can be difficult to acknowledge that our everyday behaviors can cause harm, which is why there is a tendency to push the subject of food aside and say, "If everyone else is doing it, it must be normal and okay." It takes courage to think otherwise and to recognize when "bad" has become "normal."

How did this happen? With rare exceptions, people empathize with animals and oppose animal cruelty. A recent Gallup poll found that 97 percent of Americans believe that animals should be protected from abuse. How many times do 97 percent of Americans agree on anything? But those same people unwittingly make choices that are out of line with their beliefs. They're buying meat, milk, and eggs that come from cruel factory farms. Consumers are disconnected from the source of their food—often produced far away— and protected from seeing the abuses of factory farming. People will tell you they love animals. They do. They just haven't opened themselves up to the realities of how the animals they eat are treated.

When people do become aware of how animal agriculture works, though, their worldview changes. For example, the last person in the world you might have expected to become a vegan is Steve-O, the stunt comedian most famous for the television series *Jackass*. But not only has he become a plant-based eater, he has also become one of our spokespeople. In 2012, Steve-O narrated *What Came Before*, a short film we produced about the horrors of factory farming and the heartwarming story of three animals who found refuge at Farm Sanctuary. Steve-O transformed himself from someone who never gave a thought to the issue of factory farms to someone so concerned about animals that when he goes to buy a new pillow, he first calls us up to find out which ones are the most humanely manufactured. (Speaking of which—avoid down-filled pillows!)

Like Steve-O before he became vegan, most people don't understand how their food is produced. For the most part, no one has ever urged them to find out. That's what we want to do at Farm Sanctuary—we encourage people to understand more about their food. The alternatives are

out there, more plentiful than ever before. There is no reason today not to make compassionate choices. You won't have to sacrifice taste, comfort, fashion, style, or anything else.

Kari Nienstedt, the 43-year-old National Manager of the State Council Program is another person who faced head-on the challenge of thinking about her food.

Kari grew up with animals—cats and dogs—but ate the standard meat-filled American diet. Then, when Kari was 20, her sister gave her a book called *67 Ways to Save Animals*. It was her introduction to the concept of factory farming, and it stunned her. Soon thereafter she applied to become an intern at Farm Sanctuary, where she spent a summer digging holes for fence posts, moving hay bales, and connecting with animals. By the end of her stay, impressed with everything she saw, she became a vegan.

Kari took her experience a step further. She decided "to shift my life so that I was taking action to stop something that I opposed." So instead of entering a job in business management as planned, she began a career as an activist. Her

first foray was a walk on behalf of farm animals in Phoenix. After many years of advocating as an individual, she was asked to become the campaign manager for a ballot initiative to abolish veal and gestation crates throughout Arizona. The initiative won, gaining 62 percent of the vote. The Humane Society of the United States (HSUS) then appointed her as state director of their Arizona chapter.

As Kari told us, being able to align her life with her values means that she loves her work so much that she would do it for free.

Still another example: Dan Piraro, one of the country's top cartoonists, is renowned for the multi-award-winning comic strip *Bizarro*. Dan grew up in a world as nonbizarre as life gets, in an average middle-class family in an average city (Tulsa), where he ate an average diet of meat and potatoes. He felt a kinship with animals but that meant cats and dogs. "I always bought into the stereotype that vegetarians were hippies with too much free time," he said. "If you were a vegetarian, you were probably heavily into the zodiac as well."

But after Dan divorced his first wife and became a single dad, he started paying more attention to what his kids ate—and because he was getting older, he also started paying attention to his health. That meant no more fat-marbled beef. After he learned about pigs' intelligence, he stopped eating pork as well. But he still ate eggs and dairy products.

Then, in 2002, Dan remarried. His new wife happened to be a vegan. She made no effort to change him, but a few months into the marriage, she asked if they could visit Farm Sanctuary for her birthday. Dan agreed, and they came up to Watkins Glen.

When they checked into their cabin, Dan saw a sign that read: "Please respect our residents by not having any animal products in this room."

"Really?" he recalls thinking. "They're going to control what I eat in this cabin? I got all indignant about it, like it's going to kill someone if I have a bag of chicken nuggets on me?"

Then he took a tour of the farm, where he met Arbuckle, a blind steer living in a small, isolated pasture with his best friend, a cow named

Queenie. While Dan was learning about Arbuckle, the cow calmly walked over and nuzzled him like a dog, looking for affection.

"That was the moment my previous worldview collapsed," Dan recalled. "There was someone in there. This is not an eating machine but an animal with thoughts and feelings. If I weren't such a manly man, I would have cried. What have I been doing all these years? I wondered.

"I'm not a spiritual person," Dan continued, "but I do get a great deal of satisfaction knowing that my principles align with my lifestyle. It's a daily benefit knowing that when I teach my kids not to be cruel to animals, I'm actually living that concept myself. Every thinking person should grow throughout his or her life. I'm now in my midfifties. I don't want to be the same guy I was in high school or even in my forties. A big part of that is widening my circle of compassion."

The lessons learned at Farm Sanctuary have affected his view of the wider world, as well. He told us, "It's impossible to effectively defend the idea that humans are the only species that matter. We're not. Looking at our planet from outer space, one tiny speck among billions of others, it's impossible not to see it as a unique organism made up of many millions of species of flora and fauna. We're a small part of a large system, and each part is important."

A final example: Biz Stone, the cofounder of Twitter, grew up an oblivious omnivore. He ate whatever was placed in front of him, from hot dogs to burgers, without any thought. His family was poor and sometimes on welfare, so his food choices were often limited to blocks of government cheese or school lunches of bland, highly processed chicken patties.

Then, when Biz was 20, he met his wife-to-be, Livia McRee. Livia was a vegetarian and later a vegan. Biz, however, continued to eat meat.

Some years later, Livia decided they should visit this great animal sanctuary in the Finger Lakes region for her 27th birthday. Her friends

Farm Sanctuary's
GUIDING PRINCIPLES

Vision: A world in which humans embrace a vegan ethic and practice compassion and respect for all species.

Mission: To protect farm animals from cruelty, to inspire change in the way society views and treats farm animals, and to promote compassionate vegan living.

Values: We engage people where they are on their journey to a cruelty-free lifestyle.

We support only nonviolent and respectful methods to achieve our goals.

Ending factory farming and promoting a plant-based diet is best for animals, human health, and the environment.

Animals exist for their own purposes and are not merely consumable resources.

We support incremental change.

All human and nonhuman animals should be treated with compassion and respect.

Positive human-animal connections and interactions are an effective means of education and transformation.

had said it was fun, so they hopped on a train and then rented a car. They didn't realize how long the trip would take, however, and when they arrived it was after sunset. As they drove through a dark forest on a dirt road, the light faded and the eerie shadows of the trees grew longer. Biz became worried that they were in

"BEING VEGAN ALIGNS WITH MY BUSINESS PHILOSOPHY: A GOOD COMPANY SHOULD BE ALIGNED WITH GOOD CAUSES. IF YOU CAN NUDGE YOUR BUSINESS EVER SO SLIGHTLY TOWARD A SOCIAL CAUSE, JUST BY COMING TO WORK YOU ARE DOING GOOD."

—Biz Stone, Cofounder, Twitter

some kind of danger when, out of the blue, a naked man ran past their car.

"What the hell was that?" he wondered aloud.

"I think that's the guy that runs the place," Livia answered. Biz became even more nervous.

Finally, they found their cabin, which seemed empty and desolate. Biz had been expecting something more like a hotel or a bed-and-breakfast. Instead, he got a rustic one-room cabin inhabited by clusters of flies. The couple spent the next hour and a half catching each fly and letting it out the door. Still worried that they might be in some kind of horror movie, Biz and Livia went to bed.

The next morning, they walked over to Farm Sanctuary's People Barn—another phrase that worried Biz. There they watched a video about the horrors of factory farming, which included the image of a sick but living cow being plowed

into a hole as a form of burial. Now, instead of feeling as if he himself were in a horror film, he was watching one, and animals were the victims. He recalled, "It was as if I had flipped a switch. It just kind of popped into my head: 'Oh my God, I am eating other earthlings.'"

At that moment, he decided to become a vegan. Forever.

Biz and Livia spent the rest of the weekend getting to know our animals, spending time with the pigs, the cows, and the chickens, which they'd had no idea were so cute. (They also spent some time with me, and I assured them that though it was me they'd seen jogging on that road, I hadn't been naked—just shirtless.)

Biz later told me that becoming a vegan didn't mean that he was giving anything up. It was, in fact, the opposite. He had gained something: enlightenment. The decision not to eat animals fit his agenda of being a good person.

"I like doing good things," he said. "Who doesn't? Being vegan makes doing good things automatic. I go about my everyday life knowing I am doing something very good without even trying—it's a freebie. You're having an impact on the environment, you're helping animals, and you're helping yourself."

For all of the people whose stories I've told, and many millions more, the decision to become a plant-based eater has made them feel good about both themselves and their relationship with their fellow inhabitants of the earth. It has aligned their interests with those of others. They have come to understand that it doesn't make sense to eat food that makes us feel sick (see pages 59–76), hurts the planet (see pages 77–93), and creates a gap between our belief systems and our behavior. Why rationalize and make excuses for our bad habits? It only hinders growth and prevents us from aspiring to be better, to live in greater harmony with other animals, and to be compassionate. Why not choose kindness instead of cruelty and peace instead of violence? I have yet to meet anyone who would intentionally pick the latter over the former. Every day I meet people who have decided to make the switch from meat-eater to plant-eater. That's a big part of what Farm Sanctuary is all about.

If you decide that you, too, want to live in harmony with your values, you don't have to do it all this very minute. Many people who come to Farm Sanctuary end up making significant changes to their lives, but not all at once.

Most often, they start by making a few smaller changes. Small changes are good and tend to bring about more changes that eventually lead to big ones. It's all about momentum: That first move can start a chain reaction that leads you to places you might never have expected. But you have to pay attention and decide to participate.

One of my heroes, folk singer Pete Seeger, once said, "Participation—that's what's going to save the human race."

Participate. Just do something, even if it's small. One small step can be the beginning of an entire movement.

The Hens
HELP YOU HELP OUT

THE HENS *over at the multiaward-winning site Our Hen House (ourhenhouse.org)—my friends Jasmin Singer and Mariann Sullivan—have been working hard advocating for animals for many years. I'm a big fan of all that they do with their online magazine, television show, and podcast. Here's what they said when I asked if they would share their tips on how people can get involved in creating a new world for animals.*

Start by rethinking what an animal activist is or could be. It does not necessarily mean standing outside a slaughterhouse holding a protest sign—though it certainly could. Some of the greatest change-making can happen at the office while coworkers gather around the coffee machine in the morning. Or at a PTA meeting. Or in the classroom. Or the courtroom. There is some way for every single person who cares about animals to take a step, small or large.

1. Go vegan. The best way to start changing the world for animals is to stop consuming them. Not only will you no longer be funding the industries that profit off of animal exploitation, but you will also become an inspiration to others.

2. Ask yourself, "What am I good at?" and start there. If you're a lawyer, why not offer your services pro bono to an animal-protection charity? If you're a teacher, how about including some humane education in your curriculum? If you're a student, think about writing a term paper on egg production or other aspects of factory farming. If you're a cook or foodie, it's easy: Wow your colleagues with delicious vegan cupcakes and other vegan foods. In other words, do what you're good at and tap into your existing networks to spread the word (and the peanut butter).

3. Learn how to handle "humane meat" questions. A lot of well-intentioned people are under the impression that it's fine to consume meat as long as it is raised "humanely." In order to respond to these claims, it's important to know your stuff. But it's not particularly effective to jump down people's throats. Instead, start by asking them a few simple questions, such as: What standards do these "humane" companies meet? Maybe your friends don't know that humane certification programs differ. Some don't even require that the animals get to go outside. Most allow crowding and even permit some standard mutilations common to factory farming, like cutting the beaks off laying hens. Also ask if they understand that terms like "free range" mean very little, legally speaking. Do they realize how much land would be needed to allow

all animals used for food to graze freely—land that could be used to grow food for humans or for wildlife habitat? Are they aware that, if we were to continue our current consumption habits while allowing animals even barely adequate space, we would need several more planets to accommodate them? Or maybe they don't realize that even the smallest egg producers usually get their chicks from hatcheries, where these babies never see their mothers and the males are destroyed and thrown in the garbage. They might not know that hens don't lay eggs for their entire lives, so unless people with backyard chickens want a bunch of pet hens, they're going to have to kill them eventually.

4. Learn how to talk about milk. In order to lactate regularly, dairy cows must give birth every year. Their calves are quickly taken away so that people can use the milk instead. That's just how milk production works, no matter what kind of farm it's from.

5. Change the world through food. The single most effective way to change the world for animals is by preparing and sharing delicious vegan food. Make it, eat it, donate it, photograph it; and then make and share it again. For example, bring vegan cookies to your local school's bake sale (and provide the recipe).

Bake some vegan brownies for the common area at your office. Plan ahead for family get-togethers—make sure that next Thanksgiving (or Fourth of July, Passover, or Christmas) you've made a ton of delicious vegan food, enough for everyone to have a taste and to bring some home for their families and friends to try.

One person I know who's taken many steps is Jon Camp, who first came to Farm Sanctuary as an intern in 2001. Today Jon works at Vegan Outreach, for which he has personally handed out educational booklets to more than one *million* people in almost every state in the country and four Canadian provinces! I suspect he may hold the record for the most pamphlets ever given out for any cause, *ever*.

If full-time advocacy isn't for you, here's what Jon has to say on other ideas for getting the message out.

"There are many ways to help farm animals. See if there is a group in your neck of the woods with whom you can volunteer. If not, many organizations engage in outreach tours; maybe you can help their employees the next time they swing through your city or town. You can find out when such groups will be passing through by asking your favorite animal advocacy organizations. Or you can order booklets from them and hand them out at a local event.

"Another approach is to continue working full-time in your chosen profession but donating a portion of your salary to organizations doing good work for animals. Nonprofit advocacy groups would be unable to exist if not for generous individuals who are willing to give back.

"Once you find a form of advocacy that works for you, fit it into your routine. Perhaps you'll get out and leaflet a college campus every other week. Or you'll set up film screenings or educational dis-plays at your library once a month. What's important is that you schedule your volunteer work into your calendar. By making farm animal advocacy a regular part of your life, you'll accomplish more and can feel proud about giving what you can to make the world a better place."

Engage in a Mindful Connection with Animals

TaterTot was a 10-month-old pit bull scheduled to be euthanized at the Minneapolis Animal Care and Control Center in 2013. Just hours before the dog's death sentence, a woman named Christi Smith swooped in to save him and find him a good home. She soon realized that the perfect home was her own.

One night, not long after settling in to the Smith household, TaterTot began barking and acting strangely, running back and forth between the bedroom of Christi's 4-year-old son Peyton and Christi's room. Finally Christi went to check on her son and found TatorTot barking and pawing at the boy. Christi quickly realized that Peyton was barely breathing. She rushed her son to the emergency room where doctors discovered that his blood sugar was dangerously low. Fortunately, they were able to stabilize him. According to the doctors, TaterTot had saved Peyton's life.

In 2013 alone, several dozen news stories appeared about animals who rescued their human companions—in many different and sometimes strange ways. TaterTot's case is not unusual, though; it's long been known that animals can detect hypoglycemia in humans. For instance, a 2013 Queen's University, Belfast study found that 65 percent of participants with insulin-dependent diabetes reported that their pets alerted them to the onset of a hypoglycemic episode by whining, barking, and licking them.

Other recent news stories involve animals who rescued their companions from fires, kept lost children warm at night, or spotted cancer and other illnesses. Then there's the case of the German shepherd who saw his companion, a 63-year-old Frenchwoman, walk into her backyard with a .22-caliber rifle, fire a few shots in the air, and then turn the gun on herself. The shepherd jumped up and knocked the weapon out of the woman's hands, saving her life. And there's the story of a parrot named Wunsy, an African gray who took action when his companion, who was taking him for a walk, was accosted by a stranger in a London park. (Yes, some birds like to go for walks.) Wunsy flapped his wings and squawked like a maniac, causing the attacker to flee in panic.

"THE ASSUMPTION THAT ANIMALS ARE WITHOUT RIGHTS, AND THE ILLUSION THAT OUR TREATMENT OF THEM HAS NO MORAL SIGNIFICANCE, IS A POSITIVELY OUTRAGEOUS EXAMPLE OF WESTERN CRUDITY AND BARBARITY. UNIVERSAL COMPASSION IS THE ONLY GUARANTEE OF MORALITY."

—Arthur Schopenhauer, Philosopher

For millennia, humans have enjoyed the benefits of bringing animals into their lives—not as food but as friends. Dogs were domesticated as long as 20,000 to 30,000 years ago. Cats arrived in humans' lives about 9,500 years ago. Other animals have become human companions as well, although the majority of those we share our homes with today are canines and felines. And they've helped us. Dogs have protected us from larger beasts, assisted us in domesticating other animals, and have always provided warmth and companionship. The later-arriving cats helped rid newly formed agrarian societies of the rodents that were destroying food supplies.

Throughout our history, humans have enjoyed having animals around because they've been true friends—serving us well, keeping us company, and providing love. No one has to tell us that animals are good for our heart and soul. But over the last 4 decades, medical science has started to investigate why this is so.

And now we have empirical proof that animals enrich our lives. One of the first landmark studies, performed in 1980, came out of the University of Maryland, where researchers examined the mortality rates of patients 1 year after they were discharged from a coronary-care unit. The data indicated that patients who had animal companions were more likely to be alive 1 year after release than those who didn't.

Since that study was completed, hundreds of others have been conducted, all showing similar results: Animals are good for people—emotionally, spiritually, and mentally. One study from the National Institutes of Health involving 420 married couples found that those who had animal

companions also had lower heart rates and lower blood pressure than those in human-only households. Likewise, studies comparing people who had animal companions with those who didn't found that the former were less likely to be obese, were more likely to survive a heart attack, had increased mobility during their senior years, had lower cholesterol, and were generally more relaxed.

Another study—the National Health and Nutrition Examination, presented in 2008 by the Stroke Research Center at the University of Minnesota—followed more than 4,000 cat owners more than 10 years. Researchers discovered that living with a cat dramatically reduced the subjects' chances of dying from heart disease. People who had *never* had a cat living with them were 40 percent *more* likely to die of a heart attack, as well as 30 percent more likely to suffer from other cardiovascular disorders.

It's not just cats who are good for humans' hearts. A 2007 study by the psychology department at Queen's University, Belfast showed that people who live with dogs tend to have lower blood pressure and cholesterol than those without canines.

What is particularly interesting about these data is that many of the health benefits associated with sharing our lives with animals are similar to those we experience after switching to a plant-based diet. Both lower cholesterol and blood pressure and help to prevent heart disease.

This finding points to a fundamental truth surrounding the Farm Sanctuary lifestyle: When you stop eating animals and start living peacefully among them, health-saving and life-enhancing benefits result.

Snowy and Shotzie

SNOWY AND SHOTZIE are ducks who, like cats, have lived several lives.

Snowy was abandoned, found all bloody and maimed on a park fence in Queens, New York. She'd been attacked by dogs, abused by rock-wielding teens, and ignored by passersby. Eventually, a caller alerted New York City Animal Care and Control to her plight, and a humane agent intervened, ending her abuse and bringing her to safety. She came to our New York Shelter the first week of April 2007.

Shotzie had come to Farm Sanctuary earlier that year after being left behind following the death of his caretaker. Shotzie's cohorts were removed from the property, but for some reason this young duck was forgotten and found wandering around a neighbor's yard. The neighbor called us, and we brought Shotzie to our shelter. When we examined him, we discovered a heart murmur—he wouldn't have survived much longer on his own, especially in the bitter February cold.

Both of these animals adapted to life on the farm, but they got really lucky when Farm Sanctuary members Karen Hollands and Drea Alary fell in love with them and brought them to their central New York home one snowy spring day. After the snow melted, the ducks' new lives began. Snowy and Shotzie began exploring their world in earnest, spending hours in the yard dabbling and swimming in a huge puddle. But the duo would soon set their eyes on a bigger prize: the pond.

Nestled between Karen and Drea's house and that of their neighbors, the pond was an irresistible beacon. And once settled on the water, Snowy and Shotzie refused to leave. The new parents pulled out every trick in the book to coax them back to their duck house. Drea provided room service to the stubborn ducks, bringing them nourishing homemade meals. Karen even dunked herself in the frigid pond water, swimming out in an effort to herd their babies home. But Snowy and Shotzie would have none of it. Neither food nor company could convince the two to leave. Today, if you look at the pond next to Karen and Drea's house, you will see two birds enjoying life to the fullest, and their proud parents building a new duck house on the edge of the water to help them do just that.

At the core of these healthy benefits is the prevention of one of our modern era's greatest afflictions—stress. Besides eating an unhealthful and unbalanced diet, a high-stress lifestyle is a leading cause of cardiovascular and other diseases. But the Farm Sanctuary lifestyle can help. It improves your health and can even reverse the negative effects of your previous lifestyle. Eating plants instead of animals also reduces the inconsistency and stress that occur when we feel conflicted about consuming foods from a factory farming system whose practices we abhor. Being around animals is a healthy habit, and various studies show they help us reduce stress and become more psychologically well adjusted.

For example, an ongoing study at the University of Texas Health Science Center by Mara M. Baun, who has been studying the positive effects of animals for decades, found that the presence of dogs greatly increased interactive behaviors among Alzheimer's patients. Having dogs around also decreased these patients' irritation level, improved their appetite, and increased their physical activity.

The Life Care Center of Nashoba Valley, Massachusetts, has been using chickens to calm patients with dementia. And an organization in England called HenPower installs chicken coops at nursing homes. It even coined its own phrase for senior chicken-lovers (riffing on the British term *pensioner*): hensioners.

How exactly do animals prevent or reduce stress? For one thing, their presence significantly reduces anxiety, the precursor to stress. This process was demonstrated in a study that examined the anxiety levels of patients who were about to undergo surgery. Those who spent a short amount of time with a dog before their operation experienced a 37 percent decrease in their anxiety levels once their procedure began.

In addition to lowering blood pressure, the presence of an animal companion has been linked in many studies to lower levels of cortisol, an important but potentially dangerous hormone that regulates our stress response. Not only does animal contact reduce cortisol levels, but it also increases levels of another hormone, oxytocin, which is linked to positive feelings.

A heartening bonus: These studies show that the human-animal relationship is good for the animals as well—and not just because we're not

eating them. A study undertaken at the Life Sciences Research Institute in Pretoria, South Africa, investigated six neurochemicals associated with decreased blood pressure in both humans and dogs before and after they interacted with one another. The findings showed increased levels of these neurochemicals in both species after they interacted, leading to a mutually beneficial reduction in blood pressure.

Although canines and felines make up the bulk of the research on human-animal connections, a number of studies have also been done on the benefits of watching fish. One study by scientists at the University of Pennsylvania found that quietly watching fish swimming in a home aquarium eases stress and may even offer a means of treating high blood pressure.

While the extensive research on the health benefits of connecting positively with animals is compelling, the reason behind this phenomenon is surprisingly simple—our need for companionship. This basic impulse is what attracts us to animals and is why that attraction lowers our blood pressure and relieves our stress.

Companionship with animals is an important means of combatting loneliness, especially in a world where social, structural, and family dynamics are changing constantly. All too often, people find themselves living alone, eating alone, and working alone. But by living on or near an animal sanctuary, or by sharing our home with domestic animals, we can avoid or assuage our loneliness and anxiety— with the added benefit of providing nurturing love and care for those animals in return.

All the evidence shows that we don't share our lives with animals just because we want to. We do it because we need them.

> "IF PEOPLE WERE SUPERIOR TO ANIMALS, THEY'D TAKE BETTER CARE OF THE WORLD."
> —BENJAMIN HOFF, AUTHOR, *THE TAO OF POOH*

Pets and Popularity

Being around animals can not only make a difference in your health, it can also make a difference in your popularity. That's what a study published in the journal *Anthrozoos* found. Scientists looking into the effects of an animal's presence on people's perceptions gave study subjects a test called the ATAT (Animal Thematic Apperception Test). The subjects were shown scenes picturing humans in a natural environment, some of them featuring animals and some not. Subjects were asked to rate the scenes and the people in them. On the whole, the scenes and the individuals pictured were perceived as "significantly more friendly, less threatening, and happier" when animals were included than when animals were not present.

Being kind to animals benefits both animals and humans. This is because the stronger our connection with nonhuman animals, the more likely we are to empathize with other people. Cognitive neuroscientists have discovered connections in the brain known as empathy neurons. These neurons let humans experience another person's situation as though it were their own. Many social scientists believe that the ability to empathize with another creature is an important part of human evolution and that as billions more humans populate the earth, this trait will continue to be necessary if humanity is to survive.

Cruelty-Free Fashion

AWARD-WINNING FASHION DESIGNER JOHN BARTLETT *has long championed animal rights and animal welfare, but it's not always easy for someone who works in an industry that favors fur, hides, and other less-than-compassionate fabrics and trims. John is a great, loyal friend to Farm Sanctuary and has designed several T-shirts for us that feature images of chickens, cows, and pigs. I love wearing them. I also ask him for fashion advice, which he shares here.*

When I decided to go vegan in 2010, one of the first things I did was to give away all of my leather shoes, belts, and bags. From there, I cleared my closet of all down-filled coats, silk ties, and most of my wool suits and sweaters. My friends were thrilled with my vegan giveaway and reaped the rewards gladly, but they were concerned that I would morph into a "crunchy granola," hemp- and Croc-wearing caricature of myself. I admit that my first year on a plant-based diet found me scouring the Web for any and all slogan T-shirts proudly announcing my veganism. My favorite—and one I still wear today—has a great illustration of a pig and the words "Bacon had a Mom." Who says we vegans don't have a sense of humor?

For the style-minded vegan, dressing with a sense of compassion can be a challenge. It can feel overwhelming trying to navigate through all of the seasonal trends and must-haves of the moment. Many fashions include some use of animals, from a coat's fur trim to a shoe's leather uppers. And while there are alternatives to these animal-based components, trying to express one's style as well as one's belief in nonviolence is a personal journey. Here are a few general rules.

1. Avoid wearing leather, suede, fur, and any exotic hides including snakeskin and python (usually used in luxury handbags). More alternative materials are coming through the fashion pipeline every day, which makes it easier to find accessories that have a leather- or suede-like appearance but are actually produced from man-made alternatives. Some of the most forward-thinking mills in Italy are coming out with incredible animal-free leathers that can be found in designer Stella McCartney's handbags, for example, and in the men's vegan brand Brave GentleMan.

I personally feel liberated without leather and suede as a wardrobe staple. It sparks a renewed sense of the "hunt" in me as I search out animal-free footwear, belts, and backpacks that add style and compassion in equal doses. In my own designs, I have worked with the recycled microfiber product Ultrasuede to create motorcycle biker jackets and have used heavy waxed cotton as a leather substitute for my collaboration with shoe designer Ruthie Davis. And I now wear cloth tennis shoes with just about everything—even fine suits. It definitely makes me stand out in the fashion crowd!

Fur, the cruelest form of fashion, has been actively promoted of late and is being worn by younger and younger people. It is increasingly found on many coat trims to add a touch of perceived luxury to an otherwise everyday garment. If you want to wear the look of fur without harming animals, always be sure that the item you are interested in wearing is properly labeled. Sadly, many items that are labeled as faux fur turn out upon closer inspection to be real fur. So please be careful when you purchase anything that features a "synthetic fur" trim. My honest advice? Skip the fur interpretations altogether to avoid confusion.

2. As a stylish compassionista, you should also avoid wearing wool, down, and silk. Although I kept a few of my wool pieces for sentimental reasons, I am much happier now wearing cotton-suits, shirts, and ties and have no real need anymore for a heavy wool coat.

Today down-free outerwear is plentiful. I have found incredible inspiration at upscale sporting goods stores that carry the latest in high-tech, cruelty-free skiwear that is as cool on the ski slopes as it is on Fifth Avenue. For a more urban downtown feel, my friend Leanne Mai-ly Hilgart creates fashionable, weatherproof, and wool-free coats out of high-tech performance fabrics for her label Vaute Couture.

Silk, meanwhile, is largely used in men's neckwear and finer women's dresses. I've switched to wearing cotton or linen ties and, if I can find them, quality polyester ones. My hipster vegan friends also find a lot of their silk-free neckwear in vintage stores. And for women's soft dressing, there are so many wonderful, upscale synthetics available that wearing silk is no longer chic.

3. Shun angora sweaters, socks, and other items. Angora is harvested from the Angora rabbit, often using very painful methods. More and more companies are being alerted to the unnecessary suffering involved, and the demand for angora is, thankfully, decreasing. If you do see a brand using angora, I always recommend writing a note on their Facebook wall to educate them and their followers about the cruel process of producing such garments.

4. Find your own style! True style is most successful if it captures the essence of your individuality. So I encourage everyone to celebrate a compassionate life with color, creativity, and the courage to wear your beautiful heart on your sleeve in any way that looks and feels good to you.

Embracing a cruelty-free life has definitely informed my own style. While in the past I was obsessed with luxury items using animal products, I am now equally obsessed with exploring both plant-based and man-made technology in fabrics and designs. I find it fun to create my own rules that venture outside tradition. For example, I love to mix plaids and patterns in a signature look. I typically wear a brushed-cotton flannel plaid lumberjack shirt with a cotton plaid tie and possibly a corduroy vest over that. When I add a layer of great eco-chic outerwear pieces over them, they keep me as warm as any caveman's pelt.

According to social theorist Jeremy Rifkin, reexamining human history through the lens of empathy has led social scientists to discover "previously hidden strands of the human narrative that suggests that human evolution is measured not only by the expansion of power over nature, but also by the intensification and extension of empathy to more diverse others across broader temporal and spatial domains.

I believe that humans are a fundamentally empathic species and that this empathy has helped us evolve in the past and will be a key to our future evolution as well. The more humans understand and respect other creatures on earth—and the earth itself—the more likely we all are to survive.

So it isn't just for our own health that a human-animal relationship is good. It may be indicative of health for the planet and the future of all species on earth. As Rifkin and others have pointed out, complex rela-

> "ASK THE EXPERIMENTERS WHY THEY EXPERIMENT ON ANIMALS, AND THE ANSWER IS: 'BECAUSE THE ANIMALS ARE LIKE US.' ASK THE EXPERIMENTERS WHY IT IS MORALLY OKAY TO EXPERIMENT ON ANIMALS, AND THE ANSWER IS: 'BECAUSE THE ANIMALS ARE NOT LIKE US.' ANIMAL EXPERIMENTATION RESTS ON A LOGICAL CONTRADICTION."
>
> —CHARLES R. MAGEL, PHILOSOPHY PROFESSOR

tionships exist between all living creatures (as well as between living creatures and the biosphere we call earth), and we are all dependent on each other.

Our empathy is awakened when we connect with other living beings. That's part of the magic of Farm Sanctuary. Visitors who have a dog or cat at home are often surprised by how quickly they form an equally strong bond with a cow, pig, duck, or chicken. This bonding happens so often that our staff has grown accustomed to dealing with the constant outbursts from visitors: "I had no idea that turkeys had such personalities!" "I never knew that sheep could be so sweet!" "Are goats always so playful?"

As our visitors learn, once you discover the love of a pig, the friendship of a lamb, or a connection with a goat, you also understand how similar they are to the cats and dogs with whom we already share our homes. Our empathetic instinct applies to farm animals, too. Hundreds of people of different ages and from many backgrounds come to Farm Sanctuary each month, and nearly everyone experiences some type of animal-bonding experience. What makes us happiest is to hear them say as they leave, "I'll never look at farm animals the same way again."

The best part: They don't.

This is why I encourage you to visit Farm Sanctuary. You may arrive thinking you love animals, but you will leave knowing perhaps for the first time how deeply you really do.

I'll leave you with a story that illustrates the process of forging a mindful connection with animals, as told to me by a farmer named Bob Comis. I first learned about him by reading some of his online posts, which poignantly described his struggle between treating animals with compas-

sion and slaughtering them for food. I have seen farmers wrestle with this inconsistency numerous times over the years, but many of them are scared of change—just like consumers hooked on the standard American diet who commonly give in to custom and convenience. Bob was different: He had the courage to look squarely at his quandary. When he did, he quit eating animals and began putting a plan in place to stop killing them for meat and start growing plant foods instead.

The Panoply of Beings Is Infinite

by Bob Comis

In my second year of raising hogs to kill so that we can eat their meat, I got a group of seven pigs. One of them was a runt. At first the farmers offered to give the runt to me for free. I balked. But then I realized that having a runt, who might be prone to health problems, might teach me a thing or two about raising pigs, so I accepted him. It wasn't more than a week or two after I got the pigs home that I regretted my decision. The runt wasn't growing. In fact, he was shrinking, becoming increasingly gaunt. His hair, which should have been smooth and shiny, was rough and dull. I wasn't prepared to take care of a sick pig. I had just started out raising livestock, with no farming background, and I knew absolutely nothing about it. I didn't even know anything about healthy pigs. I was just a suburban kid caught up in the burgeoning interest in living the small-farm dream. I was totally winging it.

As the runt got worse, I became increasingly paralyzed. I tried not to see him when I fed and watered the group three times a day. I pretended not to notice when his backbone began to protrude and his ribs began to stick out. I averted my eyes when the sun shined on the sharp angles of his hips. I blocked out the deep hollows of his cheeks.

One morning I was walking from the barn to the pig paddock carrying two buckets, one of feed and one of water. The six big pigs came bounding hungrily out of their shelter when they saw me. The runt was nowhere to be seen. I pretended not to notice as I fed and watered the other pigs. I was sure the runt was dead, but I couldn't deal with the idea. Just as I was turning to leave, I caught movement out of the corner of my eye. It was the runt, in the tall grass. He was lying down, but wasn't still. His body was rocking forward and back. After a big rock forward, the runt heaved himself up onto his feet and stumbled a step or two. Then he stood still, wobbling. He took another unsteady step and collapsed. He rocked, heaved himself back up again, took a couple of steps, and collapsed. He was trying to make his way over to the food.

When I had first approached the paddock and noticed that the runt was missing, I had begun to prepare myself for the fact that he had died. I had prepared myself so well, in fact, that I felt disappointed that he was still alive. Why couldn't he just have been dead, already? Why was he struggling, making this Herculean effort? And, then, in a rush of energetic emotion that washed over me, I shocked myself when I slowly whispered the answer aloud: "Because he wants to live."

My God, I thought, *what have you done?* How could you have just ignored his suffering day after day, a suffering that had been so, so very obvious? I was riddled with guilt. Then, in an instant, I truly understood the responsibility I had taken on when I decided to raise animals to be killed for their meat. The runt's life, every aspect of it, was my responsibility. I could no longer ignore what I had been shielding myself from. I did not care that it was likely too late. I was going to try to save him.

I hurried back to the barn and grabbed a large plastic pet carrier and jogged back across the street, ducking through the hedgerow instead of following the path back to the paddock. I stepped over the fence and walked over to where the runt was lying in the grass. He was still. I thought he had died in the few minutes it had taken me to run to the barn and back. Then he breathed. I knelt down on the ground next to him. I looked at his face. He was staring right at me. I could see fear, but I could also see, and perhaps I was imagining it, imploration. I believed he knew that he was dying, that he didn't want to die,

and that out of the depths of his eyes—barely distinguishable in shape, color, and richness from human eyes—he was asking me to help him, to keep him alive.

I picked him up. He squealed weakly. I slid him, snout first, into the carrier and picked it up. As I walked toward the fence line, it was hard to keep the carrier level. The runt was sliding back and forth. Then he started to moan. Though he was weak, it was a deep, forceful, plaintive moan. It lasted for a second or two, and then he stopped. Then he moaned again. He did it a few times as I approached and stepped over the fence and faced the paddock.

What I now saw and heard shocked me. All six of the big pigs had left the feed trough and were standing in a single, straight row inches away from the fence, grunting rapidly and rhythmically, in cadence with each other. I looked more closely at the pigs. Their snouts were up, sniffing. Their eyes were on me and the carrier. The runt moaned again. The big pigs increased the rhythm and volume of their grunts.

I knew that I was seeing something special, and I knew what it was. It was something that I had been taught is outside the realm of the lives of animals. It was

empathy, elicited by the plaintive moans of a herd mate. And not only were the pigs displaying empathy, they were communicating with the runt; their empathetic grunts rose and fell with the runt's moans. It was as if they were saying, "We hear you. We are with you."

I hurried back to the barn and put the runt on a bed of hay in an empty horse stall. I had no idea what to do to make him better. The only thing that I could think of was food and water, so I got a bucket of water and wet some grain. I held the mash in front of the runt's nose. He tried to raise his head, but it only came up an inch or two and then flopped back down. With my free hand, I raised his head up a bit and placed the feed in front of his snout. He took a few bites and then stopped, his snout resting heavily in my hand. I withdrew my hand and let his head down gently onto the hay.

I left him to go get a syringe to try and give him some water. Back in the stall, I placed the tip of the syringe against the side of his mouth and pressed very gently on the plunger so that only a drop or two of water came out. As soon as it touched his tongue the runt started licking. He was thirsty, so I squeezed out some

(continued)

more water. I held up his head again and offered him some more food. Just like before, he took a few bites and then stopped. This time, however, the way he stopped, midbite, I thought he had died. His eyes were closed. But, then he breathed. I realized he had passed out.

I left him for an hour. Then I fed him again and dribbled some water into his mouth. I fed and watered him every hour for a few days, and then every few hours for a few more days after that, and finally a few times a day, just like normal. Each time, he got stronger. After 10 days, he was healthy. His backbone no longer showed, nor did the curve of his ribs. When I entered his stall, he would leap up and run around, eager for his food, which he ate with gusto.

On the 11th day, I reunited him with the other pigs. For the next 4 months, I fed the runt separately from the other pigs to make sure that he was getting his fair share. As the runt ate, I rubbed his back and scratched him behind the ears. If I reached down and rubbed his belly, he would stand perfectly still, practically purring with pleasure.

Then one day, it was time. I struggled a little bit with having the runt killed, but I had committed to raising the animals for meat while providing them with a high level of welfare, even though that meant that they would be killed in the end. While I did not take that lightly, I was confident that what I was doing was okay. I believed that I was doing good— by the people who ate the pork because it was free from chemicals, and especially by the pigs, whose lives on factory farms are miserable.

The day of slaughter, the runt hopped right up into the trailer. The others had been apprehensive, but seeing the runt jump in put them at ease. One by one they lumbered up. I closed the trailer door and then drove off to the slaughterhouse. Two weeks later, I returned to the slaughterhouse to pick up the pork, neatly packaged and boxed up, which I distributed to myself and my customers after I got home.

Over the past 10 years, I have raised 2,000 pigs. During that time, I have witnessed many dis-plays of empathy. I have witnessed frustration, anger, joy, sorrow, and depression. I have seen pigs look at me with a knowledgeable wariness out of the corner of their eye. More than anything, I have seen, with my vision encompassing the attitudes, emotions, and behaviors of each of those 2,000 pigs as one whole, the entire range of what it means to be a pig. What I have found is that there is much, much more to being a pig than we generally admit. Pigs are *beings*, in the richest, most profound sense of the word.

After 10 years of raising pigs to kill them so that we can eat their meat, I am not going to do it anymore. I am not going to raise them. I am not going to kill them. I am not going to eat them. I am not going to eat flesh of any kind, as I have become a vegetarian. Those 2,000 pigs taught me that no matter how happy and carefree their lives might be, nor how quick and painless their deaths, it is not okay to kill them. Beings are sacred, and I know now that the panoply of beings is infinite.

How to "Adopt" from Farm Sanctuary

One of Farm Sanctuary's goals is to make everyone aware of the wonderful relationships that are possible between humans and other animals, and the benefits associated with these relationships.

Having a relationship with animals doesn't mean you have to build a barn or own a pasture, although some people do physically adopt our animals and bring them home. Instead, you can join our Adopt a Farm Animal Program, which allows you to provide care for a rescued farm animal even if you live in a small studio apartment in a city.

To adopt a farm animal, choose the type of animal who's right for you and complete the sponsorship registration form on the Farm Sanctuary Web site. By doing this, you will be making a yearlong commitment to a shelter animal. You will receive a certificate with a color photograph of your adopted friend, along with other benefits depending on the animal. You will also have visitation privileges and can even arrange to have a private tour to see your sponsored animal.

So far, more than 20,000 people have participated. Join in!

Liz, Nick, and Sebastian

Liz Dee is a fifth-generation candy maker. Her grandfather, already a second-generation candy man, emigrated from England in the 1940s and founded Smarties, the very successful hard-candy company. Liz attended Wesleyan University, where she met Nick Garon. Both of them went on to Columbia University for their graduate degrees. Five years ago, Liz joined the family business, where she is now co-owner and vice president of communications.

A few years ago, Liz was doing some research to determine whether Smarties were a vegan food, and that's what turned her into a full-time plant-based eater. The more she learned about veganism, the more she wanted to adopt the life-

How to Adopt an Animal in Your Home

SOME PEOPLE ARE LUCKY enough to have the space and the knowledge to bring home an adopted Farm Sanctuary animal. Our Farm Animal Adoption Network (FAAN) is a national farm animal rescue project that matches rescued farm animals with loving homes. The program has been in existence since 1986 and has helped arrange thousands of happy matches between wonderful animals and caring humans.

If you're interested, please go to the Farm Sanctuary Web site and complete an adoption application. You must meet certain qualifications, such as a commitment to animal protection and not eating animals, as well as having the income to provide rescued animals with proper care and housing plus references from qualified veterinarians. (You must also have access to an experienced farm animal veterinarian.) Certain other regulations and rules may also apply; see the Farm Sanctuary FAAN site for more information.

style. So in 2011, she did. (And Smarties, it turned out, are 100 percent vegan.)

A few weeks later, Nick, in a moment of nuptial solidarity, offered to become a vegan, too. He watched the documentaries *Forks Over Knives* and *Earthlings* and was soon committed for life. Not long afterward, Liz's parents watched *Forks Over Knives* and made the switch as well.

Liz and Nick first heard about Farm Sanctuary while watching *The Ellen DeGeneres Show*. They made their first visit in the summer of 2012, and the moment they learned about our adoption program, they signed up. Soon they'd adopted Little Peanut, a

"YOU PUT A BABY IN A CRIB WITH AN APPLE AND A RABBIT. IF IT EATS THE RABBIT AND PLAYS WITH THE APPLE, I'LL BUY YOU A NEW CAR."

—Harvey Diamond, Author

goat; Clementine, a chicken; Conrad, a cow; and Sebastian, a pig. They love them all, but Sebastian in particular. The moment they first met him, he rolled over for a belly rub as though they were already old friends. Liz and Nick also fell for their bright-orange chicken, Clementine, the bravest hen on the farm when it came to approaching humans.

Liz says the best part of adopting these

animals was that it made them more invested in all creatures. "Until we visited Farm Sanctuary, our interaction with farm animals was limited. We had no idea farm animals were just like companion animals—sweet, affectionate, and intelligent, with highly individual personalities. Because of these adoptions, we intend to visit Farm Sanctuary at least once a year to have more experience with our animals. It's really important to touch base with them—rather this than experience farm animals only on other people's plates."

Herschel and Ian

Samantha and Doug Robinson live in Tampa, Florida, with their 9-year-old son, Ian, and their 5-year-old daughter, Olivia. Five years ago,

Samantha's doctor told her she had high cholesterol and recommended she take statin medications. But Samantha's mother had read T. Colin Campbell's *The China Study* and shared it with Samantha, who decided to try a plant-based diet instead of drugs. It worked. In just a month, her cholesterol level dropped a remarkable 100 points. She soon became a vegan long term.

Samantha first heard about Farm Sanctuary when she saw a small ad for it online. She noticed that the Watkins Glen farm was near where her in-laws lived, so she and her family decided to visit. Ian was 4 at the time, and when Samantha read about the adoption program, she called ahead to say that she wanted to adopt an animal that Ian could play with during their visit.

Meanwhile, a very sweet sheep named Herschel arrived at Farm Sanctuary. One of our investigators, Dan D'Eramo, came upon a New York State farm where 70 animals were living in misery, with frozen water buckets and no food. Most of the animals were rescued, and many came to Farm Sanctuary, where animals like Herschel were lucky enough to find a loving home.

The first time Ian met Herschel was in the winter of 2009. When the sheep were being fed, all of them except Herschel scattered to go eat. He stayed behind, seeming to enjoy the attention of the little boy. Herschel remained by Ian's side in the barn for several minutes before leaving for his dinner.

In a short time, a magical bond was formed. The family now feels as close to Herschel as they do to their two rescue dogs. They keep in touch, and we've sent them photos of the sheep when he gets his hair cut or does something funny. They have photos of Herschel all over their house. Their nonvegan friends think it's a little odd, but Samantha says that their adopted sheep is a great opener for talking to others about animals in a new way. "Instead of nameless pork chops, we're talking about individuals whom we love and care about," says Samantha.

The Robinsons' relationship with Herschel has been so gratifying that they've adopted nine other animals, including Aflack, a duck; Fiona, a pig (who comes running whenever Ian calls her name across a field); Lily and Blitzen, cows; and five turkeys. The Robinsons travel to Watkins Glen at least twice a year to connect with their animal friends but particularly to see Herschel. Each time, Ian brings a new baseball cap to pose for a photo with his friend, whom he can pick out from far away in a pasture. Ian says, "Herschel comes when I call him, like a little puppy! I love him because he's sweet, nice, and woolly!"

Tony the Rooster

TONY WAS RESCUED and brought to live at our New York Shelter in November 2005. A Farm Sanctuary staff member had spotted the bantam rooster walking down the street near her home in New York City. She wasn't sure where he had come from, but she guessed he might have escaped from a nearby poultry market. She gently captured him and called Farm Sanctuary for help. A short time later, Tony arrived at our shelter. Although he had a bad case of leg mites, he was healthy and very friendly, and grew to love spending time with his caregivers. His favorite was Alan, an intern who became Tony's best friend. The two became inseparable—Tony loved to perch on Alan's shoulder, even when Alan was doing chores such as washing dishes. No one was surprised when Alan and his wife, Jo, a Farm Sanctuary staff member, applied to adopt him. In February 2006, they took Tony home to join their family. He made the successful journey from almost becoming someone's dinner to becoming someone's beloved companion.

Amy, Barclay, Santa, Charlotte, Baby Goat, and OTHERS

AT FARM SANCTUARY, we are fortunate to know people like Amy Schuchat and her husband, Barclay Prindle. Animal lovers, Amy and Barclay live at Home Farm in Sharon, Connecticut, where they share their 40 acres with various homeless and neglected animals.

Although the number keeps changing, today they can count 30 chickens, two ducks, five cows, two steers, three pigs, three horses, two donkeys, two goats, and a rooster—many of whom they adopted from Farm Sanctuary.

Amy first contacted us about 10 years ago after she heard from a friend that Farm Sanctuary had rescued two pigs who needed homes. Amy decided that pigs would be perfect for her backyard, so after being accepted as an adoptive parent, she took on Santa and Charlotte.

A few years later, Farm Sanctuary called Amy to see if she might take in two calves who needed homes. The steers, Amigo and Sasha, arrived as babies but today weigh about 1,700 pounds each.

Next came the goats. "We were expecting to take in just one goat, but we ended up taking in a second, very small one who's now known as Baby Goat." Amy said. "He had run away from a slaughterhouse and was picked up running down a road somewhere, so they put him on the trailer along with the others."

Then came more cows.

But as many animals as they've adopted, Amy knows that if another animal needs a home, there's likely more room in the pasture. And since her 13 cats, four dogs, and many ducks and chickens all get along with the other animals, all is peaceful. "I will never need antidepressants," Amy says, "because no matter what my day is like, as soon as I get to the backyard, I am level again."

In order to share their healing farm with others, Amy and Barclay invite special-needs children to visit every Thanksgiving. "The animals are so happy to see the kids, and the kids give back all the love they can. I just start crying," says Amy.

One day Amy and Barclay had a visit from a friend and his son, who was disabled and required a wheelchair. "My friend was worried that the cows might be clumsy, but his son wanted so much to see them that the man put him on his shoulders and we walked into the fields. The animals slowly came over to us. They were so careful, it was as if they knew how fragile this little boy was. They just stood there, so gentle, and let him pet them and hug them. I don't understand how, but they knew this was a fragile child. Watching him laugh and hug the animals was a memory I will never forget.

"The difference an animal can make in a human being's life is amazing."

TENET 3:
Engage in a Mindful Connection with Your Food

Too often, we Americans eat on the run—literally. It's common to see people dashing from one place to another, grabbing something on the way and wolfing it down as they go. I, too, am guilty of this, especially when I'm rushing to catch connecting flights at the airport. But I'm working on it.

This is not the way it should be. Our food is among the most intimate connections we make with the earth. Food contains life-sustaining nourishment and, as it courses through our bodies, the nutrients we ingest are absorbed into our very cells. To a major degree, we literally are what

we eat. So the source of our food matters. If we're consuming produce grown in rich, organic soil, our bodies will be nourished with a balanced complement of healthful vitamins, minerals, and micronutrients. Healthy soil yields healthy plants, and all of us benefit.

If, on the other hand, we consume foods grown on depleted soil with petrochemical fertilizer, pesticides, and herbicides, we miss valuable nutrients and ingest harmful chemicals. And if we eat factory-farmed animal products, we also swallow hazardous substances such as hormones,

antibiotics, and fecal pathogens. Did you know that chickens are routinely fed arsenic and cattle manure? I believe many of our nation's health problems can be traced directly to our sick food production system. We can't continue this way!

At Farm Sanctuary, we encourage people to eat mindfully. At all our special events, we serve wholesome food, and we aim to make our meals leisurely and celebratory: peaceful, delicious, and touched by happiness. The food is always vegan, but we welcome everyone to join us—vegans and nonvegans alike. (Vegans are glad they don't have to ask about the ingredients, while people who still consume animal products get to try amazing new dishes.)

This more conscious approach to food inevitably leads us to select more healthful, sustainable, and responsible ingredients. It helps improve our physical and mental well-being, and connects us to the source of our sustenance. It promotes local, seasonal choices that are nutrient rich and ecologically sound.

There are many other advantages to a conscious approach to food, including simple enjoyment. The more you're aware of your food, the more likely you are to take pleasure in its flavor, texture, and other qualities. A cool, juicy peach is refreshing on a hot summer day, while a hearty root vegetable soup provides warm comfort on cold winter evenings. Try it: Instead of wolfing down a quick meal, slow down and try to savor every ingredient, every seasoning, every flavor. Notice the texture as the food dissolves in your mouth. Mindful eating leads us to pause and appreciate real food, to live in the moment, and to

"I BECAME A VEGETARIAN BECAUSE WHEN I ATE THAT WAY I FELT BETTER PHYSICALLY, AND I COULDN'T STAND THE IDEA THAT I WAS, IN SOME SMALL WAY, SUPPORTING THE EXTREME CRUELTY OF FACTORY FARMING."

—CASEY AFFLECK, ACTOR

practice an engaged awareness that benefits our lives in so many ways.

One of the best ways to be mindful about food is to prepare and eat it with other people. At Farm

Famous Vegan Creations

WE ENCOURAGE RESTAURANTS and other food-related businesses to come up with new meals that are inventive and tasty. We root for plant-based places like Vegan Treats, the award-winning cupcake bakery in Bethlehem, Pennsylvania; Sticky Fingers, a Washington, DC, bakery and winner of the television show *Cupcake Wars*; and Vedge restaurant in Philadelphia, which recently won first prize on the cooking program *Chopped*. We're also excited about companies like Beyond Meat, whose plant-based "meat" was recently featured in a taste test on the *Today* show. (The hosts couldn't tell the difference between the plant-based meat substitute and animal meats.)

Sanctuary events, we work with caterers and chefs to develop wonderful vegan meals served in a caring, sanctuary setting. For many, these Farm Sanctuary meals are the first time they've seen and shared so many different kinds of plant foods—and with others, to boot. At our hoedowns, for example, we promote this experience by installing 60-foot-long tables that run the entire length of our People Barn. The air fills with the buzz of people excited to eat after a day out on the farm.

This kind of eating fosters community. People who are new to vegan living can sometimes feel isolated—especially if their friends are still meat-eaters—so breaking bread with others who aspire to this lifestyle makes for an engaging, empowering, and bonding experience.

Being a mindful eater means becoming aware of where your food comes from and how it was produced. If you are still eating animal products, pause to consider where these animals came from. How were they treated during their lives? How do you feel about that? Perhaps these thoughts will lead you to wonder more about why you eat animals in the first place and to make more plant-based choices.

Being a mindful eater also means eating slowly. It means eating socially. It means eating appropriately. And it means eating thoughtfully. As we've discussed, these steps not only lead to kinder and more emotionally fulfilling choices, but also better health. In other words, you are doing yourself a real favor when you eat mindfully.

Eating Slowly

Over the last decade, numerous scientific studies have concluded that eating slowly, with purpose, is more healthful. One such report, published in the *Journal of the Academy of Nutrition and Dietetics,* placed random test subjects in a specially designed room called a metabolic kitchen, which allowed the researchers to document each calorie the subjects consumed. Participants were instructed to eat a meal, with randomly selected individuals told to eat either more quickly or more slowly than usual. The results? The slow-eating group ate less, and they were also less hungry an hour after the meal.

At the Plaza

OUR FARM SANCTUARY DINNERS are festive and joyous, and they are also persuasive. As part of our outreach, we sometimes hold black-tie dinners. The very first of these was held at the Plaza Hotel in Manhattan in 2001. It was a magical event because that night, we debuted a selection of gourmet plant-based menu items created by a prestigious chef, Marc Felix. When we came to him and explained the kind of food we wanted to serve, his first response was skepticism. "We can't do that," he insisted. "We have a reputation to maintain!"

But because he's not just a great chef but also an open-minded person, Marc worked with us to create our vision. He became so enthusiastic that on the night of the dinner, he brought his entire kitchen crew—15 people—out on the stage to take a bow. And he announced that he would never again serve veal. Even better, Marc went on to give vegetarian cooking classes at the Whole Foods Market headquarters in Austin, Texas!

This also meant they were less likely to put on excess weight—another excellent reason to eat mindfully!

The reason for the seeming paradox of eating less and feeling more satiated is that it takes 20 minutes for the chemical process that creates a feeling of fullness to be completed. So when we spread our eating over a longer period, the mechanism that tells our body we've had enough to eat has had enough time to kick in, meaning we don't overeat.

If eating slowly is good, eating quickly is bad—and there's just as much data to prove it. For example, researchers in Japan studied the effects of eating quickly on body mass index (BMI) as well as a host of other health measures. Their experiment was similar to the one above. But instead of placing subjects in a lab and having them eat, researchers found subjects who regularly ate at one of five predefined speeds: very slow, relatively slow, medium, relatively fast, and very fast. After gathering their measurements, the scientists found that the slower the subjects ate, the lower their BMI was.

These same researchers conducted a similar study related to insulin resistance—the physiological precondition for diabetes—and found an almost identical correlation linking slow eating speed with better health measures.

For most of human history, obtaining food took time, effort, and cooperation. To run a self-sufficient farm required many hours of hands-on labor. Entire families of farmers worked the land, often joining with neighbors who pitched in to help.

That kind of farming was replaced by industrial agriculture, and our relationship to the land and animals changed. We exerted greater power and control over the natural world. Eventually factory farming became the dominant means of producing food, and along with it came a more callous attitude toward farm animals.

Luckily, the negative impacts of this approach are now widely condemned, and more traditional farming is making a comeback. It is encouraging to see a burgeoning interest in farmers' markets, community gardens, and community-supported agriculture (CSA), along with a growing popular interest in sustainable agriculture. In addition to consuming better food, people are becoming more engaged in growing it. Check out WWOOF-USA (wwoofusa.org), which connects organic farmers with volunteers willing to help out on their farms and who want a chance to learn about farming.

At Farm Sanctuary, we draw inspiration from the sustainable agriculture movement and incorporate its best elements into our own 21st-century farm community. As mentioned, one of these traditions is eating communal meals. As author Michael Pollan has written, "The shared meal elevates eating from a mechanical process of fueling

the body to a ritual of family and community, from the mere animal biology to an act of culture."

We encourage our visitors to cook communally when they return home. Picture it: Vegetables pulled from the very dirt you walk on are brought into the kitchen, cleaned, and rinsed off, exposing gorgeous natural colors and ripe, healthy shapes. Responsibilities are shared

"TURKEYS ARE AMONG THE MOST ABUSED ANIMALS ON EARTH. THE HORRORS THESE SMART, SENSITIVE BIRDS ROUTINELY ENDURE BEHIND CLOSED DOORS ON OUR NATION'S FACTORY FARMS, ALL SO THAT THEIR TORTURED BODIES CAN BE THE CENTERPIECE OF A HOLIDAY CELEBRATION ABOUT GRATITUDE, ARE APPALLING AND INCONGRUENT WITH MOST AMERICANS' VALUES OF COMPASSION."

—JOHN SALLEY, FOUR-TIME NBA CHAMPION AND WELLNESS GURU

among the group, and everyone gets to work performing the necessary tasks that will result in a stupendous home-cooked meal. Every step of the way, you become aware of the core elements of the meal. You can't help but notice each ingredient and wonder where it comes from if, like an exotic spice or unusual grain, it did not come from your own backyard. When the cooking process is over, each of those individual ingredients, some of them inedible in their natural state, come together to form one incredible whole: a big, healthful meal full of vegetables, legumes, and whole grains—the best food Mother Nature has to offer.

Preparing, cooking, and eating a communal meal can bring tremendous joy and satisfaction as you cooperate and converse. It also provides a larger perspective that exposes us to helpful information from others about food. As we harvest or purchase ingredients for the feast, it gives us an opportunity to learn more about where and how our food is grown. Finding and sharing recipes offers new ways to prepare and serve it. We can also discover fresh, seasonal foods and when and where they are available, be it a farmers' market, a neighbor's garden, or even on bushes or trees along your street.

When I run or ride my bike along the Potomac River near Washington, DC, in the summer, I often stop to pick mulberries along the path. Others see me reaching into the trees and nibbling the fruit, and some stop to enjoy the sweet berries as well. You can feel the warm sun in the fruit, and the juice turns your fingers purple as it trickles out. It is a delicious, nutritious snack—the original fast food.

There's a surprising amount of food to be found in suburbs and cities. The Web site fallingfruit.org maps the culinary bounty growing in cities around the globe. There are also urban farms where you can pick your own fruit and vegetables. The city of Seattle has even established a food forest, where people are encouraged to forage for free plums, apples, nuts, herbs, and berries. All of these local food experiences help people appreciate, and take comfort in, the abundance around us.

Jessie the Calf

IN 1986 WE STARTED our Adopt-a-Turkey project, through which people were able to save, rather than serve, a turkey on Thanksgiving. This program has become one of our most popular.

Twenty years ago we were driving across the country, bringing turkeys to homes and promoting the Adopt-a-Turkey program. As we were going through Colorado, we spotted a limping calf on the side of the freeway. Because the poor animal had fresh cuts and scrapes all over her body, we figured she had just escaped from a truck by jumping out of it. We stopped to rescue her.

As we were carrying her back to our van, a trucker came running down the highway. The man, who was on his way to the stockyards, had noticed the calf had disappeared and had pulled over to see if he could find her.

Even though we were driving a beat-up old van with Delaware license plates, we told the man we were animal officers and that the calf had a broken leg, so he couldn't sell her. Instead, we offered to take the animal off his hands.

"How much will that cost me?" he asked.

"Oh," we said, "we'll do it for free."

We then found a vet who was able to treat the calf, and, with her in back, we continued on our way to California. The calf, who was named Jessie, lived a long and happy life—although oddly, she did break her leg one other time. But she never had to jump out of a truck again.

Eating Thoughtfully

The next time you go out to eat, take a look around and notice if any young children are present at the restaurant. It's great to see multigenerational gatherings around meals. But today, it's far too easy to be distracted by smartphones and electronic games and to lose sight of the immediate present. If this occurs pre-mealtime, the implication is that eating is not important.

Eating *is* important. Too often we think of it as a task to be accomplished, rather than an activity in its own right. Starting now, try thinking more about your food—not just about eating it, but everything involving it. The first step you can take is to eat out less often. Stop relying on fast food and takeout. Instead, rely on yourself: Prepare your own food whenever possible. Shopping may not even be necessary. Just take a look at what's in the cabinet and imagine some different combinations. If you have a vegetable, a grain, and a protein, you may already have enough. If you have both canned and fresh foods, try combining them for a simple, quick meal. You can mix beans from a can with salsa or tomatoes, for example. One of my friends makes his meals interesting by combining prepared dishes with whatever he has around the house. He might buy a salad and then add in an avocado, nuts, or tofu. Dinner with him is always a bit of a scavenger hunt, and yet it always tastes good! (Using what you have on hand is also a great way to avoid wasting food.)

Another method: Pull out a cookbook. You may find it much simpler to prepare a home-cooked meal than you ever thought possible.

When your meal is ready, take time to appreciate it. Lay out a tablecloth if you have one. Place a pitcher of water on the table or light a candle. When serving the food, put out real dishes, not disposables (which are terrible for the environment). Arrange the meal on the plate in a way that is pleasing to you. You may decide to situate the different servings by color, flavor, or even shape. Remember, the more colors you see, the healthier that meal is likely to be and the better it will look. Become the Van Gogh of your dining room!

When you sit down to eat, clear the table of distractions. No books, newspapers, cell phones, or technology of any sort. Focus on the person you're with, or, if you are alone, focus on yourself. Use mealtime as a reflection period for the day. Give yourself time to just be, without doing, except to eat.

When you begin eating, focus your senses on that singular experience. Notice the food. Indulge in the smell of the freshly cooked ingredients.

Finally, take a bite, close your eyes, and focus on the flavors. They may be complicated, subtle, even surprising. Every bite has something to offer. This is the way food should be eaten—as an experience in and of itself, beyond just its nutritional value.

Consider the following:

"Eat only at the table, only sitting down. Never eat out of cartons. Use real plates and decent napkins, if you have them, to emphasize the seriousness of the activity. Eat slowly, chew properly. . . . Do not watch television or read the paper. Think only about what you are eating, smelling and savoring every bite. Practice putting down your utensils between every few bites, describing to yourself the flavors and textures in your mouth."

This sounds much like the Farm Sanctuary philosophy, but it's actually a quote from the international bestseller *French Women Don't Get Fat* by Mireille Guiliano. The evidence is strong and clear around the world that slow and mindful eating is good for us.

Sweety the Blind Cow

SWEETY, A BLIND COW, started her life at a Canadian dairy farm where she was kept on a concrete floor inside a bleak industrial building with no access to the outdoors. Once she was old enough to be impregnated, Sweety entered production. Like all dairy cows, she endured an unrelenting cycle of insemination, pregnancy, and birth, because in order to produce milk, dairy cows are forced to have a calf every year.

In large industrial farms, dairy cows are typically sent to slaughter after about 4 years in production. Sweety was kept on the dairy for 8 long years, which is unusual. After enduring several medical problems, she became emaciated, sick, and exhausted, and was slated for slaughter. The slaughter line is awful for all animals, but it is especially terrifying for those who are blind.

Then an animal rescuer named Rose heard about Sweety's plight and persuaded the dairy to spare the cow. Sweety soon arrived at Farm Sanctuary, where she met another of our rescued residents, Tricia. Tricia is a dairy cow who is also blind, saved from slaughter by a retired dairy farmer who sent her to Farm Sanctuary. When Tricia first arrived, we introduced her to Linda, a cow with a hip injury. Both cows had disabilities that kept them from living with our larger main herd, and they quickly befriended each other, forming one of the closest bonds we've ever witnessed. After Linda passed away from cancer, Tricia sadly mourned her friend. Companionship is profoundly important to cattle, so the hope was that Sweety might be able to take Linda's place.

Sweety was given a pen filled with fresh hay near Tricia and could immediately sense Tricia nearby. Tricia circled and mooed, eager to get acquainted. When it was time for the introduction, we led Sweety into Tricia's stall. Tricia was busy enjoying some hay, and it took her a moment to realize that the newcomer was beside her. As Sweety leaned in for a sniff, however, Tricia perked up and began investigating. Within moments, the two cows were gently nuzzling one another and sharing a meal. By evening, they were nestled together for a night of quiet comfort—and a beautiful new friendship had formed.

The Farm Sanctuary way of eating, then, honors the best traditions involving the way food is meant to be consumed. It benefits our health, our families, our communities, and the animals with whom we share the planet. I firmly believe that the more we think about our food, the more we consider what it is, where it comes from, and how we eat it, the more likely we are to choose a plant-based diet and a lifestyle that supports it. It just makes so much sense.

Farm Sanctuary Celebrations Menus

CELEBRATION FOR THE TURKEYS

Gourmet Vegan Menu

Watkins Glen, New York

HORS D'OUVRES

Roasted garlic and fava bean pâté on crostini with sun-dried tomato chutney

Curry poached potato stuffed with mushroom and roasted cauliflower ragout

Crackers and bread with artisan vegan cheese provided by Dr. Cow and Ste Martaen

STARTERS

Massaged red and green kale salad with roasted nuts and dried cranberries

Butternut squash soup

Rolls with vegan spread

ENTRÉE

Tofurky roast with cranberry chutney and caramelized onion gravy

Garlic mashed potatoes

Sautéed green beans with slivered almonds and bread crumbs

Roasted root vegetables with spinach leaves

Cranberry sauce

DESSERT

Pumpkin cheesecake with maple-walnut topping and vegan whipped cream

 farmsanctuary
rescue · education · advocacy

TENET 4:
Eat Plants . . . for Your Health

Here's a news flash: You don't need to eat animal foods to be healthy and strong! Consuming animal foods actually contributes to serious health problems. Our bodies are best suited to consume plant foods.

Biologically, humans are more like herbivores than carnivores. Carnivores have short intestinal tracts, which allow putrefying flesh to pass through them quickly. In contrast, humans have long, winding intestinal tracts. It can take days for meat, which is void of fiber, to make its way through. Can you imagine what a rotting piece of meat looks like after 48 hours in a moist 98.6-degree environment?

We don't have fangs or claws for tearing hide and flesh like carnivores, nor do we have the stomach acid for digesting meat. Our front teeth are suited for biting into fruits and vegetables, and our back teeth are designed for breaking down fibrous plant material. Carnivores' jaws move up and down like those of cats and dogs who also swallow large chunks of food. But vegetarian animals' and humans' jaws also move side to side to allow us to chew and grind plant foods. Finally, if we were natural meat eaters, we'd salivate at the sight of dead or injured animals—something few of us would ever do.

On the topic of cows' milk, do we really need to drink the milk of another species? Why not drink dogs' milk or gorillas' milk? Cows' milk is the perfect food for baby calves who will grow to weigh over a thousand pounds. It is not good for human infants or adults for that matter. Like other species, human babies are best suited to consume their own mother's milk.

Over the years, countless people have told me that by switching to a plant-based diet, they feel so much better. It's very satisfying to eat healthful food. It's delicious on your palate, and you can feel the goodness of the nutrients it contains. Unlike junk food, whole plant foods don't catch up with you later, making you feel bloated or nauseated. The food is good at the point of contact, and it continues to be good as it travels all the way through your system.

Eight Reasons Why a Plant-Based Diet Is the Most Healthful

I admire cardiologist Robert Ostfeld because he understands how important a plant-based diet is to overall health and preventive medicine. Rob received a bachelor's degree from the University of Pennsylvania, his medical degree from Yale

"THERE IS NOBODY THAT IS WILLING TO EAT A LIFELESS AND A DEAD THING AS IT IS; SO THEY BOIL IT, AND ROAST IT, AND ALTER IT BY FIRE AND MEDICINES, AS IT WERE, CHANGING AND QUENCHING THE SLAUGHTERED GORE WITH THOUSANDS OF SWEET SAUCES, THAT THE PALATE BEING THEREBY DECEIVED MAY ADMIT OF SUCH UNCOUTH FARE."

—PLUTARCH, GREEK HISTORIAN AND BIOGRAPHER

University, and a master of science in epidemiology from the Harvard School of Public Health. He then completed his medical internship and residency at Massachusetts General Hospital, and has practiced at New York's Montefiore Medical Center for more than 10 years.

Rob's diet was not always plant-based, but he made the switch after reading Dr. T. Colin Campbell's best-selling book *The China Study*. Then Rob decided to create a wellness program at Montefiore, where he counsels his patients to eat an exclusively plant-based diet. The program's success has been phenomenal. So far, more than 150 patients have joined the program, and many have seen extraordinary results in as little as 3 months. Some have lost more than 70 pounds; others have seen their LDL, or bad cholesterol, drop by up to 120 points.

I asked Rob to share his thoughts on the benefits of eating all plants, all the time. Here's his list. A plant-based diet:

1. **Protects your heart.** Heart disease is the leading cause of death for adult men and women in the United States. In fact, nearly two heart attacks occur each minute. By reducing and potentially reversing multiple risk factors for heart disease, a plant-based diet can profoundly lower your risk of having a heart attack. It may even shrink the cholesterol blockages already present in your blood vessels.

2. **Lowers blood pressure.** High blood pressure has been labeled the silent killer because, although you don't feel it, it can kill you. If you are a 55-year-old living in the United States, your lifetime risk of developing high blood pressure is about 90 percent. But a diet rich in vegetables and fruits can improve blood vessel health, make your arteries more flexible, and, in the process, may lower both your blood pressure and your risk of developing hypertension!

3. **Reduces your risk of developing diabetes.** Unfortunately, diabetes is common and increases your risk for a heart attack, stroke, kidney disease, erectile dysfunction, blindness, and other things you do not want. A plant-based diet can reduce your risk of developing diabetes and may even reduce or reverse it if you already have it.

4. **Reduces cancer risk.** Populations eating a plant-based diet have a reduced risk for a variety of cancers. Best-selling author and pioneering cardiac disease specialist Dr. Dean Ornish has published many studies that demonstrate a healthier diet can improve the prognosis for those with early prostate cancer. Other studies have demonstrated that animal protein can *increase* the spread of liver cancer.

5. **Protects your brain.** Alzheimer's disease and stroke can be devastating. By improving vascular function and reducing inflammation, a plant-based diet may reduce your risk for both.

6. **Improves bone health.** Animal products, including milk, may actually increase your risk for developing osteoporosis. Such products acidify the blood, which can leech minerals, including calcium, from your bones as your body tries to buffer that acid. A plant-based diet is more alkaline. Accordingly, studies demonstrate that plant-eaters have a decreased risk for osteoporosis.

Monet and Matisse

WE'LL NEVER KNOW HOW Monet and Matisse ended up at our New York farm—an anonymous rescuer left them there one night and then disappeared. But there was plenty of evidence to suggest where they had come from.

Monet and Matisse are Moulards, a breed of duck used by producers of *foie gras*, French for "fatty liver." *Foie gras* is created by force-feeding ducks large quantities of corn and fat through a pipe shoved down their throats over the course of 2 to 3 weeks, swelling each one's liver to 10 times its normal size. As they approach the point of slaughter, the birds increasingly struggle to walk and to breathe. They suffer lacerations and punctures from the feeding pipes. They choke on the feed or their own vomit. They contract foot and leg infections. Their other organs begin to fail. Many die before the period of force-feeding is complete.

When they showed up at our doorstep, Monet and Matisse were very young, but they had already been subjected to this type of abuse. Both arrived with sores on their bills from the feeding pipe. The cuts, scrapes, and broken feathers on their bodies testified to rough handling and lives spent in filthy, cramped enclosures used to hold struggling birds while feed is pumped into their bodies.

Monet and Matisse were so terrified when they arrived that it was difficult for us to get near them. Ducks rescued under other circumstances may be wary at first but eventually grow comfortable with occasional handling. Most *foie gras* ducks, however, never fully lose their fear of being touched and held by humans. Luckily, Monet and Matisse had already developed a lifelong friendship with each other that helped them feel secure—and they are beginning to trust humans, too.

Plant-Based, Protein-Packed Foods

NO MEAT MEANS NO protein, right? Wrong! The plant-based diet's staples offer rich, tasty, and easy-to-find sources of protein.

1. Whole grains. Whole grains high in protein include quinoa, spelt, wheat, bulgur, and brown rice.

2. Green vegetables. Good sources include broccoli, kale, spinach, peas, and lima beans.

3. Soy. Unprocessed soy foods, such as tofu or soybeans, are better than processed ones. Fermented soy foods, such as tempeh, may be best.

4. Nuts. Good sources include almonds and Brazil nuts.

5. Avocados. These delicious fruits are a surprisingly good source of protein.

6. Beans and legumes. Try lentils, chickpeas, and peanuts—yes, peanuts are actually a legume.

7. Hemp. Hemp seeds are a good source of protein. You can add them to cereals, salads, oatmeal, and smoothies.

8. Seeds. Pumpkin, sesame, sunflower, and poppy seeds are good sources of protein. You can eat them plain or sprinkled on foods.

9. Nondairy milks, including soy, almond, oat, and hemp varieties.

---

7. **Lowers cholesterol.** Elevated cholesterol has been called the key risk factor for heart disease. Our body needs cholesterol to function, but we make all we need ourselves. Animal products have cholesterol, and plants have essentially none. Hence, when you eat a plant-based diet, you absorb less cholesterol (and excrete more—thank you, fiber!). That can substantially lower your cholesterol level, even without medications.

8. **Encourages weight loss.** Obesity is obscenely common, and it is associated with multiple health risks. With its lower caloric density, a whole foods, plant-based diet can lead to substantial weight loss, especially when you limit oils.

We should also acknowledge that raising animals by the billions on factory farms creates a breeding ground for disease. The vast majority of antibiotics used in the United States are fed to farm animals to keep them alive and growing in these filthy, stressful conditions. This has led to the development of new diseases and virulent pathogens that are resistant to formerly life-saving drugs. Still, animals get sick, and yet surprisingly the USDA allows diseased animals to be killed and sold for human food.

A whole foods, plant-based diet is simply and clearly the healthiest way to eat. If I were to list all the advantages here, there wouldn't be room for anything else in this book. That's how much information medical science has uncovered

about the benefits of a vegan diet. And yet many people still believe that life-threatening diseases are simply a roll of the genetic dice—despite the fact that study after study has proven that consuming animal fats and proteins increases the risk of falling prey to diseases such as cardiovascular disease, diabetes, rheumatoid arthritis, and cancer.

Heart Disease

Let's look more closely at cardiovascular disease. Not long ago, the National Heart, Lung, and Blood Institute released a report based on the 10-year findings of its Cardiovascular Health Study. The study concluded that nearly all males older than 65 years and females older than 70 who had grown up eating a typical Western, animal-foods-based diet were suffering from

Plant-Based Foods with Calcium

CALCIUM IS IMPORTANT FOR healthy teeth and bones. You do not need to drink cows' milk to get it, however. In fact, many studies show that milk, which is acidic, actually leeches calcium from your body. Trade it for any of the foods below.

1. Green vegetables, such as broccoli, kale, arugula, and collard greens
2. Blackstrap molasses
3. Fortified nondairy milks, fortified orange juice
4. Almonds
5. Tempeh
6. Tahini

some form of heart disease, the advanced stages of which kill more Americans than the next four fatal illnesses combined.

This trend is very recent: At the turn of the 20th century, heart disease was low on the list of causes of death. By the mid-2000s, however, more than 3,000 per day were dying from heart disease in the United States. Every year, nearly one million Americans die as a result of cardiac complications—and one in two Americans ultimately dies from heart disease or stroke.

The primary cause of cardiovascular disease is a sticky deposit called plaque, which has a tendency to build up in arteries throughout the body, increasing blood pressure. Over time, plaque accumulation can narrow the arterial passageways through which our blood delivers vital nutrients and oxygen. If left untreated—or, more commonly, if the unhealthy habits that promote the buildup of plaque persist—blood vessels can close off completely and cause a heart attack.

The way most people address the condition is by taking medication, which dilates arteries to help the heart receive more blood, but they do little to attack the actual problem. Wider blood vessels, after all, simply mean more room for plaque to accumulate until the vessels inevitably close off. No medication can entirely reverse the buildup of plaque.

Far better than drugs is a plant-based diet. Animal-based products are chock-full of the worst building blocks for heart disease, namely LDL cholesterol (the so-called bad cholesterol) and greasy saturated fats. This lethal cocktail thickens your blood with the dangerous plaques that can rapidly stick to your silky-smooth artery linings. Blood saturated with animal pro-tein also irritates artery linings, causing them to become sticky, inducing the LDL cholesterol found in these foods to bore into your arteries. Attempting to heal itself, the body forms the equivalent of a pimple full of enzymes around the damaged artery, which in turn may burst as blood flows through it. The blood then rapidly clots; as the clot enlarges, it can cause a heart attack.

It's not surprising, then, that according to a 2010 report published in the *Annals of Internal Medicine*, consuming animal-based fats and proteins is directly correlated with increased rates of death. The study followed more than 85,000 women and nearly 45,000 men—all of whom were health care professionals without preexisting heart disease, cancer, or diabetes—for a period of 20 to 26 years. Each participant regularly filled out a questionnaire about his or her eating habits. The study's conclusion: "A low-carbohydrate diet based on animal sources was associated with higher all-cause mortality in both men and women, whereas a vegetable-based low-carbohydrate diet was associated with lower all-cause and cardiovascular disease mortality rates."

A recent National Cancer Institute study comprising 500,000 people found that those who had consumed 4 ounces or more of red meat each day were 30 percent more likely to have died than those who had consumed less. On the other hand, a team of Harvard researchers studying a group of 110,000 people for 14 years discovered that those who averaged eight or more servings of fruits and vegetables per day were 30 percent less likely to suffer from a heart attack or stroke than those who consumed a predominantly animal-based diet.

Perhaps the best evidence for a vegan diet

(continued)

Opie

OPIE WAS BORN ON a dairy farm and was quickly sent to the Bath, New York, stockyard. It was a freezing morning, and the poor calf was still wet from birth. He suffered hypothermia, collapsed in an alleyway, and was left to die.

When we noticed him, Opie was practically comatose, unable even to lift his head. I asked the stockyard worker about Opie's future, and he replied that as soon as the animal died, he'd bury him. I offered to take the dying calf off the worker's hands and save him the trouble, and he agreed.

I took Opie to a veterinarian, who said that treating him made no economic sense, especially after she tried taking his body temperature and found that it was so low it didn't register on the thermometer. I explained that Opie wasn't an economic investment and that we just wanted to do what was right for him. The veterinarian reluctantly agreed to treat the calf and gave him IV fluids, although she said he had less than a 5 percent chance of survival.

Then we brought Opie to Farm Sanctuary and kept a 24-hour watch, monitoring his temperature and fluid intake, hoping he'd recover. He did. His body slowly warmed up to normal temperature, his eyes began to flicker with life, and his breathing became steady.

Within a couple of days, Opie was eating well and showing signs of curiosity about the world around him. He had regained a degree of physical well-being, yet there was something missing. He wasn't energetic and playful like other calves. Then it dawned on us that Opie needed to be with other cows, so we brought him to the cow barn, where the others welcomed him enthusiastically. As they gathered around his pen, mooing and nuzzling him through the fence, Opie perked up and within minutes, he was happy—he started bucking and kicking up his heels.

Opie grew into a gentle giant, weighing nearly 3,000 pounds, and enjoyed a happy, 18-year life at Farm Sanctuary. A peaceful soul, he became a favorite of cows and humans alike.

comes from *The China Study*, which reveals the results of a 3-year investigation into the dietary habits and health of 6,500 Chinese in 65 rural villages. One startling finding: American men were 17 times more likely to die of heart disease than rural Chinese men. An even more dramatic discovery: In the most isolated regions of China, where residents ate only plant-based diets, researchers could not identify a single victim of heart failure among more than 100,000 people. Ironically, as millions of Americans eating a typical animal-based diet are desperately trying to lower their cholesterol with a battery of expensive prescription drugs, the cholesterol level for participants in the China Study was low, averaging between 81 and 135.

"TO PROTEST ABOUT BULLFIGHTING IN SPAIN, THE EATING OF DOGS IN SOUTH KOREA, OR THE SLAUGHTER OF BABY SEALS IN CANADA, WHILE CONTINUING TO EAT EGGS FROM HENS WHO HAVE SPENT THEIR LIVES CRAMMED INTO CAGES, OR VEAL FROM CALVES WHO HAVE BEEN DEPRIVED OF THEIR MOTHERS, THEIR PROPER DIET, AND THE FREEDOM TO LIE DOWN WITH THEIR LEGS EXTENDED, IS LIKE DENOUNCING APARTHEID IN SOUTH AFRICA WHILE ASKING YOUR NEIGHBORS NOT TO SELL THEIR HOUSES TO BLACKS."

—PETER SINGER, PHILOSOPHER

This may be all well and good for people lucky enough to have been raised on a plant-based diet, but what about those of us who have eaten meat our entire lives—is it too late to reverse the damage?

Happily, the answer is a resounding no. An extensive 2-year study by Caldwell B. Esselstyn Jr., MD, the internationally renowned surgeon, researcher, and clinician at the Cleveland Clinic, has shown how a plant-based, whole foods diet can not only prevent heart disease but reverse it. After 5 years on Dr. Esselstyn's diet, the average cholesterol level of his group—all of whose members started the study with advanced coronary heart disease—dropped from a dangerous 246 to a healthy 137. Moreover, of 17 patients who had previously suffered from 49 separate cardiac events, not a single participant experienced heart failure in a 12-year period after starting Dr. Esselstyn's plant-based program.

What makes a whole foods, plant-based diet so effective?

First and foremost, this way of eating naturally minimizes intake of fat and cholesterol, which are the cornerstones of heart disease. Without this plaque-producing cocktail inundating your bloodstream with every meal, over time the body's natural healing processes can stabilize and gradually metabolize existing plaque buildup. And because a pure plant-based diet contains healthy unsaturated fats, protein, and antioxidants, it helps reduce cholesterol and allows arteries and other blood passageways to relax naturally.

Simply by eating fewer animal products, you can improve your health.

Avoid heart disease. Don't eat animals!

Unexpected Health Benefits of Eating Plants

According to Dr. Ostfeld, many recent studies examining the plant-based diet have found that several unexpected health benefits may arise. Here are six of them.

1. **Improved athletic performance.** By improving the efficiency of the body's mitochondria, which enable the body's ability to produce energy, plant foods can lead to higher achievement in sports. (Carl Lewis, the champion Olympian, did his best times on a vegan diet.)

2. **Healthier joints.** In general, there are two types of arthritis. The more common, wear-and-tear kind is called degenerative arthritis, or osteoarthritis. The autoimmune kind, in which the body attacks itself, is called rheumatoid arthritis. A plant-based diet may be helpful to both types. It's thought that the reduced inflammation and weight loss prompted by decreased meat consumption help prevent or relieve degenerative arthritis. And the same reduction in inflammation, plus the changes to our gut flora when we eat only plants, may decrease our immune system's propensity to attack our joints and thereby reduce both the incidence and symptoms of rheumatoid arthritis.

3. **Improved sexual function for men and women.** Up to 40 percent of men age 40 and older—and up to 70 percent of men 70 and older—have some degree of erectile dysfunction. Achieving an erection is a psychological, neurological, and vascular event. So by improving blood vessel health, a diet high in vegetables, fruits, nuts, and beans may also improve erectile function. Similarly, several studies have also shown that a plant-based diet can improve sexual satisfaction in women.

4. **Improved lung function.** Asthma and chronic obstructive pulmonary disease (COPD) are two common forms of lung disease. People with asthma have increased airway reactivity and may become dangerously short of breath in the face of a variety of lung irritants. A diet rich in vegetables and fruits, with their high concentration of antioxidants and ability to reduce inflammation, has been associated with both a lower incidence of asthma and improved lung function in those with the disease. COPD, commonly found in smokers, can also lead to profound shortness of breath and a reduced quality of life. Of course, quitting cigarettes is most important here, but a diet rich in antioxidants can improve COPD, too.

5. **Less constipation.** Animal products contain no fiber. Plant products have plenty. Fiber keeps our system moving and can help relieve constipation. Consequently, a vegan diet is associated with a higher frequency of bowel movements compared with diets composed mainly of meat and dairy foods.

6. **Better-looking skin.** Who doesn't want to improve their appearance? Numerous studies have shown that a plant-based diet full of nutrients called carotenoids may improve skin health. It may even help with acne!

I'll add a seventh health benefit: a happier you. Several studies have demonstrated that a diet high in fat and animal protein may be linked to depression. One of them, published in *Nutrition Journal* in 2011, showed that vegetarians had significantly fewer negative emotions than omnivores.

Strokes

Next let's consider another cardiovascular disease. Strokes often occur with few to no warning signs and result in death nearly 25 percent of the time for the 700,000 Americans who suffer from them annually. A stroke is similar to a heart attack, but it affects the brain—typically in one of two ways. The first type, known as ischemic stroke, is the result of plaque narrowing the arteries leading into the brain and causing a clot that eventually cuts off bloodflow. The second type, hemorrhagic stroke, occurs when an artery leading to the brain ruptures entirely, which can suddenly halt bloodflow and cause oxygen-starved nerve cells in the brain to die.

Although strokes can be massive and sudden like a heart attack—full-blown strokes commonly cause paralysis and death—they can just as frequently be small and imperceptible. These ministrokes, known as TIAs (transient ischemic attacks), can last from 1 to 24 hours, slowly but surely ravaging the brain by sapping vital oxygen and killing off nerve endings that control everything from fine motor function to memory.

As with heart disease, a predominantly animal-based diet inundates the blood with grease, fat, and cholesterol. These bad guys promote the buildup of either large plaques that gradually narrow arterial walls until they close up entirely or smaller plaques that can suddenly rupture and create a clot. Keeping your blood pressure at safe levels is the most effective way to prevent stroke, but an animal-based diet composed of meat, dairy, and eggs can raise blood pressure in two significant ways. First, the saturated fats so prevalent in animal products thicken the blood, which invariably increases blood pressure, especially when arterial walls are already constrained with plaque. And second, animal products can be high in sodium, which has the effect of forcing the body to retain excess fluid—again, causing an increase in blood pressure.

Can a plant-based diet reduce the risk of stroke, just like it does heart disease? Yes, as proven by the Framingham Heart Study, a 60-year, ongoing investigation into the dietary habits of 5,209 men and women in the town of Framingham, Massachusetts. Since 1948 participants have regularly undergone detailed physicals, blood tests, and lifestyle interviews to help scientists better understand the causes of heart disease, stroke, cancer, diabetes, and other chronic diseases. These researchers discovered that a typical animal-based diet drastically increased the risk of stroke, but that a proper plant-based program reduced that risk by 22 percent for every three additional servings of fruits and vegetables consumed daily. Furthermore, according to a 10-year study presented on behalf of the American Heart Association, female survivors of stroke could significantly minimize their future risk simply by consuming higher proportions of carrots, spinach, and other fruits and vegetables.

Avoid strokes. Eat a plant-based diet!

Cancer

Then there's cancer, the second-leading cause of death each year in the United States. According to the American Hospital Association, cancer will surpass heart disease as the number one cause this decade. A quarter of all Americans will die from it. In 2011, cancer killed 1,500 people a day.

Cancer begins at the microscopic level, as billions of cells are born, grow, divide, and die—over and over and over. Occasionally, cells may mutate due to chemical, environmental, or nutritional factors. These mutated cells then divide incessantly, spreading throughout the body as they clump together to form tumors, destroying tissue and sapping vital nutrients.

There's a widespread misconception that one's likelihood of developing cancer is predicated entirely on genes. Your vulnerability to the disease depends only partly on genetics. Certain cancers, like lung cancer or colon cancer, are commonly the result of specific environmental factors such as smoking or eating meat. Your diet and lifestyle make a difference.

The reality is that cancer cells flourish on specific ingredients: meat, dairy, eggs, oils, tobacco, processed sugars, and alcohol. Most animal-based products are riddled with saturated fats and are high in calories. That combination encourages cell

Eight Plants
WITH UNEXPECTED HEALTH BENEFITS

1. Avocados may help prevent birth defects. They contain a high level of folate, an important B vitamin that combats a common condition called neural tube defect.

2. Beans can be a benefit to those with diabetes. They are highly nutritious but low on the glycemic scale, so they don't cause blood-sugar spikes.

3. Flaxseeds can improve women's health. They reduce the risk of breast cancer by safely metabolizing estrogen and can reduce hot flashes in menopausal women. Flax can even help regulate the menstrual cycle.

4. Kale is great for detoxing. Its high fiber and sulfur content supports the health of your liver.

5. Swiss chard contains more vitamins and antioxidants than nearly any other plant. Its nutrient contents include omega-3 fatty acids, B folates, copper, sodium, potassium, iron, manganese, calcium, phosphorous, and vitamins A, C, and K. It also helps fight colon and prostate cancer.

6. Beets improve sexual vitality. They contain high levels of boron, which is linked to the production of human sex hormones.

7. Celery can relieve joint pain. It's a natural anti-inflammatory.

8. Arugula is loaded with nutrients and has been recommended as a performance enhancer for athletes, without any negative side effects.

division in both healthy and cancerous cells. This means that microscopic cancer cells that might ordinarily take decades to manifest themselves into tumors can reproduce and spread far more rapidly.

An 8-year study that followed more than half a million individuals, conducted in association with the AARP (American Association of Retired Persons), revealed that older individuals who frequently consumed meat were far more likely to develop specific cancers including those of the lung, esophagus, liver, and pancreas.

Dairy products in particular generate a potentially carcinogenic hormone known as IGF-1, which can radically alter the body's hormonal balance. In women, it can escalate estrogen levels, and high estrogen is linked to breast and ovarian cancers. In men, IGF-1 can increase testosterone levels, which can promote prostate and testicular cancers.

Eggs contain an abundance of cholesterol and animal proteins. These proteins tend to create an acidic environment in the bloodstream that can promote the division of cancerous cells. A 20-year study published in the *Journal of the American Medical Association* found that women who consumed eggs 3 or more days a week were three times more likely to die from ovarian cancer than women who consumed less than one egg weekly. Even egg whites, supposedly a healthy alternative, rank among the most concentrated forms of animal protein.

Can a plant-based diet truly help prevent cancer? Yes. Besides lacking cholesterol and animal protein, a proper plant-based diet is free of the other ingredients that can cause cancerous muta-

"GOD LOVED THE BIRDS AND INVENTED TREES. MAN LOVED THE BIRDS AND INVENTED CAGES."
—JACQUES DEVAL, FRENCH PLAYWRIGHT AND DIRECTOR

tions: processed sugar and fatty oils. Studies routinely prove that when fats exceed 15 percent of our daily caloric intake, the likelihood of developing cancer increases. Unlike a typical Western diet, a plant-based lifestyle cuts out the high-fat oils and sugary, processed foods on which cancer cells thrive.

Furthermore, a healthy plant-based lifestyle doesn't just cut out the ingredients that cause cancer—it can actively ward off cancer. Fruits, vegetables, legumes, and leafy greens are loaded with fiber and phytochemicals that promote healthy, normal cell division and encourage regular bowel movements. Bowel movements, in turn, remove toxins and carcinogens through the digestive tract. In addition, a plant-based diet contains an abundance of antioxidants that help neutralize dangerous free radicals that can cause cancerous mutations in cells.

Avoid cancer. Go vegan!

A plant-based diet can help prevent more than just these three diseases. There's also evidence that it can help you avoid Alzheimer's disease. At the 2000 World Alzheimer's Congress, researchers released the results of a study showing that on average, "people who remained free of any form of dementia had consumed higher amounts of beta carotene, vitamin C, vitamin E, and vegetables than the people in the study who developed Alzheimer's."

Similarly, the United States is facing a dramatic increase in type 2 diabetes. But research has

(continued on page 76)

Susie Loves Larry

OVER HER 15 YEARS at Farm Sanctuary, our national shelter director, Susie Coston, has mentored hundreds of other sanctuary directors and workers across the country. In this role, she teaches them how to provide the best care for rescued farm animals. Nobody understands animals better than Susie. She loves them, and they love her—which is why she shares her home with nine cats, two dogs, and various farm animals who need special care. In addition to providing them healing and love, Susie helps their personalities come to life. She's always full of engaging stories. Here's one.

Although I'm fond of all the animals, most of my strongest relationships have been with cattle. I never would have expected that—my background was in caring for pigs. And of all the cattle I've known, my truest love was Larry, a 3,000-pound steer.

Larry wasn't the head of the herd; he wasn't the most beautiful or the most outgoing; he didn't stand out in any way. But he and I became remarkably close. He was gentle, he was kind, and he had this wonderful, almost silent moo—like a whisper.

It's hard to explain why you become so close to certain animals. It's like explaining human relationships—who understands them? A few of the creatures you may never bond with, but they'll develop a close relationship with another staff member. Some are so frightened of people you have to love them from a distance. Some, though, become yours. When they do, they look forward to seeing you as much as you do them. And you can't just pick one out. The process has to be mutual: You love them, they love you. It just happens—as it does with any friends.

I loved Larry.

All spring and summer, the cattle are regularly rotated between pastures. One time, I had been off for a weekend, and when I returned, I went to see the cattle herd. Even though there were dozens of cows in front of me, I knew immediately that Larry wasn't there. It turned out someone had left him in the wrong pasture. I yelled his name. Despite his tiny little moo, I could hear it from far away, and when I found him all the way up the hill, he was so excited to see me that he started to bound around, bouncing his head back and forth, feet springing off the ground.

Whenever we spent time together, he would rub himself all over me and lick me, and I would scratch his chin. He used to rest his massive head on my head or on my shoulder. He was just so happy that we were together. They buck when they're that excited. I was almost ready to buck, too.

A few years ago, Larry, then 18, began to falter. He could no longer walk, and he developed hip degeneration. Even on the highest doses of pain medications, he was having trouble. We knew that as his hips broke down, he would have more and more difficulty getting up, and that eventually we'd have to put him down.

On the last day of our life together, one of the caregivers heard him grinding his teeth, as cattle do when they're in severe pain and distress. Even with assistance, he could not get up. He was done.

I called the veterinarian, and she came right over. She gave him an injection, and he lay there with his head on my lap and basically fell asleep, forever, as we cried over his dormant body.

As he fell into his final rest, I flashed on all the wonderful memories Larry and I had together. I pictured him nuzzling me, looking for me when I was walking to find him, and I remembered how he always walked alongside me up a hill—never behind me or ahead of me. Always right next to me.

While we were still sitting with Larry, another steer named Kevin came up and licked him. Cattle mourn the loss of one of their own, and, in Larry's case, they surrounded him in death, quietly paying their respects. Kevin was Larry's best friend and the head of the cattle herd. When, late in life, Larry developed heart issues and had to be pulled from the main herd and placed in the special-needs cattle section, Kevin would reach over the fence that separated the two groups and lick him. They stayed·close. Eventually Kevin lost his position and stopped traveling with the group, so we moved him to our special-needs area, too—next to Larry. He'd spend all day across the fence from his friend, so eventually we let him move in.

Kevin died just 8 months after

Larry. One day he was fine, the next he had an aneurysm and passed away. I want so much to think that Larry and Kevin are together again, playing, caring for each other, and being the friends they always were. Even more, I picture myself with them someday—I dream about that all the time. Perhaps after I die, I'll have this same job, but whether it's where it's warmer or cooler, I don't know. I just hope we are all together.

shown that people who consume a diet centered on healthy, high-carbohydrate plant foods have the lowest rate of diabetes in the world. Moreover, Neal Barnard, MD, president of the Physicians Committee for Responsible Medicine and author of *Dr. Neal Barnard's Program for Reversing Diabetes*, has demonstrated that a simple plant-based diet can prevent, control, and even reverse the disease.

There are many other medical problems that a plant-based diet can address. The facts are clear: A low-fat, plant-based diet is the ticket to good health.

TENET 5:
Eat Plants . . . for the Health of the Earth

Two degrees Celsius; 565 gigatons; 2,795 gigatons. According to longtime environmental activist Bill McKibben, these are the three most fundamental statistics when it comes to global warming and climate change.

The first figure is the maximum number of

degrees the earth's atmospheric temperature can safely rise before catastrophic climate change and more intense natural disasters occur around the world.

The second figure is the maximum amount of oil we can safely extract from the earth's crust before our atmosphere rises by 2 degrees Celsius or more.

The third figure is the amount of untapped oil currently owned by the globe's major oil companies, which must remain in the earth to avoid catastrophic climate change.

These numbers paint a dire picture: If we don't drastically reduce our greenhouse gas emissions by burning less fossil fuel, then droughts, hurricanes, floods, tsunamis, and other extreme weather events are likely to be more intense and frequent—transforming the earth's climate as we know it.

As McKibben warns, energy companies are preparing to extract nearly *five times* the amount of oil it would take to raise the earth's temperature well beyond 2 degrees. Since it's virtually unthinkable that major corporations will voluntarily abandon reserves they've already paid for and could make money from, aren't the calamitous effects of climate change a certainty? After all, we citizens have no direct control over oil and gas companies and their incessant thirst for profit. So how can we possibly prevent this major source of global emissions from being extracted?

We can control what we eat.

Food production has a giant "carbon footprint" that we can help shrink. Scientists calculated McKibben's figures assuming the world's other sources of greenhouse gases remain constant. And according to the Food and Agricultural Organization (FAO) of the United Nations' 2006 report

"Livestock's Long Shadow," the livestock sector is among the "top two or three most significant contributors to the most serious environmental problems," including climate change. Animal agriculture is responsible for more greenhouse gas emissions than the entire transportation industry with all cars, trains, boats, and planes combined.

So even though eating isn't as dramatic as rising up en masse against the oil companies, we can actually change the math of climate change simply by adopting a vegan diet. The livestock industry represents a significant proportion of the emissions we create, and we can choose not to support it. So if you're looking to reduce greenhouse gas emissions, look no further than your dinner plate! A 2008 *New York Times* article entitled "Rethinking the Meat-Guzzler" found that it took 16 times more fossil fuels to produce a meat meal than a vegetarian meal.

Scientists from various disciplines have been making progress on ways to replace fossil-fuel-based power sources and modes of transportation—and perhaps, someday, everything will run on solar, wind, and other cleaner forms of energy. On the other hand, the world's demand for meat and dairy is increasing along with its human population. Global meat production is expected to double, from 229 million tons in 2001 to nearly 465 million tons by 2050. Milk output is projected to nearly double, from 580 to 1,043 million tons.

This is not good. The FAO's 2013 report estimates that 14.5 percent of total global greenhouse gas emissions is a direct result of the livestock industry. This figure includes the various energy-intensive activities that are required to sustain the world's demand for dairy and meat: the production and processing of food for livestock, such as corn and grain (45 percent of the industry's total emissions); outputs of greenhouse gases (primarily methane) during digestion by cows and other ruminants (39 percent of emissions); manure decomposition (10 percent of emissions); and transportation and meat processing (6 percent).

The FAO's estimate of 14.5 percent is actually considered conservative by many experts. They place a much higher percentage of blame on animal agriculture. For instance, researchers at the World Bank and the International Finance Corporation (IFC) suggest that the FAO's number is missing some key factors: CO_2 produced by livestock respiration; understated methane emissions; and deforestation required to open new land on which to feed animals for slaughter. Because trees absorb CO_2, deforestation reduces the earth's capacity to store carbon dioxide.

After considering these factors, World Bank and IFC scientists have estimated that livestock contribute 51 percent of global greenhouse gas

emissions. This means more than *half* of the problem is the result of what we're putting in our stomachs. Just think about that the next time a friend tells you she can't decide whether she should order the veggie burger or the double patty bacon cheeseburger.

Clearly it's a matter of scientific fact, not opinion, that consuming animals—especially in the current industrialized fashion—is terrible for the environment. But the emissions caused by animal agriculture are only one aspect of the problem. Equally important is how much of the vast resources we currently spend to raise, kill, and transport animals could be better employed elsewhere.

Reclaiming the Land

Besides being cooler, what would our world look like if we weren't exploiting animals for food?

Less crowded, for one thing. The clearest example of livestock's effect on our environment is the space they inhabit. Although we take their presence for granted, livestock didn't exist in such great numbers until very recently. Today, an unprecedented 35 percent of the ice-free surface area of the earth is devoted to rearing livestock or growing their food. That's more than one-third of the planet! A Cornell University study found that in the United States, about 32 million acres of land are used to grow vegetables, rice, fruit, potatoes, and beans for human consumption. Yet 746 million acres are devoted to grazing and growing food for livestock—that's about 23 times more land devoted to feeding farm animals.

The United States isn't alone. In South America's Amazon Basin, nearly 70 percent of deforested land is used for grazing. In the process, delicate and complex forest ecosystems are being destroyed, and the toll of excess carbon dioxide in the atmosphere is being exacerbated.

Some people ask: Wouldn't promoting a plant-based diet only intensify deforestation? Wouldn't more trees have to be cut down to make more room to grow crops? Absolutely not. Plant-based agriculture is inherently more efficient and requires fewer resources than animal agriculture.

Nearly 260 million acres of land in the United States have been appropriated to grow feed for farm animals. More than 70 percent of all corn and more than 90 percent of the soybeans grown are devoted to feeding animals for slaughter. An estimated 80 percent of agricultural land is exploited either to graze or grow food for livestock.

A 2005 report in *New Scientist* estimated that while driving a hybrid car could save about 1 ton of CO_2 emissions per year, adopting a vegan diet in place of a comparable animal-based diet would save nearly 1.5 tons. That's a 50 percent additional savings! Meat, milk, and eggs have between a 4:1 and 54:1 energy input-to-protein output ratio; in other words, the process of

"NOTHING WILL BENEFIT HUMAN HEALTH AND INCREASE THE CHANCES FOR SURVIVAL OF LIFE ON EARTH AS MUCH AS THE EVOLUTION TO A VEGETARIAN DIET."

—ALBERT EINSTEIN, NOBEL PRIZE-WINNING THEORETICAL PHYSICIST

harvesting food to feed animals reared for slaughter is significantly less efficient than harvesting the same crops for human consumption directly.

Studies have also shown that people sustaining themselves on animal products require ten times more land than those who simply grow vegan food. An average *family* in Bangladesh eating a diet of fruits, vegetables, rice, and beans uses less than an acre of land to fulfill its dietary needs. The average American *individual* requires 20 times that amount of land, largely because of the 270 pounds of meat he or she consumes annually.

Water

Then let's consider water use. Water is a precious and increasingly scarce resource that is emerging as a major global issue. Experts are predicting a decline in the availability of clean water, a major and fundamental problem that may soon be the subject of international conflict. Best-selling author and environmental activist John Robbins has calculated that it takes 60, 108, 168, and 229 pounds of water to produce 1 pound each of potatoes, wheat, maize, and rice respectively. A liter of milk? Some 2,200 pounds. A pound of beef? More than 20,000 pounds.

An average North American hog farm with 80,000 pigs consumes nearly 75 million gallons of fresh water each year. A larger farm, which might have a million or more pigs, needs as much water as a city. And what about burgers? The US Environmental Protection Agency (EPA) estimates that 1 pound of processed beef requires 2,464 gallons of water to produce. Contrast that with the 250 gallons required per pound of soy or 25 gallons per pound of wheat. Moreover, the EPA concluded that livestock consume water in amounts roughly equal to the total consumed by every other water user in America.

How many farm animals are gobbling up all these resources? In 2014, there were more than 17 billion livestock on this earth, just about triple the human population. According to the United States Geological Survey, 13 percent of this nation's fresh water is used for domestic activities including showers, baths, toilets, and so on. Approximately 40 percent is used solely for the purposes of irrigating crops raised for livestock consumption. With the 2,464 gallons needed to produce just 1 pound of beef, you could take a 7-minute shower every day for 6 months.

A few years ago, the Stockholm International Water Institute teamed up with researchers from the FAO and the International Water Management Institute to quantify the effect of all these animals on the world's water supply. They predicted that, given the projected growth of the world's population by two billion people, in 2050, continued livestock production will cause intense competition for water. Though the report's figures seem dire, the researchers also note that a solution is within reach. While animal protein currently accounts for 20 percent of most people's diets, we could feed these two billion added mouths by dropping the proportion to 5 percent while still saving water. In other words, shifting only 15 percent of the calories we now get from meat to plant foods could drastically alleviate the pressure on our water supply.

Waste

Exhausting our natural resources is one problem. Poisoning them is another. Many of the vast tracts of land harvested exclusively for animal feed are riddled with the pesticides and fertilizers

used to grow GMO (genetically modified organism) crops as rapidly as possible. Unfortunately, many of these man-made chemicals seep into groundwater and eventually flow into rivers and oceans, generating toxic plumes that kill native plants and animals and threaten natural ecosystems. Industrial-scale farming has also depleted our nation's rich topsoil, leaving it devoid of healthy microbes, nutrients, and other organic matter.

Meanwhile, the billions of animals exploited every year produce enormous amounts of manure and urine, which in turn pollute our environment. In the United States alone, we produce annually nearly 2.7 trillion—yes, *trillion*—pounds of manure, or 5 tons of waste per animal. That's ten times more waste than is produced by all American humans combined. A single dairy cow produces more than 100 pounds of waste every day. Animal excrement significantly alters the pH levels of water sources because livestock are typically reared in extremely concentrated numbers in feedlots and at factory farms. Their waste is also a source of pathogens, including antibiotic-resistant bacteria, which have been found in groundwater downstream from factory farms. It also contains the antibiotics and other toxic chemicals, like arsenic, that are fed to farm animals to promote growth rates.

So what happens to all that waste? Some of it is spread on fields, which can create runoff that poses a threat to the environment. Often, to store vast quantities of the waste that the land cannot absorb, farmers build so-called lagoons that, in theory, hold the waste and prevent its spread. But they often leak, overflow, or burst. In 1995, for instance, 25 million gallons of manure and urine spilled from a North Carolina manure lagoon into the New River, killing 10 million fish and devastating nearly 365,000 acres of coastal wetlands. In addition, the waste from factory farms emits plumes of harmful gases, particularly ammonia, methane, and hydrogen sulfide. It is estimated that animal farms are responsible for 73 percent of ammonia released into the air each year, which can interact adversely with other atmospheric gases to cause acid rain, smog, and respiratory problems.

Biodiversity

Possibly the most chilling effect of the livestock industry alters our planet in ways that change its

"IT SHOULDN'T BE THE CONSUMER'S RESPONSIBILITY TO FIGURE OUT WHAT'S CRUEL AND WHAT'S KIND, WHAT'S ENVIRONMENTALLY DESTRUCTIVE AND WHAT'S SUSTAINABLE. CRUEL AND DESTRUCTIVE FOOD PRODUCTS SHOULD BE ILLEGAL. WE DON'T NEED THE OPTION OF BUYING CHILDREN'S TOYS MADE WITH LEAD PAINT, OR AEROSOLS WITH CHLOROFLUOROCARBONS, OR MEDICINES WITH UNLABELED SIDE EFFECTS. AND WE DON'T NEED THE OPTION OF BUYING FACTORY-FARMED ANIMALS."

—JONATHAN SAFRAN FOER,
AUTHOR, *EATING ANIMALS*

composition forever. Duncan Williamson, food policy manager at the World Wildlife Fund, UK, estimates that approximately 30 percent of global biodiversity loss can be attributed to aspects of livestock production. Our planet is rich in biodiversity, meaning it hosts an enormous variety of life-forms. And healthy ecosystems comprise a complex system of millions of interrelated species. Insects, bats, and birds pollinate flowers and feed on pests. Microbial species live on, and in, plants and animals, and are especially abundant in soils. These creatures serve to maintain balance and recycle nutrients so that life can regenerate, convert atmospheric nitrogen to soil nitrogen compounds vital for plant growth, and live in association with plant roots to facilitate the uptake of water and nutrients.

How does livestock production alter biodiversity? For one, via the spread of grazing and cropland. Turning forests and savannas over to agriculture—especially animal agriculture, because it requires so much land—destroys native plant and animal species and their habitat. In addition, animal farming saps soil nutrients and pollutes the environment as waste runoff from farms causes algae blooms that consume oxygen in water, killing essential bacteria and destroying healthy ecosystems. During most summers today, between 13,000 and 20,000 square kilometers at the mouth of the Mississippi River become a "dead zone" due to agricultural runoff. Nearly 400 dead zones ranging in size from 1 to more than 70,000 square kilometers have been identified, from the Scandinavian fjords to the South China Sea.

In addition to crowding out native ecosystems and the land's natural biodiversity, modern farmers grow only a handful of crops for animal feed, which further reduces plant biodiversity. Public health scientists at Harvard University have estimated that just 15 plant species constitute more than 90 percent of those grown to support global livestock production.

The earth's ecosystems are delicate and complex, and scientists warn that such a drastic reduction in biodiversity could be catastrophic, especially when compounded by climate change. As the Harvard scientists write, "Genetic diversity in crops reduces the odds of crop failure secondary to changing weather, protects against the spread of plant diseases and attack by plant pests, and can lead to greater yields. As agriculture continues to rely on fewer and fewer species and varieties of crops and livestock, and as wild relatives are increasingly threatened, the need to preserve the genetic diversity of crop species and domestic animals for future generations grows steadily." Shifting away from animal agriculture would free up millions of acres that could be returned to their more natural state, allowing balanced, diverse ecosystems to function.

As you can see, the effects of an animal-based diet create a vicious cycle. Livestock contribute significantly to the release of gases that hasten global warming while simultaneously making our environment much more vulnerable to the effects of climate change. The livestock industry deprives the planet of water and space while making it

"I CARE NOT MUCH FOR A MAN'S RELIGION WHOSE DOG AND CAT ARE NOT THE BETTER FOR IT."

—ABRAHAM LINCOLN

impossible to accommodate the expected population growth in the coming decades.

At Farm Sanctuary, we follow a plant-based diet that seeks to reverse these ominous trends. Living in harmony with animals and the environment is not simply a matter of being in nature and communing with our fellow creatures. It's also about acknowledging that communing with animals rather than eating them is the healthiest choice that we can make for the planet and the future generations that will inhabit it. Plus it makes the animals happy (I couldn't help but throw that in there).

Helping Out the Earth

Some people think, "Okay, I've gone vegan—done!" And while it's true that adopting a vegan diet is the best thing any individual can do for the environment, there are many other things we can and should do as well.

Bruce Friedrich leads Farm Sanctuary's policy and legal efforts as well as our "Someone, Not Something" project. He is one of the most

remarkable activists I've ever met, having been involved in issues ranging from homelessness and poverty to peace and animal rights. He's thoughtful, smart (he holds degrees from Grinnell College, the London School of Economics and Political Science, and Johns Hopkins University), and is respected among peers. That is why so many people—including me—consult Bruce on how to most effectively create positive change. Here are his 10 ideas for helping the environment.

1. **Ride a bike!** Rajendra Pachauri, PhD, who chairs the Nobel Peace Prize–winning Intergovernmental Panel on Climate Change, held a press conference in which he encouraged people to avoid meat, shop frugally, and ride a bike instead of driving a car. Although it's true that meat is the number one source of greenhouse gases, cars and light trucks in the United States contribute significantly to these emissions. Riding a bike is an emissions-free form of

travel, with the added benefit of keeping your heart healthy and your waistline in check. (By the way, walking or even riding a skateboard or scooter is also great for the earth and your health.)

2. **Don't shop 'til you drop.** Dr. Pachauri's second piece of advice makes a lot of sense as well. Do you really *need* that extra pair of shoes, that fifth suit, or your 10th pullover? In addition to all the energy required to create and ship new things, most clothing is made of cotton, which (unless it's organic) uses massive amounts of pesticides and herbicides—toxic chemicals that kill insects and small animals and poison farmworkers. Don't just think "Can I afford this?" Think "Can the planet afford this?"

3. **When you do shop, consider secondhand first.** When I really do need something, I can't begin to tell you how great it feels to type exactly what I want into an eBay search form and have the perfect secondhand item pop up, often never or barely used and in the original packaging. So shop eBay and Goodwill or other thrift stores before you buy new. Save money and the earth!

4. **Borrow it.** One of the easiest ways to cut back on consumption is to share things—whether it's a car, a drill, a chess set, and so on. My suburban community maintains an e-mail listserv that allows members to send a quick e-mail anytime they need to borrow something. It's a great resource! You could create your own online group, either on e-mail or through social media. The next time you need to borrow a tool or hitch a ride, try posting a quick request on Facebook or Twitter. You might be surprised to see who responds!

5. **Try a staycation.** The airline industry likes to point out that air travel accounts for only 5 percent of our greenhouse gas emissions each year, but remember, 5 percent is still a lot! One bicoastal round trip emits 2 tons of greenhouse gases per passenger, which is as much as the average commuter (100 miles/week) will emit from her car in an entire year. So when you're thinking about a vacation, think local.

6. **When in doubt, don't throw it out.** Here's an odd fact: Some 40 percent of food produced in the United States is never consumed! Even vegan foods require land, water, and energy to produce, and transporting these foods contributes to climate change. Of course, vegan foods cause far less environmental havoc than animal foods, but given that they still require energy and resource use, the least we can do is ensure that everything we buy or raise gets eaten! So if you go out to eat, take a container with you and bring the leftovers home. When you go shopping or visit a buffet, only take as much as you're going to eat—don't worry, you can get more later. In addition to lessening your environmental impact, you'll be saving money. Americans throw away $165 billion worth of food every year!

7. **Go Luddite.** Well, not necessarily Luddite, but do you really *need* that new iPhone, laptop, or other tech gadget? These electronics are an environmental nightmare. Once thrown out, the toxins they release end up polluting unregulated landfills in the

developing world and poison people (sometimes children) who make a living by stripping them and reselling the metal they contain. So if you can go an extra few years before you replace your phone or computer with the latest model and perhaps go without the next shiny new thing, you'll be doing the environment—and poor people in the developing world—a big favor.

8. **Cut back on plastic.** Have you heard of the Great Pacific Garbage Patch (GPGP)? If not, look it up. (And then think very hard about whether you really need that bottle of water or that plastic bag for your groceries.) The GPGP covers at least 270,000 square miles of ocean. All that trash is killing sea turtles, birds, and fish. Julia Butterfly Hill, my favorite environmental activist, says: "When I hear someone say they're going to throw something away, I always wonder where 'away' is, exactly." Apparently, "away" is the Great Pacific Garbage Patch. Let's try not to make it, or other garbage dumps, worse.

9. **Develop the gift of gab.** The great French novelist Victor Hugo once wrote, "Nothing is more powerful than an idea whose time has come." I use this quote often when I'm talking about veganism, but it's also true about other environmental protection ideas. We owe it to future generations to do all we can to lessen our adverse impact on the

planet. Environmentalism has indeed arrived, and we can spread the idea more quickly if we get the message out. So don't just adopt a vegan diet and buy gently used things on eBay; post about your actions on social media. Tell all your friends what you're doing and why!

10. **Activate!** The novelist and human rights activist Alice Walker likes to say that "activism is my rent for living on the planet." As we discussed, it's important to live according to your values and to tell all your friends and family about it. But if you can also convince a corporation or a local, city, or state government to adopt an animal- or environment-friendly policy, regulation, or law, the impact can be huge. Democracy is a participatory sport, so in addition to acting when you receive alerts from Farm Sanctuary and other animal organizations, why not pick a favorite environmental group and get involved with their work, too?

Food Labels and What They Mean

Healthful, sustainable, and compassionate food choices are becoming more popular, bringing with them lots of different package labels that food companies use to increase the desirability and price tag. Often, the labels make what's inside sound better than it is. Three of the most common food labels are "natural," "organic," and "local."

Natural: While it sounds pure, this is largely a marketing term. It usually means the item has had limited processing and few or no synthetic ingredients added, but it tells us nothing about how it was produced. Meat from a steer injected with hormones and fed GMO corn and antibiotics at a factory farm or feedlot can be sold as "natural."

"ANIMALS ARE MY FRIENDS . . . AND I DON'T EAT MY FRIENDS."

— GEORGE BERNARD SHAW, IRISH PLAYWRIGHT

Organic: Unlike "natural" foods, organic foods are regulated by the USDA. Foods with the USDA organic label must undergo a certification process to prove they were grown without the use of chemical fertilizers and pesticides and without GMOs. Organic farmers must also comply with regulations defined by the Organic Foods Production Act and enforced by the USDA. However, as large food companies have entered the organic food market, standards have been weakening. Organic food is better than nonorganic, but when it comes to meat, milk, and eggs, "organic" does not mean humane.

Local: This term refers to the distance a food travels from farm to table, the time it takes to get there, and the number of production points it passes through on its journey. Like "natural," the term has no legal definition, but it generally implies

"THE SQUIRREL THAT YOU KILL IN JEST DIES IN EARNEST."

—HENRY DAVID THOREAU

that the food should have been grown within 100 to 200 miles of where it will be purchased.

The best ways to eat local? Shop at your nearest farmers' market and get to know the farmers. Sign up for a CSA or farm share, which links consumers with regional food growers and allows them to purchase a share of what the farmer grows that season. There are also farms where you can pick your own produce. But the most local choice of all? Grow your own food! Many people are replacing lawns with gardens. Even if you don't have a big yard,

Seven Foods

THAT ARE EASY TO GROW AT HOME

Basil: This tasty Italian herb can thrive in a small pot near the window. Use it in sauces and salads, or to make homemade pesto.

Carrots: These vitamin A–rich vegetables grow well in most types of soil and are extremely versatile in cooking.

Spinach and kale: As soon as their leaves sprout, they are ready to eat, cooked or in a salad. Plus, they are a great source of iron. Spinach and kale will grow new leaves as soon as the ripe ones are picked—they are the vegetables that keep on giving.

Tomatoes: One of the most popular foods to grow at home, and for good reason. There are so many varieties to choose from, and cultivating tomatoes is a wonderful way for beginners to learn about gardening. (Starter kits are available in many home and garden stores.)

Cucumbers: These viney plants are a delight to grow. Watch as your cucumbers grow bigger and bigger until they finally detach themselves from the vine. Or pick them early and make homemade pickles! Bonus—their flowers are pretty, too.

Zucchini: Similar to cucumbers, zucchini grows on a vine, and individual plants can reach tremendous sizes. Because of its high yield, this summer squash is great for feeding a family.

there are plenty of space-efficient techniques and easy-to-grow plant foods (like kale) to choose from. If you don't have a yard at all, try growing vegetables in containers on your porch or terrace.

Food-Related Ways to Help the Environment

Our daily choices and actions add up, and they have enormous impacts on our planet, especially when taken collectively. By adopting habits and behaviors that lighten our "foodprint" and enable regenerative agriculture, we can all make a positive difference for ourselves and our communities, today and for future generations.

1. **Grow at least some of your own food.**
   By cutting down on resource and energy costs and avoiding pesticides and packaging, starting a vegetable garden and/or planting fruit and nut trees is one of the most direct ways you can help the environment.

2. **Compost.** Give your food waste directly back to the earth. If you don't have a garden to compost in, see if your neighbor or community has a compost pile you can contribute to, or advocate for your city to create a composting program.

3. **Don't waste.** Avoid needlessly throwing out food by planning a few days' meals in advance and buying only the foods you actually will eat.

4. **Plan communal meals.** Save money and resources by preparing and eating meals as a group. Plan menus around dry beans, whole grains, and other inexpensive and healthy bulk foods.

5. **Buy whole foods.** Unwrapped vegetables and fruits are better for the environment because they use less plastic and undergo less processing than prepared foods.

6. **Buy in bulk.** Cut down on plastic by avoiding small packages of food. You can often buy grains, beans, nuts, and other staples in large quantities at a regular grocery store. They last a lot longer once you get them home, too!

7. **Embrace the season.** By eating foods in season, you can minimize the distance they need to travel to reach your supermarket, thereby conserving fossil fuels. Buying in season is also economical because foods are plentiful then. In summer, you can load up on berries and other fruits and freeze them for later.

8. **Reuse.** If you must buy plastic containers, don't throw them away as soon as they are empty. Jam jars, take-out containers, and other packages can be reused as cups or dishware or to store leftovers. Also, use a metal travel cup.

"THE GREATNESS OF A NATION AND ITS MORAL PROGRESS CAN BE JUDGED BY THE WAY ITS ANIMALS ARE TREATED."

—MAHATMA GANDHI,
INDIAN INDEPENDENCE LEADER

People throw away hundreds of disposable coffee cups every year, many of which are made of Styrofoam and take centuries to decompose. Or bring your own reusable mug to work and cut down on waste.

9. **Buy local.** That means food that's grown within 150 miles of your home. Shop at farmers' markets—it shortens the distance between the farm and your table, and allows consumers to meet and learn from the people who grow their food.

10. **Invest in a CSA.** Community-supported agriculture programs deliver fresh produce from the farm to your doorstep and also connect farmers with consumers. This model, in which you pay for an entire season's "share" of produce up front, reduces farmers' risks and

is great for people who can't always make it to the farmers' market.

11. **Get to know your farmers.** The US Department of Agriculture's (USDA's) online "Know Your Farmer, Know Your Food" map can tell you where your food comes from.

12. **Choose organic or sustainably produced foods.** These options don't contain man-made chemicals and thus don't introduce toxic substances into the environment (and your body). They all help sustain a healthier food system.

PART 2
FARM SANCTUARY IN YOUR KITCHEN

SETTING UP
YOUR VEGAN
KITCHEN

Eating a plant-based diet hasn't always been easy. In fact, when I went vegan back in 1985, no one could even pronounce it.

Vay-gan? Vee-gain? And even if people could say it, they didn't understand it. You won't get enough protein, they'd say. According to them, if I didn't die from the lack of protein, I'd perish from the absence of nutrients. What about vitamin B_{12}? What about calcium? What about iron? Doesn't everything larger than a squirrel have to eat meat? (No. See Tenet 1.)

But I did live, and thrive, and so have the many others who over the last few decades have made the switch to an all-plant diet. No statistics exist for the number of people who were vegans in 1985, but today an estimated three million Americans eat this way, and another seven to eight million are vegetarians. A nationwide survey by Cultivate Research in 2010 showed that an additional 15 million Americans would be willing to give up all forms of meat. And the polling data consistently show that these numbers are rising every year!

Because so many people are coming around to the plant-based diet, the range of available foods has expanded dramatically over the last 2 decades. There was a time when being a vegan meant scurrying around from health food stores to food co-ops to find specialty plant-based food. Of course, fruits, vegetables, grains, and beans were generally available at grocery stores and supermarkets. In 1985, when we wanted soy milk, we had to mix a chalky powder with water. Now you can buy cartons of soy milk—along with quite a few other nondairy options like almond, coconut, and rice milks—in mainstream supermarkets. Vegan snacks used to consist of carrot sticks and celery stalks, but now you can find all kinds of plant-based munchies. A vegan meal at a restaurant used to mean a salad or, if you were lucky, pasta with vegetables. Things have changed. Not long ago, I was in cow country—Omaha, Nebraska—and found a place that sold vegan Philly cheesesteaks.

Moreover, Web sites such as Happycow.net and Veganrestaurantfinder.com will help you locate vegan food wherever you are. And of course, there are now smartphone apps that do the same thing, including Vegman, which locates the nearest vegetarian and vegan restaurants in your area. Eating plants instead of animals has never been easier!

Personally, I think one of the best ways to enjoy the Farm Sanctuary life is simply to prepare your food at home. But not everyone has the best recipes. So I asked friends of Farm Sanctuary to contribute some of their favorite plant-based dishes, and I included one of my own as well. The result is a smorgasbord of almost 100 all new, never published recipes (starting on page 111), that anyone, whether you're a gourmet chef or a novice in the kitchen, can make at home. Surprise your friends with these delicious meals—you don't even have to tell them they're plant based. All they'll know is that the food tastes absolutely wonderful!

SETTING UP A VEGAN KITCHEN I
Kitchen Essentials

It's time to make the kitchen your kingdom! By stocking your kitchen with a few key tools, you will be armed to take on any new recipe fearlessly.

Chef's knife: A good knife is the cornerstone of your kitchen equipment. Invest in a decent knife so you can chop, dice, mince, and chiffonade away!

Paring knife: A little smaller than a chef's knife, a paring knife is good for more delicate jobs like slicing apples.

Vegetable peeler: This handy tool makes easy work of removing the skin from potatoes, carrots, and all of your favorite veggies.

Stock pot: Whether you're making soup or chili or heating up leftovers, a good-sized stock pot is a necessity. If you can invest in one 2-quart pot and one 4-quart pot, you'll be ready for anything.

Skillet: When it comes time to make Sunday morning pancakes, a skillet is the tool of choice. Also use it for sautéing and stir-fries. Nonstick ones are the best.

Baking sheet: This inexpensive tray is perfect for turning out homemade cookies or sweet potato fries.

Six Uses for Ginger

Peeled or grated on top of ice cream or other desserts

Cooked with sugar for ginger syrup, which can be made into ginger ale

Pickled and served with sushi

Candied, for a healthy dessert

Juiced with fruits and vegetables for a detoxifying drink

Boiled, for a tea that eases digestion

Casserole dish: Deeper than the baking sheet, a casserole dish is great for roasting vegetables, making a batch of dairy-free mac and cheese, or (you guessed it!) baking a casserole.

Food processor: A food processor, while a bit of an investment, is an incredible time-saver. Use it to make pesto or salsa, or to finely chop vegetables and herbs.

Blender: Easily blends up smoothies, sauces, and pureed soups (and maybe the occasional margarita!).

Box grater: Quickly shreds carrots, beets, or other favorites for salads and stir-fries.

Cutting board: Keep your counters scratch free with a cutting board. They're available in a variety of materials from silicone to wood.

Measuring cups and spoons: An essential for following recipes, measuring cups are inexpensive and ensure culinary success.

Spatulas: A silicone spatula is perfect for scraping the batter out of the bottom of the bowl or for spreading frosting. A thin metal spatula can be used for flipping pancakes, veggie burgers, or anything else in your skillet.

Whisk: Many recipes call for a whisk, whether you're getting the lumps out of a meat-free gravy or blending cocoa powder into nondairy milk for a delicious hot chocolate.

Wooden spoons: Wooden spoons are great for stirring things while they are cooking. They don't melt like plastic, and they won't get too hot to handle like metal.

Colander: Use your colander to drain the water from cooked pasta, freshly washed greens, or pressed tofu.

Containers with lids: To save time during the week, cook a big batch of your favorite entrée during the weekend and pack the leftovers in containers in the fridge. On a busy night, just grab one and heat it up for a quick meal.

Electric hand or stand mixer: This is important for making the fluffiest frostings, fillings, and nice airy cupcakes.

Plant-Based Pantry Staples

Beans: Add protein to salads, soups, and chilis with black beans, pinto beans, or your other favorites! Chickpeas are particularly great because they can be used to make hummus or smashed with vegan mayonnaise for a tasty faux-chicken salad. Have these and a few other canned varieties on hand for when inspiration strikes.

Grains: Stock up on hearty, healthy grains like rice, quinoa, and bulgur and you'll always have the building blocks for a quick, meat-free meal. Oats are great to have on hand for an easy hot breakfast.

Oils: For sautéing and to add healthful unsaturated fats to your diet, keep a few different varieties like olive oil and coconut oil in the cupboard.

Herbs and spices: Eating a plant-based diet opens up a whole new world of flavors! Stock your spice rack to be ready for any new recipe that tempts you. You can purchase prefilled spice racks that come with everything you need to get started, or you can slowly add to your collection by picking up a new spice each time you shop.

Vital wheat gluten: This wonder ingredient binds things together and is used to make seitan, a savory protein source with a delicious, meaty texture.

Nutritional yeast: Give a cheesy flavor to pasta, soups, or even popcorn with a sprinkle of nutritional yeast! Found in the bulk section, these tasty little flakes are packed with flavor and vitamin B_{12}!

Canned pumpkin and unsweetened applesauce: When baking, replace eggs with canned pumpkin or unsweetened applesauce for rich, moist brownies, cakes, muffins, and breads. Use $1/4$ cup for each egg called for. Works great for boxed mixes, too!

Ener-G Egg Replacer: A convenient powdered egg substitute, Ener-G can be used in any of your favorite baked goods.

Raw cashews: Cashews are a staple for many top vegan chefs, who use them to give amazing, creamy texture to sauces, dairy-free cheeses, and desserts. Soak raw cashews in water overnight. In the morning, drain and rinse them and then add to a blender with just enough water to cover. Blend until smooth, and you have a fabulous substitute for heavy cream in recipes!

Coconut milk: Creamy, luscious coconut milk is used in decadent dessert recipes and is the base for many exotic entrées such as Thai curry.

Vegan Worcestershire sauce: Most conventional Worcestershire sauces contain anchovies, so pick up a vegan brand like Annie's when your recipe calls for it.

Liquid smoke: When your dish needs a little bit of smoky flavor, reach for this. Liquid smoke can be used to make tempeh bacon or to add a little faux fresh-off-the-grill flavor to your meal.

Nondairy milks: There are so many delicious nondairy milk varieties out there: soy, almond, coconut, rice, hemp. Try a few and you're sure to find one you love! Keep a carton of a plain, unsweetened variety on hand for baking. Many nondairy milks are shelf stable until opened, so you can keep one in your pantry in case a recipe calls for it.

Earth Balance: Like butter, only better. This nonhydrogenated, oil-based, nondairy spread can be used in recipes, on toast, or anywhere you'd normally use butter or margarine.

Vegan mayonnaise: Try brands like Just Mayo or Follow Your Heart Vegenaise. They are great not only to spread on sandwiches but also for making dips, dressings, and sauces.

Better Than Bouillon: This concentrated bouillon paste can be used to make delicious broths for soups and sauces. Start with Vegetable Base, No Chicken Base, or No Beef Base for a hearty, comforting bowl of soup.

Agar-agar: Available as flakes or powder, this sea vegetable works just like gelatin (which is made of animal by-products). Use it to create fruit desserts or even to make your own vegan cheeses.

Hummus: The ultimate healthy vegan snack. Comes in a wide variety of savory flavors like spinach artichoke and spicy red pepper. Eat with crackers, cut-up vegetables, or pita chips.

All-purpose flour: From biscuits and breads to pies and cakes, cooking is going to be easier when you have some of this versatile flour on hand.

Baking powder: A pantry staple needed to start your day with fluffy pancakes or any other baked treat.

Baking soda: Don't forget this important addition or your baked goods will likely turn out sad and flat.

Pure vanilla extract: There are so many delicious ways to flavor your baked goods, but having some vanilla on hand allows you to always be ready to add the basics.

Miso paste: As you try new recipes, this Japanese spread made from soybeans is great to have around.

Tahini: Made from sesame seeds, tahini is great as a base for dressings and sauces.

Raw cane sugar: We prefer raw sugar so we don't have to wonder about the processing. It's great to have in the cupboard, because what's a meal without dessert?

Substitutes for Animal-Based Foods

There is a growing variety of plant-based meat, dairy, and egg products available in the marketplace that make transitioning to vegan living easier than ever. Vegan products are winning taste tests against animal foods, and new ones are coming out all the time, so you're guaranteed to find something you love.

You can search for meat, dairy, and egg substitutes online, or go to Web sites like veganstore.com, veganessentials.com, dixiediner.com, or even amazon.com, to find a wide variety of vegan foods. They are also increasingly found at supermarkets across the United States and around the world. Here are just a few examples of what's available.

VEGAN MEAT AND PROTEIN

Instead of chicken, try:

Gardein products, including Chick'n Scallopini and Seven Grain Crispy Tenders

Beyond Meat Chicken-Free Strips

Boca Chik'n Patties

Instead of turkey, try:

Tofurky (they make both deli slices and roasts, which are perfect for Thanksgiving)

Yves Meatless Deli Turkey Slices

Gardein Turk'y Cutlet

For the grill, try:

Lightlife Smart Dogs

Tofurky Gourmet Sausages

Field Roast Frankfurters or Sausage Links

Gardein Beefless Burger

Engine 2 Tuscan Kale White Bean Burgers

Engine 2 Poblano Black Bean Burgers

Amy's Bistro Veggie Burger

Sunshine Burgers

Boca Original Vegan Veggie Burgers

Instead of beef, try:

Gardein products, including Beefless Tips and Gluten-Free Beefless Ground

Nate's Meatless Meatballs

Lightlife Gimme Lean Ground Beef Style

(continues on page 106)

Five Veggie Dishes You Didn't Think You Could Prepare at Home

Curried anything: With Indian spices and a can of coconut milk from the grocery store, you can easily make dishes with amazing flavors.

Falafel: This street food favorite is deliciously fun to make using balls of spiced mashed chickpeas and a little oil.

Hummus: Mash together chickpeas, lemon juice, and tahini, and you have the perfect appetizer or snack.

Peanut sauce: Prepare pad thai in your own kitchen using peanut butter, soy sauce, and rice vinegar.

Salad dressing: Store-bought dressings can be high in fat and sugar, but homemade options are often healthier and taste better.

Five Root Vegetables
THAT ARE DELICIOUS YET OVERLOOKED

Bamboo shoots: You probably ate them the last time you had Thai food, but bamboo shoots are easy to prepare at home and do especially well in curries.

Cassava: The source of tapioca, this root can be substituted for potato but is toxic if cooked improperly.

Daikon: This big, white radish is great for pickling or stir-frying, and the leaves are edible, too.

Rutabaga: A cross between a cabbage and a turnip, this root is popular in Scandinavia, Scotland, and Canada but has yet to catch on in the States.

Water chestnuts: These aren't nuts at all but are vegetables rich in complex carbohydrates and dietary fiber.

Beyond Beef Beefy Crumbles

MATCH Ground Beef

Upton's Naturals Seitan (traditional or ground styles)

Instead of fish, try:

Sophie's Kitchen plant-based seafood selections

MATCH Crab

Gardein Fishless Filet

OTHER SOURCES OF PROTEIN

Beans: As mentioned, another tasty way to add protein to your dishes, including soups and salads, is to throw in delicious and pocketbook-friendly beans. Both canned and dry beans are easy to find at most supermarkets, and there are dozens of varieties—kidney, lentil, northern, and others—to keep things interesting. For Mexican dishes, try black or pinto beans. If you're looking for some Mediterranean flare, use chickpeas.

Tofu: This soybean-based product originated in China 2,000 years ago and has recently gained a big following in the West, showing up on the shelves of many major supermarkets. Tofu soaks up the flavor of the foods and seasonings it's cooked with, making it the ultimate low-calorie addition to stir-fries, sauces, and other meat-free dishes. If you're adding tofu to an entrée, opt for firm or extra firm. Soft and silken varieties are wonderful in dips, smoothies, and mousse desserts.

Seitan: Seitan (say-tahn) is a super protein source derived from wheat. It is sometimes served in restaurants as mock chicken or duck. Seitan makes a perfect substitute for meat in many recipes, and it can satisfy even the toughest carnivore. You can find brands like White-Wave and Lightlife in some grocery stores, or you can make your own using vital wheat gluten mixes from brands such as Arrowhead Mills (look for them in the baking aisle).

Tempeh: Tempeh is a fermented soy product with a slightly nutty flavor and a firm texture. You can find grain-based versions, too. Look for products like tempeh "bacon" to add extra oomph to your breakfast or sandwiches. Tempeh can be found in the refrigerated section of most health food stores and in the natural foods aisle of well-stocked grocery stores.

Cheese replacements: Finding plant-based cheese had been a challenge for vegans, but that has changed. Daiya cheese is now widely available online and in various markets, including at some pizza places. There are tasty artisan cheeses produced by companies like Kite Hill, Dr-Cow, and Miyoko's Kitchen, while Soy Kaas, Sunergia Soyfoods, Follow Your Heart, and GO Veggie! make great plant-based Cheddar, mozzarella, Parmesan, and feta cheeses. Vegan cream cheeses and sour cream are available from companies like Tofutti.

Milk and dairy replacements: Large dairy companies are recognizing the growing demand for alternatives to cows' milk and are now investing in plant-based milks. Almond, soy, and coconut milks are very popular and widely distributed, along with rice, oat, hemp, flax, and other plant-based milks. You can even make nondairy milk at home. Vegan creamers, commonly made from soy or coconut, are also readily found at the supermarket. Earth Balance and other plant-based margarines can replace butter, while olive oil can serve as a preferable alternative.

Eight Foods Meat-Eaters Don't Think of as Vegan—But Are

Bean burritos

Pasta with tomato sauce

Fried rice

Tortilla chips with salsa or guacamole

French fries with ketchup

Popsicles or sorbet

Salted popcorn

Peanut butter and jelly sandwiches

Egg and mayonnaise substitutes: It is easy to find egg substitutes for baking by searching online. These include applesauce, oil, silken tofu, baking soda, and flaxseeds, and you can sometimes just leave eggs out of the recipe. There are also products on the market created specifically to replace eggs, including Ener-G Egg Replacer and Bob's Red Mill Egg Replacer, or The Vegg, which was designed to replace egg yolks.

Instead of mayonnaise you can use Vegenaise by Follow Your Heart or Just Mayo from Hampton Creek, which is developing a variety of other egg substitutes. Plus Earth Balance makes several kinds of vegan mayonnaise.

Eating Vegan
and SAVING MONEY

BECAUSE ELLEN JAFFE JONES (vegcoach.com) is the author of *Eat Vegan on $4 a Day* (as well as *Paleo Vegan: Plant-Based Primal Recipes*), I thought she would have a lot of tips on how to be vegan and eat on the cheap. She does! Here they are.

1. The best way to save money is to cook from scratch—especially if you cook with beans, which are much cheaper than the cheapest hamburger meat. (A large bag of beans and grains can be stored in Mason jar–type containers, especially ones that have rubber gaskets around the lid. Be sure to change the containers at least every 10 years or so, as they can get cracked.) Beans are delicious sprouted and served atop salads. Cookbooks just about beans abound, offering hundreds of recipes. And there are so many different varieties of beans, including tiny lentils that, when cooked, mimic a burger's texture, if that's your thing. Also try giant chickpeas and lima beans, which are ridiculously cheap and very tasty.

2. If you trade out the meat and dairy for beans, you'll have plenty of money left over to buy produce. A great way to do that is to join a CSA or find a local farm by checking the Web site localharvest.org. Often, the food is organic, and if you volunteer or sign up for a work-share, you can get the produce at greatly reduced prices or even for free, depending how often you volunteer.

3. Check the unit prices. Most stores have a small red square below items stocked on grocery shelves. Take the time to crunch the numbers yourself. The price is usually per ounce, so you really can compare apples to oranges or, in this case, beans to meat. If an ounce of beans is marked as $.05, simply multiply that number by the number of ounces you will need to make a serving.

4. Shop the circumference of the store. That's where the produce and fresh foods live. And look high and low all over the shelves. Manufacturers pay big bucks to grab your attention at eye level. They know our tendency to impulse buy, and that happens most often within arm's reach. But sometimes the best bargains are near the floor!

5. Keep receipts and track prices. That's the only way you'll know when a bargain is truly a bargain, or when foods like berries are in season and at their cheapest price of the year. That's the time to stock up on them and freeze some. Produce that rots from abandonment in your refrigerator is no bargain.

   Many excellent apps are available to help you keep track of receipts and food prices. Some of the most popular for general budgeting and receipt tracking are Shoeboxed, Smart-Receipts, and Putnam Price Check & Save. For grocery store product and price comparisons, consider Shop'NCook, Mighty Grocery, Grocery Pal, Grocery iQ, Grocery Gadget, GroceryList, and Shopping List. The best of these apps have large databases so you can add items to your list. They'll also recognize your favorites. Some even have online list updating and bar code scanners. These apps are always changing, so be sure to be on the lookout for all the latest improvements.

6. Use your head, not your stomach, when you shop. It sounds obvious, but it is definitely worth a reminder that we buy more when we are hungry. Even if you just eat a banana before going through the grocery store doors, you'll do much to stave off the hunger that makes you impulse buy instead of sticking to that nice grocery list you prepared at home.

7. Buy store brands. They will almost always be cheaper than manufacturers' brands. Often, you'll find the same product inside under a different label. This is especially true for staples such as dried beans. Most supermarket chains now offer their own brand of organic foods, which makes buying organic on a budget a lot easier.

THE RECIPES

BREAKFASTS

Pancakes with Orange Moscato Syrup and Pine Nuts

Jason Wyrick, executive chef of The Vegan Taste and author of *Vegan Tacos*

Says Jason: "I created this recipe when I was leading a vegan food tour in the south of Italy. Everyone really wanted pancakes for breakfast, but I wanted to utilize some of the exceptional ingredients we had. That included a bottle of orange moscato, fresh pine nuts, and oranges picked directly from the orchard outside the villa where we stayed. It's quintessential Italian. Not a lot of ingredients so the ones that are there can really shine. Best of all, this is a fancy breakfast that doesn't take any more effort than making regular pancakes."

MAKES 4 SERVINGS
TIME TO MAKE: 15 MINUTES

3–4 tablespoons pine nuts

⅔ cup whole wheat pastry flour

¼ teaspoon salt

2 teaspoons baking powder

⅔ cup almond milk

2 teaspoons olive oil

Grated peel of 2 oranges

¼ cup agave nectar

3 tablespoons orange moscato*

In a medium skillet over medium heat, toast the pine nuts for 1 minute.

In a mixing bowl, combine the flour, salt, and baking powder, making sure they are evenly distributed. Whisk in the almond milk and oil until you have a thin batter.

Bring a medium skillet to just above medium heat. Add a very thin layer of olive oil and wait about 30 seconds for it to heat. Pour about ⅓ cup of the batter into the skillet and quickly rotate it a couple of times to get the batter to spread out. Cook the pancake for 2 minutes, then flip it and cook for 2 minutes. Remove and keep it warm. Repeat until you are out of batter.

In a medium bowl, combine the orange peel, agave, and moscato.

Plate the pancakes, pour the syrup on them, and top with the toasted pine nuts.

Skip the moscato and add 2 tablespoons fresh orange juice and 1 tablespoon white wine.

Fabulous French Toast

Fran Costigan, pastry chef, instructor, and author of *Vegan Chocolate*

Says Fran: "French toast—it's not just for Sunday breakfast, and it sure doesn't need to be made with the typical cholesterol-loaded egg-based custard or refined bread. This nutritious, delicious vegan version got enthusiastic thumbs-up from my granddaughters Georgia and Cecile, as well as their parents. Another plus: It is very quick and easy to make, using just a few pantry staples. Some of the ingredients may be unfamiliar to nonvegans, but all are easy to find. (See "Special Ingredients" on page 118.)

"I use sprouted wheat bread, but any bread, including gluten-free, is fine. The recipe makes enough of the intentionally thick custard for four average-to-large slices of bread. Make a double batch, if you prefer. Definitely try the Chocolate and Banana French Toast Sandwiches variation that follows, to serve as dessert or for a special brunch!"

MAKES 2 SERVINGS
TIME TO MAKE: 40 TO 45 MINUTES

1 cup almond milk, coconut milk beverage, or soy milk

½ teaspoon guar gum

3 tablespoons pure grade B or dark amber maple syrup

1½ teaspoons nutritional yeast powder or ¾ teaspoon flakes, optional but recommended

2 teaspoons ground black or white chia seeds

½ teaspoon ground cinnamon

Pinch of fine sea salt

4 thick slices bread (any bread of your choice)

2 tablespoons coconut oil, vegan buttery spread, or mild-tasting extra-virgin olive oil, or more as needed

In a blender, combine the milk and guar gum. Blend on high for 1 minute. The milk will be thick. Add the maple syrup, nutritional yeast (if using), chia seeds, cinnamon, and salt. Blend on high for 2 minutes if using a standard blender or 1 minute if using a high-speed blender. Taste the custard. There should be no crunch of chia. If you taste any crunch, allow the custard to rest for 5 minutes and blend for another minute.

Pour the custard (you will have about 1 cup) into a 13" x 9" baking dish. Press the bread into the custard. Wait 5 minutes and then turn each slice over with a wide spatula. Spoon some of the custard over the top of the bread. Allow the bread to soak for another 5 to 10 minutes, depending on the thickness of the bread, turning the slices over another time.

When you are ready to cook, put the oil or spread (or a combination) onto a griddle or heavy-bottom pan. Heat over medium heat until the fat begins to sizzle. Place as many slices on the griddle as will fit without touching. Cook for 5 minutes on each side, turning the slices with a wide spatula. Increase the heat and flip again if necessary to get a darker color.

Serve warm with maple syrup or confectioners' sugar.

Chocolate and Banana French Toast Sandwiches Variation (see photo) Sprinkle 1 to 2 tablespoons finely chopped vegan chocolate on 2 slices of the cooked French toast. Chop 1 banana and divide between the 2 slices, placing it on top of the chocolate. Top each with a second slice. Press down with a spatula. Cut each sandwich in half or into quarters, and serve warm from the pan, with or without a drizzle of maple syrup or confectioners' sugar.

Special Ingredients

Chia Seeds (Black or White) are tiny, gluten-free seeds that are even richer in omega-3 fatty acids than flaxseeds, and since chia seeds are so rich in antioxidants, they can be stored for long periods without becoming rancid. When mixed with water, ground chia seeds form a gel that thickens and binds, like eggs. Refrigerate chia seeds in a covered container for up to 6 months and the ground seeds for 3 months.

Guar Gum is a thickener made from a bean that grows in India and Pakistan. You'll see guar gum listed as an ingredient in almost all ice creams and many of the nondairy milks. It has seven to eight times the thickening potency of arrowroot, cornstarch, and tapioca and does not need to be cooked. I use a very small amount, but it is essential for the best-tasting result. I use guar gum from Bob's Red Mill. A bag will likely last for up to 2 years stored in a tightly closed container or jar in the refrigerator.

Nutritional Yeast (aka "Nooch") adds a hint or more of cheesy flavor and is loaded with nutrition, particularly B_{12}, folic acid, selenium, zinc, and protein. It's low in fat and gluten-free (check brands for certification), and contains no added sugars or preservatives. I use it every day for the flavor, but if you don't want to buy a jar just now, leave it out of the recipe. You'll find nutritional yeast in larger grocery stores, natural foods stores, and online.

Hakuna ("No Worries") Frittata

Alka Chandna, human rights, animal rights, and environmental activist

Alka Chandna interned at Farm Sanctuary in the mid-1990s and is a longtime vegan and activist. She says, "Conventional frittatas are made with eggs, cheese, and bacon. This frittata packs in all the hearty flavor of the brunch staple but leaves out the cholesterol-laden animal ingredients—so, no worries!"

MAKES 4 TO 6 SERVINGS
TIME TO MAKE: 1 HOUR

Bac-Os: Bacon bits fall into the "better living through chemistry" category of "accidentally vegan" products (like Oreos!). Bac-Os are good for the smoky flavor and the red color that contrasts nicely with the green of the spinach, but if you'd rather not load up on artificial flavors and colors, you can just add a couple drops of liquid smoke when you're adding the salt and pepper.

- 2 tablespoons olive oil
- 1 medium onion, diced
- 2 medium russet potatoes, washed, scrubbed, and grated
- 4 cloves garlic, minced
- 1 pound extra-firm tofu, drained and grated*
- 1–2 teaspoons salt
- ¼–½ teaspoon Indian black salt,† optional
- Ground black pepper
- ¼ cup nutritional yeast
- ¼–½ cup Daiya Cheddar Style Shreds, optional
- ¼ cup Bac-Os Bacon Flavor Bits, optional
- 1 pound frozen spinach, thawed

Preheat the oven to 350°F. Grease a 10" or 12" pie pan.

Heat the oil in a large skillet over medium-high heat. Add the onion and cook for 5 minutes, or until translucent. Add the potatoes and cook for 10 to 12 minutes, using a spatula to turn the potatoes over. Add the garlic and cook for 2 to 3 minutes. Stir in the tofu. Add the salt, black salt (if using), and black pepper to taste.

Turn off the heat and stir in the nutritional yeast, cheese (if using), and bacon bits (if using). Stir in the spinach. Pour the mixture into the pie pan.

Bake for 30 to 40 minutes, until the cheese is completely melted.

Variations: You can add whatever vegetables you like or what's in season to this frittata. Zucchini, summer squash, green onions, kale, peppers, and mushrooms are all spectacular in this frittata. And, if you're more of a soy meat person, leave out the veggies in favor of sliced Tofurky sausages, Gardein strips, or soy pepperoni.

*Gently press the tofu; it will crumble if pressed with too much force.

†Black salt has a sulfur taste that imbues an egg flavor to the frittata. You can find it in health food stores and also Indian grocery stores, where it's called kala namak. If you use black salt, make sure it's finely ground.

Gluten-Free Baked No-Egg French Omelet Soufflé with Kale and Onions

Caryn Hartglass (host of the radio show *It's All about Food* and the podcast *Ask a Vegan*) and vegan chef **Gary De Mattei**

Caryn Hartglass is one of the best vegan cooks I have ever met. She's also an ovarian cancer survivor who has lectured around the world on how a plant-based diet saved her life. She has appeared on *Dr. Oz*, *20/20*, and CNN and hosts two weekly Internet radio shows. She and her husband, Gary De Mattei, are also excellent cabaret singers, with an act called The Swinging Gourmets (in the spirit of Steve and Eydie). Here is their favorite omelet.

MAKES 6 TO 8 SERVINGS
TIME TO MAKE: 1 HOUR 10 MINUTES

Batter

- ½ block firm tofu (6–7 ounces), drained
- 1 cup unsweetened soy milk
- ½ cup frozen corn
- ¼ cup ground flaxseeds
- ¼ cup chickpea flour
- 1 tablespoon soy lecithin
- 1 teaspoon granulated garlic powder
- Salt and ground black pepper
- 1–2 tablespoons water

Filling

- 1 tablespoon olive oil
- 1 medium onion, chopped
- 1 cup chopped raw kale
- 1 teaspoon granulated garlic powder
- ⅓ teaspoon salt
- ⅓ teaspoon coarsely ground black pepper
- ½ block firm tofu (6–7 ounces), rinsed, drained, and crumbled

To make the batter: In a blender, combine the tofu, milk, corn, flaxseeds, flour, lecithin, garlic powder, and salt and pepper to taste. Blend until smooth. The consistency should be like a heavy pancake batter. Let the batter set for 15 minutes. It will thicken while it sets. Add the water, 1 tablespoon at a time, to return the batter to its previous, thinner consistency.

Preheat the oven to 425°F.

To make the filling: Place a large cast-iron or heavy ovenproof skillet on the stove over high heat for about 30 seconds. Reduce the heat to medium and add the oil. Wait until it shimmers but does not smoke. Add the onion and cook until translucent and lightly browned. Add the kale, garlic powder, and salt and pepper to taste. Cook for 4 minutes, or until soft.

Spread the ingredients evenly on the bottom of the skillet. Add the crumbled tofu evenly over the top. Do not mix!

Pour the batter on top of the filling in the skillet. Lightly move around the chunks to evenly distribute the batter, but again, do not mix! Lower the heat to a simmer and cook the mixture for 2 to 3 minutes, or until it comes to a slow boil.

Place the skillet in the oven and bake for 10 minutes, or until the mixture starts to brown slightly. You'll see it bubble occasionally. Reduce the heat to 325°F and bake for 15 to 20 minutes longer, or until it starts to move away from the sides of the pan and turns golden brown.

Serve right from the pan.

Savory Wild Mushroom Crêpes with Roasted Fingerling Breakfast Potatoes

Jason Stefanko, executive chef for Gardein

Says Jason: "My father was an excellent breakfast and brunch cook, and so I've always spent a lot of my kitchen time focused in the morning. Here I've combined my love of breakfast with my love of mushrooms to create this gluten-free, vegan breakfast recipe."

MAKES 2 SERVINGS
(2 CRÊPES PER SERVING)
TIME TO MAKE: 1 HOUR 30 MINUTES

Crêpes

1 cup chickpea flour

1¼ cups water

⅛ teaspoon baking powder

1 teaspoon chopped fresh thyme

1 teaspoon chopped fresh parsley

¼ teaspoon sea salt

¼ teaspoon ground black pepper

Potatoes

10 fingerling potatoes

1 tablespoon olive oil

1 teaspoon chopped fresh thyme

1 teaspoon chopped fresh rosemary

¼ teaspoon fine sea salt

¼ teaspoon coarse black pepper

Filling

2 tablespoons olive oil

3 cups oyster, shiitake, or cremini mushrooms, washed, stemmed, and sliced

2 tablespoons white wine

2 cups spinach leaves

¼ teaspoon fine sea salt

¼ teaspoon coarse black pepper

¼ cup vegan mozzarella

2 teaspoons truffle oil, optional

Fresh chopped parsley, for garnish

To make the crêpes: In a mixing bowl, gently whisk the flour, water, baking powder, thyme, parsley, salt, and pepper. Refrigerate for at least 1 hour.

To make the potatoes: Preheat the oven to 450°F. Wash the potatoes and drain. Cut the potatoes that are larger than 1" into halves. In a mixing bowl, combine the oil, thyme, rosemary, salt, and pepper. Toss the potatoes in the mixture. Transfer them to a nonstick baking pan.

Roast for 15 minutes. Turn the oven to broil and cook for 10 minutes, or until they are browned well and crispy.

(continued on page 124)

To make the filling: In a nonstick pan, add the oil and mushrooms and cook over high heat for 8 minutes, or until caramelized and cooked through. Deglaze the pan by adding the wine and quickly stirring. Add the spinach. Cook for 1 minute or until the spinach is wilted. Add the salt and pepper.

To assemble: Preheat a nonstick crêpe pan or 9" pan over medium-high heat. Coat with olive oil and add ½ cup of the crêpe batter. Spread the batter evenly in the pan. Cook for 2 to 3 minutes, or until it is browned and crispy, then flip it. Add one-quarter of the mozzarella and one-quarter of the mushroom-spinach filling. If desired, drizzle ½ teaspoon truffle oil onto the filling before rolling the crêpe.

Roll the crêpe and garnish with the parsley. Repeat with the remaining batter, filling, cheese, and truffle oil (if using). Serve with the potatoes.

The Best Tofu Scramble You've Ever Had

Gene Baur

I still remember the wonderful Sunday morning family breakfasts of bacon and eggs when I was growing up. I loved them. So when I stopped eating animal foods, breakfast was one of the most difficult meals to plan. I missed the large, hearty weekend fare. But it wasn't long before I discovered that scrambled tofu is a good alternative to scrambled eggs. This scramble is one of the first plant-based meals I ever prepared, and it remains one of my favorites. It is also high in protein and very low in fat.

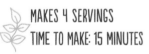

MAKES 4 SERVINGS
TIME TO MAKE: 15 MINUTES

1 medium red onion, chopped

1 red, orange, or yellow bell pepper, chopped

3 cloves garlic, finely chopped

8 ounces sliced white mushrooms

1 pound firm tofu, rinsed, drained, and crumbled

1 cup nutritional yeast

1½ teaspoons salt

1 teaspoon ground black pepper

1 teaspoon ground turmeric

5 cups fresh spinach

In a cast-iron skillet over medium-high heat, add about 2 tablespoons water and cook the onion, bell pepper, and garlic. Stir frequently and add a ⅛" layer of water (it will steam off) to prevent the veggies from sticking. When the onion is translucent, add the mushrooms. Continue stirring and adding water as necessary.

When the mushrooms boil down to approximately half their original size, reduce the heat to medium and add the tofu, nutritional yeast, salt, and pepper. Continue stirring frequently, mixing and adding water as necessary.

When the tofu, spices, and veggies are mixed well and heated evenly, after about 5 minutes, add the turmeric and continue stirring and adding water to prevent sticking.

After the tofu attains a uniform yellowish color, mix in the spinach, which will boil down to a fraction of its original size. Then enjoy!

Variations: Feel free to add other veggies or more of the veggies listed above, which will make the dish less protein dense. You can also add vegan sausage, like Tofurky or Field Roast, if you want a heavier dish.

Peppery Cardamom Rolls

Jason Wyrick, executive chef of The Vegan Taste and author of *Vegan Tacos*

Says Jason: "I love cinnamon rolls. If you put a dozen cinnamon rolls in front of me, you will be missing 12 cinnamon rolls by the time you get back to the table. I wanted to do something a little different one morning, though, and I had a cup of chai in front of me. Most chai masalas (that's the spice mix used in chai) have both cinnamon and cardamom, so I simply took the idea of cinnamon rolls and slid them over into cardamom rolls. Chai also features black pepper, so it made a natural kick to this off-the-beaten-path version of cinnamon rolls. If you want to turn them into chai rolls, just add a healthy amount of freshly grated ginger, some cinnamon, and a dash of cloves, but I very much enjoy the simple combination of cardamom and pepper (and sugar, of course)."

MAKES 10 ROLLS
TIME TO MAKE: 2 HOURS
(MOSTLY FOR THE DOUGH TO RISE)

Dough

- 1 teaspoon yeast
- 1 cup almond milk, warmed
- 1 tablespoon granulated sugar
- 3 tablespoons vegan margarine, melted and warm
- 3 cups all-purpose flour
- ¼ teaspoon salt

Filling

- ¼ cup vegan margarine, melted, or almond oil (I prefer almond oil, but it's also more expensive)
- ½ cup turbinado or brown sugar, loosely packed
- 1 teaspoon coarse black pepper

Frosting

- 1½ cups confectioners' sugar
- 1½ teaspoons ground cardamom
- 3 tablespoons almond milk
- ¼ cup sliced almonds, toasted
- Coarse black pepper

To make the dough: In a bowl, combine the yeast, almond milk, and sugar. Wait for the yeast to foam, about 5 minutes. Stir in the melted margarine. Add the flour and salt and stir until you have a tacky dough. Lightly flour a working surface and knead the dough until it is no longer sticky. Lightly oil the dough to keep the outside from drying out, place it in a bowl, cover it, and let it rise for 1 hour.

Lightly flour a working surface again. Roll the dough out into a ¼"-thick rectangle. The rectangle should be about 12" long and at least as wide.

To make the filling: Brush the dough with most of the margarine or almond oil. Sprinkle the turbinado or brown sugar and pepper about two-thirds of the way up the dough in the direction in which you will roll it closed. Roll the dough closed. Wet your knife and gently cut the dough into 10 discs. Flip them on their sides so you can brush the outside with a little more melted margarine or almond oil. Place them on a baking sheet and let rise for about 15 minutes.

Preheat the oven to 350°F. Oil a baking sheet. Place the rolls on the baking sheet and place it in the oven. Bake for 25 minutes.

To make the glaze: In a medium bowl, combine the confectioners' sugar, cardamom, and almond milk until you have a thick glaze. As soon as the rolls come out of the oven, spread the glaze on top, then sprinkle with the slivered almonds and pepper.

Better-Milk Biscuits with Chipotle Greens and Maple Beans

Rip Esselstyn, former firefighter and author of *The Engine 2 Diet*

Longtime plant-based advocate Rip Esselstyn actually got his entire firehouse in Austin, Texas, to go vegan! If you know firefighters, you know this was not easy. But it was food like this that did it. In this recipe, there is no buttermilk, just better-milk: oat, almond, soy, or hazelnut milk! They are much better than the cow-based thing. Smother these biscuits with maple beans and a side of garlicky chipotle greens, and even the most ardent nonvegan—and even firefighters—will come calling for breakfast.

MAKES 4 SERVINGS
TIME TO MAKE: 20 MINUTES

Biscuits

- 2 cups white whole wheat flour + ½ cup for dusting the board
- ¼ teaspoon baking soda
- 1 tablespoon baking powder
- ½ teaspoon salt
- ⅔ cup raw unsalted cashews or walnuts
- 2 tablespoons water
- 1 cup oat, almond, soy, or hazelnut milk

Greens

- 2 large bunches chard, sliced into ribbons
- 8 cloves garlic, sliced
- 1 chipotle chile in adobo sauce, minced
- ⅓ teaspoon salt

Beans

- 2 cans (15 ounces each) pinto beans with liquid
- ¼ cup water
- ¼ cup maple syrup
- ½ teaspoon salt

To make the biscuits: Preheat the oven to 400°F. Line a baking sheet with parchment paper or use an aerated pan.

Combine the 2 cups flour, baking soda, baking powder, and salt in a bowl. In a food processor, blend the cashews and water until they form a dry clump of cashew butter. Remove it from the food processor (no need to clean it yet!), and place it in a small bowl.

Add the flour mixture to the food processor. Crumble the cashew butter uniformly on top of the dry ingredients. Pulse the food processor, starting with about 8 quick pulses, until the mixture has a mealy consistency. Add the milk and mix until just combined but no more.

Turn the dough out onto a board dusted with the ½ cup flour. Gently pat the dough out with your hands—not a rolling pin—until it is ½" thick. Gently and lightly fold the dough about 5 times over itself. Gently press down on the dough until it is 1" thick. Using a round cutter or even a drinking glass, cut the dough into 2" to 2½" rounds. Knead the scraps together to make more rounds and use up all the dough. If you prefer soft sides on your biscuits, place the biscuits on the baking sheet touching each other. If you prefer crusty sides, place them about 1" apart.

Bake for 11 minutes. Once they come out of the oven, poke a toothpick into the center of one of them. If it comes out clean, the biscuits are done. If there is moist batter stuck to it, bake the biscuits for 2 minutes longer.

To make the greens: In a large skillet or medium saucepan over medium heat, cook the chard, garlic, chile, and salt for 10 minutes, or until the greens are completely wilted.

To make the beans: Combine the beans and their liquid, water, maple syrup, and salt in a small pot. Warm them over medium-low heat for 10 minutes. Smash them a few times with a potato masher until you have a very rough sauce.

Pour the bean sauce over the biscuits and serve the greens on the side.

Lemon-Blackberry Muffins

Madelyn Pryor, chef and national culinary instructor for The Vegan Taste

Says Madelyn: "These were created after a local news channel wanted to feature me and my cooking classes on air. They wanted me to create what I was making that night, plus provide a lot of 'healthy produce.' Knowing that all produce is healthy, I grabbed what looked good including a lot of berries. After getting only a few hours of sleep the night before, I raced down to the studio, set up… and after 45 minutes they told me I was canceled and to leave. I packed up my food, including the blackberries that became these muffins, and left to get a nap before my cooking class that night."

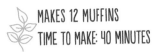

MAKES 12 MUFFINS
TIME TO MAKE: 40 MINUTES

1¾ cups gluten-free baking mix

2 teaspoons xanthan gum

2 tablespoons cornstarch

2½ teaspoons baking powder

½ cup + 2 tablespoons granulated sugar

⅓ cup vegetable oil

¼ cup lemon juice

1 tablespoon grated lemon peel

1 cup nondairy milk

½ teaspoon lemon extract

1 cup large fresh blackberries

Line a 12-cup muffin pan with muffin papers. Preheat the oven to 400°F.

In a bowl, stir together the baking mix, xanthan gum, cornstarch, and baking powder. In a separate bowl, cream together the ½ cup sugar and oil. Add the lemon juice, lemon peel, milk, and lemon extract. The mixture will be thick but you will still be able to spoon it into the muffin papers.

Place a small layer of batter in each muffin paper, then top with the blackberries. Repeat 2 more times, creating layers of blackberries and batter. Once the muffin tins are full, sprinkle the tops of the batter evenly with the 2 tablespoons sugar.

Bake for 25 minutes. Remove the pan from the oven, allow the muffins to cool slightly, then remove from the pan. Allow them to completely cool before removing them from the papers.

Orange-Basil Green Smoothie

Christy Morgan, chef, vegan fitness trainer, and author of *Blissful Bites*

If you've never had basil in a smoothie, you are in for a treat!

MAKES 1 SERVING (16 OUNCES)
TIME TO MAKE: 5 MINUTES

1 frozen banana

Small handful of fresh spinach

½ cup nondairy milk

½ cup orange juice

1 scoop vegan protein powder

1 tablespoon chopped fresh basil

In a blender, combine the banana, spinach, milk, juice, protein powder, and basil. Blend until smooth and no chunks remain. Serve immediately.

Emily Deschanel's Green Juice

Emily Deschanel, actress, television and film producer

Says Emily: "We don't have time to cook much in my house, but my 3-year-old loves making green juice. This is Henry's favorite green juice. You need a juicer, but this is so simple, healthy, and refreshing!"

MAKES 1 SERVING
TIME TO MAKE: 5 MINUTES

2 cucumbers

4–5 ribs celery

Handful of fresh spinach or kale

1 lemon, peeled

1 piece fresh ginger (2")

Small handful of fresh mint or cilantro, optional

In a juicer, combine the cucumbers, celery, spinach or kale, lemon, ginger, and mint or cliantro (if using). Juice away!

Confetti Oatmeal

Laura Theodore, author, host of the PBS cooking show *Jazzy Vegetarian*

Colorful cranberries, raisins, and bits of coconut offer a festive change to the typical morning bowl of oatmeal. A touch of sugar on top makes this porridge a sweet way to start the day!

MAKES 2 SERVINGS
TIME TO MAKE: 15 TO 20 MINUTES

1 cup rolled oats

3 tablespoons unsweetened shredded dried coconut

2 tablespoons dried cranberries

2 tablespoons raisins

1 heaping tablespoon wheat germ

2 cups + 2 scant tablespoons filtered or spring water

1 heaping tablespoon brown sugar or Sucanat + more as needed

Nondairy milk, optional

In a medium saucepan, combine the oats, coconut, cranberries, raisins, and wheat germ. Stir in the water. Cover and bring to a simmer over medium-low heat. Cook, stirring occasionally, for 7 minutes, or until all of the liquid is absorbed.

Remove from the heat and gently stir. Sprinkle the brown sugar over the top. Cover and let stand for 5 minutes.

Serve with nondairy milk, if desired, and more brown sugar on the side.

Giddyup Raw Apple Cereal

Kayle Martin of the Web site Cowgirls and Collard Greens

What's better than making your very own cereal? It tastes incredible, it's fresh, and the flavor is better than anything you can get out of a box! No additives or preservatives—just fresh ingredients from nature that are filling and delicious.

MAKES 2 SERVINGS
TIME TO MAKE: 10 MINUTES + AT LEAST 2 HOURS TO SOAK THE ALMONDS

½ cup raw almonds

2 organic apples, grated

2 ripe organic bananas, chopped

½ cup shredded coconut

½ cup raw hulled sunflower seeds

2 teaspoons Bee Free Honee or agave nectar

Dash of nutmeg

Nondairy milk (I prefer coconut or almond), optional

Soak the almonds in water for at least 2 hours or, if time allows, overnight. Rinse and finely chop them.

In a medium bowl, mix together the almonds, apples, bananas, coconut, sunflower seeds, Bee Free Honee or agave, and nutmeg. Add a splash of milk, if desired. Since this is a totally raw dish, it's best eaten as soon as possible.

Superfood Dark Chocolate Granola

Deb Gleason, certified holistic nutritionist and vegan lifestyle coach

Says Deb: "Chocolate for breakfast is probably the best idea I have come up with, and why not? Cacao is loaded with antioxidants and complements this delicious granola recipe perfectly. Add some almond milk and savor the healthy decadence."

MAKES 5 TO 6 SERVINGS
TIME TO MAKE: 25 MINUTES

3 cups rolled oats

½ cup unsweetened shredded coconut

½ cup chopped almonds

¼ cup whole chia seeds

¼ cup raw cacao nibs

¼ cup hemp seeds

2 tablespoons raw cacao powder

¼ teaspoon sea salt

3 tablespoons coconut oil

½ cup maple syrup

1 teaspoon vanilla extract

Preheat the oven to 350°F. Line a large baking sheet with parchment paper.

In a large mixing bowl, mix the oats, coconut, almonds, chia seeds, cacao nibs, hemp seeds, cacao powder, and sea salt.

In a small saucepan, heat the oil over low heat until it is just melted. Remove from the heat and add the maple syrup and vanilla extract, stirring to combine. Add to the dry ingredients and stir until well combined.

Evenly spread the granola on the baking sheet. Bake for 15 minutes, then stir the granola and bake it for 5 to 10 more minutes, or until the granola begins to brown at the edge of the baking sheet. Remove from the oven and allow to cool fully on the baking sheet. Once cool, store in airtight containers.

SALADS

Blood Orange, Olive, and Basil Salad

Jason Wyrick, executive chef of The Vegan Taste and author of *Vegan Tacos*

Says Jason: "This salad, typically made with whatever fresh oranges are on hand and made with blood oranges here, is a popular winter dish throughout the south of Italy. Fennel and red onion are popular additions, but my favorite version (this one) concentrates on the interplay of the sweetness of the oranges, the saltiness of the olives, the pop of the basil, and the smoothness of the olive oil. It showcases one of the quintessential elements of Italian cuisine, namely that you don't need complicated recipes to make outstanding food. You only need outstanding ingredients and the willingness to let them speak for themselves."

MAKES 2 SERVINGS
TIME TO MAKE: 10 MINUTES

- 4 blood oranges or oranges of your choice, peeled and carefully chopped into bite-size pieces
- 3 tablespoons chopped oil-cured pitted black olives or ¼ cup chopped pitted kalamata olives
- ¼ cup finely sliced basil leaves
- ¼ teaspoon ground black pepper
- 2 tablespoons good-quality extra-virgin olive oil (preferably with a peppery finish)
- ¼ cup thinly sliced fennel, if in season, optional

In a large bowl, toss together the oranges, olives, basil, pepper, oil, and fennel, if using. Let the salad sit for 5 minutes before serving. Make it low fat by omitting the oil.

Grilled Thai Cabbage Salad with Almond Chile Sauce

Chad Sarno, vegan chef, instructor, and bestselling author

The freshness of Thai herbs paired with the earthiness of the charred cabbage makes this salad a flavor-packed dish. Says Chad: "When head lettuce, bitter greens, or cabbage are grilled, it takes the ingredients to a whole other level. This grilled cabbage is celebrated with the trinity of Thai herbs—cilantro, basil, and mint—and creamy spiciness of . . . almond chile sauce, [which] has been a go-to sauce for years for me." Serve this hot as a side dish.

MAKES 6 SERVINGS
TIME TO MAKE: 20 MINUTES

Salad

- 1 small white, green, or red cabbage, cut in 6 large wedges
- 2–3 tablespoons olive oil
- Sea salt and ground black pepper
- ¼ cup ripped or coarsely chopped fresh mint, loosely packed
- ¼ cup ripped or coarsely chopped fresh basil, loosely packed
- ¼ cup ripped or coarsely chopped fresh cilantro, loosely packed + additional for garnish
- ½ cup Asian bean sprouts
- 3 green onions, sliced into 1"–2" pieces
- 1 lime, cut in small wedges

Sauce

- ½ cup almond butter
- 2 tablespoons lemon juice
- 1 tablespoon rice wine vinegar
- 3 tablespoons maple syrup or 5 pitted dates
- 1 tablespoon chopped fresh ginger
- ½ small serrano chile, minced
- 2 cloves garlic, coarsely chopped
- 2 tablespoons reduced-sodium tamari
- ¼ teaspoon sea salt
- ¼ cup coconut water or plain filtered water

To make the salad: Preheat a grill to medium-high.

Drizzle the cabbage wedges with the oil and gently toss with salt and pepper, to taste, making sure not to break the wedges. Place the wedges on the grill and grill all 3 sides of each wedge until they have grill marks all around.

In a bowl, add the mint, basil, ¼ cup cilantro, bean sprouts, and green onions and gently mix by hand. Coarsely chop the grilled cabbage and toss with the herb mixture.

To make the sauce: In a blender, combine the almond butter, lemon juice, vinegar, maple syrup or dates, ginger, chile, garlic, tamari, salt, and water. Puree until smooth.

To dress and garnish the salad: Drizzle the salad with a generous amount of Almond Chile Sauce before serving. Garnish with the lime wedges and cilantro.

Watermelon Salad

Allyson Bedene, owner of
A Friend of the Family catering
company

Says Allyson: "This watermelon
salad elevates a simple summer-
time pleasure into a treasure. To
further elevate it, you may add a
salty brined (feta-type) vegan
cheese. This is dedicated to the
memory of Jorge 'George' Hernan-
dez, a dear friend and very tal-
ented chef who taught me this
recipe and the value of mint, salty
flavors, and lime juice. He passed
away in 2013."

MAKES 6 SERVINGS
TIME TO MAKE: 10 MINUTES

1 seedless watermelon, cubed

Juice and grated peel of
2 or 3 limes

½ cup fresh mint leaves

Salt

In a large bowl, combine the watermelon, lime juice and peel, and mint.
Season to taste with salt and serve.

Sweet and Sour Salad

Victoria Moran, author of *Main Street Vegan* and *The Good Karma Diet* and director of Main Street Vegan Academy

Says Victoria: "I created this recipe to serve at Main Street Vegan Academy, a weeklong live program in New York City to train and certify vegan lifestyle coaches and educators. We get students from around the world and people who have a variety of dietary preferences—oil free, gluten free, soy free—so I try to come up with recipes that meet all these needs, can be easily doubled and tripled for a large group, contain reasonably priced ingredients, and are colorful and pretty on a buffet table. This one meets those criteria, as well as providing some unique taste thrills—sweet and tart. It's also a nutritional treasure trove with the dark, leafy greens, legumes, berries, and seeds. Maybe I should have called it 'Superpowers Salad!'" Seasoned rice wine vinegar is surprisingly rich and "dressing-like" all by itself.

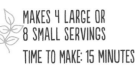

MAKES 4 LARGE OR
8 SMALL SERVINGS
TIME TO MAKE: 15 MINUTES

5 ounces mixed baby greens or baby romaine (about 6 cups)

5 ounces fresh arugula (about 6 cups)

1 can (15 ounces) chickpeas, drained

1 cup halved grape or cherry tomatoes or chopped whole tomatoes

½ cup raw pumpkin seeds

½ cup dried cranberries

Italian-style vinaigrette dressing or seasoned rice wine vinegar

In a large bowl, combine the greens, arugula, chickpeas, tomatoes, pumpkin seeds, and cranberries. Toss with the dressing or, for an oil-free salad, rice wine vinegar (found in the Asian aisle at the supermarket).

Variations: Toss in steamed broccoli florets or steamed sweet potato chunks that have been cooled, and make it a full meal. If dried cranberries are unavailable, substitute raisins, currants, or chopped dates.

Roasted Root Salad

Deb Gleason, certified holistic nutritionist and vegan lifestyle coach

Says Deb: "Root vegetables give me a warm mental image of pigs methodically rooting in the dirt in search of these delectable finds. When I think of pigs, I think of Nikki, the sweetest pig at Farm Sanctuary. In 2008 I was part of the team who rescued Nikki and her piglets from the flooded banks of the Mississippi River. She was a beautiful mother who continues to show the power of love with her adult kids at Farm Sanctuary to this day."

**MAKES 6 SERVINGS
TIME TO MAKE: 50 MINUTES**

Salad

4 cups diced beets (½" cubes)

4 cups sweet potatoes, diced into ½" cubes

1 bulb fennel, diced

2 teaspoons balsamic vinegar

Dressing

2 tablespoons balsamic vinegar

¼ cup water

2 tablespoons tahini

1 tablespoon dried dill

½ teaspoon sea salt

1 clove garlic, minced

Ground black pepper

To make the salad: Preheat the oven to 375°F. Line a baking sheet with parchment paper.

In a bowl, toss the beets, sweet potatoes, and fennel with the 2 teaspoons balsamic vinegar. Place on the baking sheet and cover with foil. Roast for 30 to 35 minutes, or until the veggies have softened but are still somewhat firm.

To make the dressing: In a small bowl, mix together the 2 tablespoons balsamic vinegar, the water, tahini, dill, salt, garlic, and pepper to taste.

Transfer the cooked vegetables to a serving bowl and toss them with the dressing.

Sprouted Buckwheat Tabbouleh

Matteo Silverman, Sonoma, California–based executive chef of Chalk Hill Cookery

Instead of using bulgur wheat, this tabbouleh recipe uses sprouted buckwheat groats. Sprouting buckwheat increases its nutritional content and digestibility and makes this recipe gluten free. It is a simple recipe to prepare, but you will need to plan ahead in order to soak and sprout the buckwheat. Everything else comes together quickly. The flavors remain classic with a tangy olive oil and lemon dressing. The mint and parsley add freshness and harmony to the dish.

MAKES 6 SERVINGS
TIME TO MAKE: 15 HOURS 10 MINUTES

1 cup buckwheat, soaked for 6 hours in filtered water

2 cups seeded and diced tomatoes

2 cups diced cucumber

¾ cup chopped fresh parsley

¾ cup chopped fresh mint

½ cup sliced green onions

½ cup olive oil

¼ cup lemon juice

¼ teaspoon ground black pepper

¼ teaspoon sea salt

Pinch or two of cayenne

Drain the buckwheat in a sieve and allow it to sit overnight to sprout. The next day, dry the buckwheat with a clean towel to remove excess moisture.

In a large bowl, combine the sprouted buckwheat, tomatoes, cucumber, parsley, mint, and green onion. In a small bowl, whisk together the oil, lemon juice, black pepper, salt, and cayenne until emulsified. Pour the dressing over the buckwheat mixture and toss it all together. Serve immediately or marinate up to 1 hour prior to eating.

Waldorf-Style "Chicken" Salad

Wendy Matthews, education and outreach manager for Farm Sanctuary

With so many incredible (dare we say superior) chicken and mayo alternatives on the market, this take on the classic Waldorf salad adds a key component that was missing from the original—a healthy dose of compassion. With a delectable mix of sweetness, creaminess, and crunch, we're sure it won't just be the animals that are happy with this recipe on the table; your diners will be, too.

MAKES 6 SERVINGS
TIME TO MAKE: 10 TO 15 MINUTES

½ cup Vegenaise (more if you prefer)

1 teaspoon vegan Worcestershire sauce

Sea salt and ground black pepper

3 cups diced Beyond Meat Chicken Grilled Strips, brought to room temperature

1 cup halved seedless red grapes

1 cup finely sliced celery

¾ cup chopped pecans

½ small red onion, finely chopped

Pitas, lettuce, and avocado, optional

In a large bowl, whisk together the Vegenaise, Worcestershire sauce, and salt and pepper to taste. Add the Beyond Meat, grapes, celery, pecans, and onion and toss until evenly coated and combined.

Serve on pitas with lettuce and avocado, if desired.

Arugula Pear Salad with Walnut-Crusted Gardein Chick'n

Jason Stefanko, executive chef for Gardein

Says Jason: "Four years ago, I represented Gardein at the national restaurant show in Chicago. It was in Chicago that we met a very important chef from Disney named Gary Jones. Gary put Gardein and me in front of every executive chef from Disney in Orlando, Florida. We teamed up with Chef Jens Dahlmann to create Epcot International Festival's Food and Wine first-ever vegan food pavilion. For 6 weeks in late September through October, Gardein has two menu items and vegan wine showcased at a kiosk named Terra. For the last 2 years, those menu items have been Trick'n Chick'n Curry over Basmati Rice, and Beefless Tips Chili Colorado with Jalapeño Cashew Cheese Drizzle and Fresh-Made Kettle Chips. This salad recipe comes from cooking classes that I hosted at Epcot during the food and wine festival."

MAKES 4 SERVINGS
TIME TO MAKE: 20 MINUTES

Chick'n

- ¾ cup walnuts
- ¼ cup bread crumbs
- 3 tablespoons nutritional yeast
- 1½ teaspoons dried basil
- 1½ teaspoons dried rosemary
- ¾ teaspoon salt
- ½ teaspoon ground black pepper
- 1 cup all-purpose unbleached flour
- 1 cup soy milk
- 1 package Gardein Chick'n Scallopini

Dressing

- ¼ cup olive oil
- 1 tablespoon minced shallots
- 2 teaspoons white wine vinegar
- ¼ teaspoon sea salt
- ¼ teaspoon Dijon mustard
- Ground black pepper

Salad

- 6 cups baby arugula leaves
- 2 Anjou pears, cored and thinly sliced
- ½ cup quartered dried Mission figs
- ¼ cup chopped candied walnuts
- ½ wheel Kite Hill White Alder cheese, chopped into ½" pieces

To make the Chick'n: In a food processor, pulse the walnuts, bread crumbs, nutritional yeast, basil, rosemary, salt, and pepper until the walnuts are coarsely ground. Do not overprocess into flour.

Place the flour, soy milk, and walnut breading each into 3 separate bowls. Dredge the Chick'n Scallopini in the flour, then the soy milk, and finally in the breading to coat. Coat a large nonstick skillet with oil and heat to medium-high. Add the scallopini to the pan and cook for 2 to 3 minutes on each side, or until crispy. Drain on a paper towel.

To make the dressing: In a small mixing bowl, mix together the oil, shallots, vinegar, salt, and mustard. Season to taste with the pepper.

To make the salad: In a large bowl, toss the arugula, pears, and figs. Pour on the dressing and toss together.

Place about 1½ cups of the arugula salad over each Chick'n. Garnish each salad with the candied walnuts and cheese.

Glazed Carrot Salad

Bryant Terry, author of *Vegan Soul Kitchen* and *Afro-Vegan*

This dish is a mashup of glazed carrots, which are popular in the South, and Moroccan carrot salad. The savory coating is rich, intense, and delicious, and makes for a gorgeous dish.

MAKES 6 TO 8 SERVINGS
TIME TO MAKE: 40 MINUTES

10 medium carrots (about 1½ pounds), ends trimmed

1 tablespoon plus ½ teaspoon coarse sea salt

2 tablespoons peanut oil

1 tablespoon freshly squeezed lemon juice

2 teaspoons maple syrup

1 teaspoon ground cinnamon

1 clove garlic, minced

1 teaspoon cumin seeds, toasted

¼ cup packed chopped cilantro

2 tablespoons crushed roasted peanuts

2 tablespoons chopped fresh mint

Preheat the oven to 425°F. Line a large roasting pan with parchment paper.

Put about 12 cups of water in a large pot and bring to a boil over high heat. While the water is heating up, cut the carrots into sticks by cutting them in half crosswise, trimming away the edges of each piece to form a rough rectangle, then quartering each rectangle length-wise. (Compost the scraps or save them for another use.)

When the water is boiling, add 1 tablespoon of the salt, then add the carrots and blanch for 1 minute. Drain the carrots well, then pat them dry with a clean kitchen towel.

Put the oil, lemon juice, maple syrup, cinnamon, garlic, cumin seeds, and the remaining ½ teaspoon salt in a large bowl and mix well. Add the carrots and toss until evenly coated. Transfer to the lined pan (no need to clean the bowl). Cover with aluminum foil and bake for 10 minutes. Remove the foil, gently stir with a wooden spoon, then bake uncovered for about 10 minutes, until the carrots start to brown.

Return the carrots to the bowl. Add the cilantro and toss gently to combine. Serve garnished with the peanuts and mint.

HANDHELD MEALS

Tacos with Salted Grilled Plantains, Salsa Verde, and Pepitas

Jason Wyrick, executive chef of The Vegan Taste and author of *Vegan Tacos*

Says Jason: "If the tortilla is the soul of a taco, then the filling is the body, and fresh lime and spicy salsa are the life of it. It's the fusion of all three of these components that makes tacos the perfect hand-held meal. Because the traditional tortilla for a taco is only about 5½" in diameter, one serving is usually two or three tacos—or four if you're hungry!"

MAKES 12 TACOS
TIME TO MAKE: 25 TO 35 MINUTES

Chef's Tip: You can use pre-made tortillas. Warm them on the grill for 5 seconds per side before filling them, to make the tortillas pliable. If you are using full-size torti-llas, you will end up with about 8 tacos. Also, you can cook these on the stovetop by chopping the plantains, then tossing them in the oil, and cooking them for 7 to 8 minutes over medium heat. Once you're done, toss them in the lime peel, lime juice, and salt and top your tortillas.

- 2 cups fresh masa (corn dough for making tortillas) or 12 small premade corn tortillas
- 2 medium semiripe plantains, peeled
- 1 tablespoon garlic-infused oil
- Grated peel and juice of 2 limes
- 1 teaspoon salt
- 1 teaspoon ancho chile powder
- 1½ cups salsa verde
- ¾ cup toasted pepitas
- 2 cups shredded red cabbage

Heat a grill, preferably using mesquite wood. If using a gas grill, bring to medium heat and add soaked mesquite chips in the smoking box.

While the grill is coming to temperature, make the tortillas. Bring a griddle or comal to medium heat. Lay plastic wrap over the bottom flap of your tortilla press.

Take 2 to 2½ tablespoons of the masa and form it into a ball. Lay this on the plastic wrap, just slightly off center toward the hinges of the press. Lay a sheet of plastic wrap at least the size of the tortilla press flap over the masa ball. Press down firmly until the masa is flat and you have a tortilla ready to be cooked. This takes a little practice, so if your first few tortillas don't turn out right, simply re-form the dough into a ball and press it again. Make as many uncooked tortillas as your griddle can handle before laying them on the hot griddle. Typically this will be 2 to 4 tortillas. Make sure to press each tortilla in its own plastic wrap and keep them in the wrap until you are ready to lay them on the griddle.

Remove the top layer of the plastic sheet. Flip the tortilla over and remove the other layer. Gently lay it on your griddle. Cook the first side for 30 sec-onds to 1 minute, or until you see the edges of the tortilla change color. Flip the tortilla over and cook for 1 minute. Flip it back over one more time and cook it for another 30 seconds. Remove the tortillas from the heat, stacking them and keeping them covered so they don't dry out.

Brush the plantains with the oil. Grill them until they are heavily browned on both sides. Remove them from the grill and chop into bite-size pieces. Immediately toss them with the lime peel and juice and then the salt and chile powder.

To each tortilla, add the plantains, 2 tablespoons of the salsa verde, 1 tablespoon of the pepitas, and the cabbage.

Reef Tacos

Nanci Alexander, owner of Sublime Restaurant in Fort Lauderdale, Florida

Says Nanci: "I live on Fort Lauderdale Beach and love to take early morning walks along the ocean. One day I wondered how we could get the smell of the ocean, the feeling of the beach, and the sensation of eating seafood without actually using sea animals. Sublime experimented with tofu, nori, and made a creamy sauce using cilantro—and this is the result."

MAKES 4 TACOS
TIME TO MAKE: 15 TO 20 MINUTES

Tempura Batter

- 4 sheets nori
- 1 cup all-purpose flour
- 1 cup rice flour
- ¼ teaspoon baking soda
- ¼ teaspoon baking powder
- ¼ cup dulse flakes
- 2 cups carbonated water

Cilantro Cream Sauce

- 1 cup Tofutti sour cream
- ⅓ bunch fresh cilantro
- ¼ cup pickled jalapeño chiles, drained
- 2 tablespoons fresh lime juice

Asian Cabbage Slaw

- ⅓ cup shredded Napa cabbage
- ⅓ cup shredded green cabbage
- ⅓ cup shredded red cabbage
- ⅓ cup shredded carrots

Filling and Toppings

- Oil
- 8 (1" thick) slices extra-firm tofu, drained, sliced to the length of your tortillas
- 4 corn or flour tortillas
- ½ cup pico de gallo, divided
- 8 tablespoons minced chives (garlic chives preferred)

To make the batter: Toast the nori sheets over an open flame or in a 375°F oven for 5 minutes, or until golden green and very brittle. Crush the nori with your hands until the flakes are the same size as the dulse flakes. In a medium bowl, sift together the flours, baking soda, and baking powder. Stir in the nori and dulse flakes. Whisk in the carbonated water until the batter is smooth.

To make the sauce: In a blender, combine the sour cream, cilantro, chiles, and lime juice. Puree until smooth.

To make the slaw: In a medium bowl, combine the cabbages and carrots.

To finish preparing: Add enough oil to a heavy pot, wok, or deep fryer to cover your tofu by 1". Bring the oil to 375°F. Dredge the tofu through the tempura batter and drop it in the oil. Cook for 3 to 4 minutes, or until golden brown.

Grill the tortillas for a few seconds on each side. Spread 1 teaspoon of the cilantro cream sauce onto each tortilla. Place two strips of tofu on each tortilla, then top each taco with 1 tablespoon of pico de gallo. Garnish with the slaw, more cream sauce to taste, and finally, the garlic chives.

Jamaican Barbecued Seitan Sandwiches with Coleslaw

Tamasin Noyes, coauthor of *Vegan Finger Foods* and *Vegan Sandwiches Save the Day!*

Says Tamasin: "Packed with addictive island flavors, this savory sandwich will keep you coming back for more. The complex flavors of the barbecue are offset by the mild coleslaw. We'll admit to sometimes spiking the slaw with hot sauce or, conversely, substituting a jalapeño pepper for the scotch bonnet. Play with it to cook to your taste, too!"

MAKES 4 SANDWICHES
TIME TO MAKE: 40 TO 45 MINUTES

Seitan

2 tablespoons olive oil, divided
½ cup chopped onion
¼ teaspoon sea salt
1 scotch bonnet chile, chopped
2 cloves garlic, minced
1½ teaspoons grated fresh ginger
1½ teaspoons ground cardamom
1½ teaspoons ground cumin
¼ teaspoon cayenne, or more to taste
¼ teaspoon ground allspice
¼ teaspoon ground black pepper
2 tablespoons tamari
1 can (14.5 ounces) fire-roasted crushed tomatoes
2 tablespoons white wine vinegar
1 tablespoon blackstrap molasses, or more to taste
1 can (6 ounces) tomato paste
12 ounces seitan, cut into strips
4 buns, toasted

Coleslaw

3 cups grated cabbage
¼ cup chopped green onions
3 tablespoons grated carrots
¼ cup vegan mayonnaise
1 tablespoon white wine vinegar
1 teaspoon sugar, or more to taste
1 teaspoon fresh lime juice, or more to taste
¼ teaspoon dried thyme
Salt and ground black pepper

To make the seitan: Heat 1 tablespoon of the oil in a large saucepan over medium heat and add the onion and salt. Cook, stirring occasionally, for 3 to 5 minutes, or until softened.

Add the dried spices. Cook and stir for 2 minutes, or until fragrant. Add the tamari, crushed tomatoes, vinegar, molasses, and tomato paste. Bring to a boil, then reduce to a simmer and cook for 10 minutes, stirring occasionally. Blend with an immersion blender (or transfer to a blender) until smooth.

Pour the remaining 1 tablespoon oil into a large skillet and heat over medium-high heat. Add the seitan strips and cook for 3 to 4 minutes, or until browned. Add the barbecue sauce and simmer for 5 minutes.

To make the coleslaw: In a medium bowl, stir together the cabbage, green onions, carrots, mayonnaise, vinegar, sugar, lime juice, thyme, and salt and pepper to taste.

Divide the barbecued seitan evenly among the buns and top with coleslaw.

Just Mayo Chickpea Salad Sandwiches

Hunter Clark in conjunction with Hampton Creek

I love what the people at Hampton Creek are doing to bring compassionate choices to the masses—they are creating delicious foods that do not need eggs, from mayonnaise to cookie dough. This recipe from them is a tasty, uncomplicated meal (two of my favorite things) that can be made in just a few minutes.

MAKES 6 SANDWICHES
TIME TO MAKE: 10 MINUTES

1 carrot

3 ribs celery

½ yellow onion

¼ cup fresh parsley

2 kosher dill pickles (Bubbies brand are my favorite)

2 cans (16 ounces each) chickpeas, rinsed and drained

½ cup Just Mayo + additional for spreading

2 teaspoons lemon juice

Salt and ground black pepper

12 slices sourdough bread

1 large tomato, thinly sliced

In a food processor, combine the carrot, celery, onion, parsley, and 1 pickle. Pulse until they are minced. Add the chickpeas and pulse approximately 4 times, scraping the sides after each pulse. Be careful not to smash the chickpeas too much. It is okay for there to be some chickpeas left whole.

Remove the chickpea salad from the food processor and stir into it the ½ cup of Just Mayo, lemon juice, and salt and pepper to taste.

For each sandwich, place 2 slices of bread together and toast them so that only the outside surfaces of the bread gets lightly toasted.

Spread a bit of Just Mayo on the inside of each slice of bread. Thinly slice the remaining pickle and add a few slices to half the bread slices. Top the other slices of bread with the tomato. Add a bit of chickpea salad to every slice of bread and combine to form 6 sandwiches. Cut in half and enjoy!

Vegiterranean Tempeh Sandwiches with White Bean Rosemary Spread

Julieanna Hever, MS, RD, CPT, author of *The Complete Idiot's Guide to Plant-Based Nutrition* and *The Vegiterranean Diet*

This is a hearty sandwich with Mediterranean flavors and sweet undertones. Use your preferred whole grain bread or roll, or try it as a wrap in a whole grain tortilla.

MAKES 4 SANDWICHES
TIME TO MAKE: 1 HOUR TO 1 HOUR 10 MINUTES

Tempeh

1 package (8 ounces) tempeh

¼ cup fresh lemon juice

2 tablespoons balsamic vinegar

1 tablespoon pure maple syrup

½ teaspoon dried basil

½ teaspoon dried oregano

½ teaspoon dried rosemary

¼ teaspoon crushed red-pepper flakes

8 slices whole grain bread or 4 whole grain tortillas

Romaine lettuce leaves

Sliced fresh tomatoes

Spread

¼ cup vegetable stock

2 cloves garlic, minced, optional

1 teaspoon minced fresh rosemary

1 can (15 ounces) cannellini or other white beans, rinsed and drained

2 teaspoons fresh lemon juice

Salt and ground black pepper

To make the tempeh: Slice the tempeh into 8 pieces. In a square baking dish, stir together the lemon juice, vinegar, maple syrup, basil, oregano, rosemary, and pepper flakes. Carefully place each piece of tempeh into the marinade, coating both sides well. Cover the tempeh and refrigerate it for at least 30 minutes.

Preheat the oven to 350°F. Transfer the tempeh to the oven and bake the tempeh for 20 minutes. Flip the tempeh over and bake for 10 minutes.

To make the spread: Meanwhile, in a medium pot, bring the stock, garlic, and rosemary to a boil over medium-high heat. Cook for 5 minutes, or until the garlic and rosemary are soft. Add the beans and reduce the heat to a simmer. Simmer for 3 to 5 minutes, or until the beans are completely softened. Add the lemon juice and salt and pepper to taste and stir to combine. Turn off the heat. With an immersion blender (or after transferring to a blender), puree for 5 to 10 seconds, or until smooth.

Lightly toast or warm the bread or tortillas. For each sandwich, use a quarter of the bean spread, dividing and spreading it evenly on both slices of bread. If you are using tortillas, spread a quarter of the bean spread on each tortilla. Place 2 pieces of tempeh on the bottom slice of bread or on the tortilla. Add the lettuce and top with the tomato.

Po-Lentil Curry Burgers

Steven Todd Smith, master Reiki teacher and community manager for *Forks Over Knives*

Says Steven: "I never really cooked much until I went vegan. Soon I was discovering new foods and new ways to approach meals that got my creative juices flowing. One day, while making a simple meal of black beans and tempeh, I got bored and started mixing and mashing everything together until it formed one cohesive mixture. I had a lightbulb moment, adding my favorite spices and some other fun ingredients, formed the mixture into patties, threw them in the oven, and 20 to 30 minutes later I had my first homemade bean burgers. Not only were they tasty, but I had a great time playing around to make the meal."

MAKES 8 TO 10 BURGERS
TIME TO MAKE: 50 MINUTES

Burgers

- 1½ cups cooked brown lentils
- 1 can (15 ounces) low-sodium chickpeas, rinsed and drained, or 1¾ cups cooked
- 1 can (15 ounces) low-sodium cannellini beans, rinsed and drained, or 1¾ cups cooked
- 9 ounces polenta (about ½ tube)
- 2 tablespoons yellow curry powder
- 1 tablespoon garlic powder
- 1 tablespoon onion powder
- ½ tablespoon smoked paprika
- 3 tablespoons ketchup
- ¼ cup diced white onions, optional
- ¼ cup nutritional yeast
- Hot sauce
- Salt
- ¼ cup whole wheat bread crumbs or panko
- ¾ cup rolled oats
- 8–10 whole wheat hamburger buns

Topping Combo 1

- 2½ cups sliced cremini mushrooms
- 1 cup ketchup
- 2 avocados, pitted and sliced
- 1 cup spicy brown mustard, optional

Topping Combo 2

- 4 cups torn kale leaves or mustard greens
- 1 cup ketchup
- 1½ cups shredded carrots
- 1 cup spicy brown mustard, optional

To make the burgers: In a medium or large bowl, mash the lentils, chickpeas, cannellini beans, and polenta, but leave a little chunky for added texture. Add the curry powder, garlic powder, onion powder, smoked paprika, ketchup, onions (if using), nutritional yeast, and hot sauce and salt to taste. Stir until combined. Add the bread crumbs and oats and mix one final time. Cover the bowl with plastic wrap and refrigerate for 10 to 20 minutes.

Preheat the oven to 400°F. Cover a baking sheet with a light coat of nutritional yeast and bread crumbs.

(continued on page 166)

Remove the burger mixture from the refrigerator. Pat into eight to ten ¾"-thick patties and spread them out on the baking sheet. Bake for 12 to 15 minutes, flip them, and bake for 12 to 15 minutes longer.

To make the topping combo: While the burgers are baking, prepare either topping and toast the buns.

For topping 1, in a dry pan over medium-high heat, cook the mushrooms, stirring occasionally, for 7 to 8 minutes, or until they are well browned. Spread about 2 tablespoons of the ketchup on the bottom buns, then place the burgers on the buns. Top with the mushrooms and sliced avocado. Spread the mustard, if using, on the top bun.

For topping 2, in a large pot, steam the kale or mustard greens for 10 minutes. Spread 2 tablespoons of the ketchup on the bottom buns, then place the burgers on the buns. Top with the shredded carrots and then the steamed greens. Spread the mustard, if using, on the top bun.

Close the burgers and eat!

Herbed Portobello Burgers

Laura Theodore, author and host of the PBS cooking show *Jazzy Vegetarian*

Slathered with all the classic fixings, these burgers are the perfect solution for a compassionate summer barbecue or a fun family supper. Serve them up with the works, and you will satisfy vegans and omnivores alike!

MAKES 4 BURGERS
TIME TO MAKE: 4 HOURS 35 MINUTES

12 large fresh oregano leaves, finely chopped (about 1 teaspoon)

8 large fresh basil leaves, finely chopped (about 1 tablespoon)

2 large fresh sage leaves, finely chopped (about 1 teaspoon)

4 cloves garlic, minced

2 tablespoons reduced-sodium tamari

2 tablespoons filtered or spring water

4 teaspoons Dijon mustard

2 teaspoons dried Italian seasoning blend or your favorite all-purpose seasoning

¼ teaspoon cayenne

4 portobello mushrooms, washed, with stems removed

4 teaspoons ketchup

4 teaspoons Dijon mustard

4 teaspoons relish, optional

4 whole grain hamburger buns or crusty rolls, cut in half

1 large beefsteak tomato, cut into 8 slices

4 large romaine lettuce leaves

In a small bowl, briskly whisk together the oregano, basil, sage, garlic, tamari, water, mustard, Italian or other seasoning, and cayenne. Place the mushrooms, gill side up, on a plate. Distribute the marinade evenly over each mushroom. Cover and refrigerate for 3 to 4 hours.

Preheat the oven to 375°F. Line a baking dish with unbleached parchment paper.

Arrange the mushrooms, gill side up, on the baking dish. Pour any excess marinade over the mushrooms. Cover with foil and bake for 15 minutes. Remove the foil from the baking dish and bake for 15 to 17 minutes, or until the mushrooms are tender and slightly browned.

Spread the ketchup, mustard, and relish (if using) on the bun tops. Add the mushrooms to the bun bottoms, top with 2 tomato slices and a lettuce leaf, close the buns, and serve immediately.

Pizza Buns

Wendy Matthews, Farm Sanctuary education and outreach manager

On Fridays our staff has a plant-based potluck dinner. Some of these meals are better than others—not all workers are great chefs. But there are certain dinners that are always winners. This easy-to-prepare recipe is one of the favorites. It's inexpensive, filling, and even nonvegans can't get enough of it.

MAKES 12 BUNS
TIME TO MAKE: 25 TO 30 MINUTES

Buns

16 ounces prepared pizza dough (homemade or store bought)

½ teaspoon dried basil

½ teaspoon dried oregano

2 cups marinara sauce

1 bag (8 ounces) Daiya Mozzarella Style Shreds

Your favorite pizza toppings (sliced mushrooms, chopped spinach, fresh basil, Tofurky Pepperoni Slices, etc.)

Garlic Butter Topping (optional)

¼ cup Earth Balance spread

3 cloves garlic, minced

½ teaspoon dried parsley

Vegan Parmesan cheese, optional

Warmed marinara sauce, optional

To make the buns: Preheat the oven to 450°F. Grease a 13" x 9" baking dish with a small amount of Earth Balance or olive oil.

Flour a working surface. Roll and stretch the pizza dough into a large rectangle approximately ½" thick. Sprinkle the dough with the basil and oregano. Spread the marinara evenly onto the dough using a rubber spatula or spoon. Sprinkle the mozzarella on top in an even layer. Distribute the toppings evenly over the cheese. When spreading these ingredients onto the dough, leave a 1" uncovered short edge. Roll closed, starting from the covered edge and roll toward the uncovered edge.

Starting with the short edge, roll the dough into a log shape and pinch the seams to seal it. Using a bread knife, cut the log into 12 slices approximately 1" wide. Place the slices in the baking dish, cut sides up. There should be a little space between the rolls before baking, but they will rise to fill the dish when baked. Set this aside while preparing the garlic butter topping, if using.

To prepare the topping: In a small skillet over medium-low heat, melt the Earth Balance spread. Add the garlic and cook for 1 minute, or until fragrant and slightly golden. Stir in the parsley and immediately remove the pan from the heat. Using a pastry brush, brush the top of each pizza bun with a small amount of the garlic butter. Sprinkle the tops with the Parmesan, if using. Bake for 10 to 15 minutes, or until the dough is risen, golden, and cooked through. Serve warm marinara sauce for dipping, if desired.

SOUPS

Bangkok Butternut Squash Chowder

David Silver, restaurateur and vegan food industry consultant

Says David: "I created Bangkok Butternut Squash Chowder for a restaurant in Hell's Kitchen back in the early '90s. It was inspired by the Pan Asian theme of the restaurant. At the time, I used fish sauce. Upon becoming vegan, I modified the recipe with umeboshi paste (evolution at work!). This soup was on the menu year-round for a decade at my former cafe, Second Helpings in Brooklyn, and has appeared at Woodstock Farm Animal Sanctuary twice for their Thanksliving event. One critic said that it was so good it was like sex in a bowl."

MAKES 8 SERVINGS
TIME TO MAKE: 1 HOUR 15 MINUTES

Chef's Tip: Make this simple. Instead of peeling, seeding, and chopping butternut squash, you can often find already chopped butternut squash at the store. Alternatively, you can use 4 cans of unsweetened pureed butternut squash.

3 tablespoons coconut oil

3 tablespoons Thai red curry paste*

2 yellow onions, chopped

3 cloves garlic, minced

6 cups chopped butternut squash or 3½ cups puree

3 carrots, coarsely chopped

2½ cups coconut milk

2½ cups water

1 teaspoon salt

2 teaspoons umeboshi paste, optional

3 cups corn

In a large pot over medium heat, melt the oil. Add the curry paste and fry it for 2 to 3 minutes. Add the onions and cook for 6 to 8 minutes, or until they are translucent. Add the garlic and cook for 3 to 5 minutes.

Add the squash, carrots, coconut milk, water, salt, and umeboshi paste and stir until the curry paste disseminates throughout the soup. Bring to a simmer and cook for 30 to 45 minutes, or until all the ingredients are soft. Then puree the soup in a blender until it is smooth.

Bring a dry skillet to a high heat. Add the corn and cook, stirring, for 5 to 7 minutes, or until it browns. Add to the soup and serve.

*Many red curry pastes are not vegan as they contain fish and shrimp paste, so take care and check the label.

Spring Vegetable Cioppino

Rich Landau and
Kate Jacoby, owners and
executive chefs of Vedge
Restaurant in Philadelphia

I love this robust "catch-of-the-day"
tomato soup, because here the
catch isn't fish, it's wild mushrooms, peas, leeks, and fennel.
Served with a slice of toasted sourdough bread, this is a compassionate version of a San Francisco
classic.

MAKES 4 TO 6 SERVINGS
TIME TO MAKE: 45 MINUTES

1 pound fresh or frozen
   shelled mixed peas and/or
   beans (English peas, fava
   beans, chickpeas, limas,
   etc.)
4 tablespoons olive oil
2 medium trimmed leeks,
   finely sliced (about 1 cup)
2 tablespoons minced garlic
1 small bulb fennel, finely
   sliced (about 1 cup)
½ cup dry white wine
2 cups sliced wild mushrooms
3 cups vegetable stock

1 can (16 ounces) diced San
   Marzano tomatoes
1½ teaspoons salt
1 teaspoon ground black
   pepper
1 tablespoon seafood
   seasoning (Old Bay
   preferred)
1 tablespoon chopped fresh
   thyme or oregano leaves
½ teaspoon red-pepper flakes
4 slices grilled or toasted
   sourdough bread

In a large stock pot, bring salted water to a boil. Add the peas and/or
beans and blanch them for 3 minutes, then shock them in ice water to
prevent further cooking. Drain.

In the same stock pot, heat 2 tablespoons of the oil over medium heat
until it ripples. Add the leeks and garlic, and cook for 3 to 5 minutes, or
until they are browned.

Stir the fennel, then the wine, into the pot. Bring the wine to a boil, then
simmer for 2 minutes. Add the mushrooms, stock, tomatoes, salt, pepper,
and seafood seasoning. Simmer over medium-low heat for 15 minutes, or
until the mushrooms are tender and the fennel is soft. Stir the thyme or
oregano, blanched peas and/or beans, and red-pepper flakes into the
soup.

Ladle the soup into bowls. Drizzle with the remaining 2 tablespoons oil, if
desired, and serve with the bread.

Hearts of Palm Bourdetto

Rich Landau and
Kate Jacoby, owners and
executive chefs of Vedge
Restaurant in Philadelphia

Another great recipe from Vedge
and an innovation on what is
classically a seafood stew. And
another reason why it's one of
the most popular restaurants in
Philadelphia.

MAKES 4 TO 6 SERVINGS
TIME TO MAKE: 30 MINUTES

4 tablespoons olive oil

½ cup finely diced onions

½ cup finely diced red bell
pepper

2 tablespoons minced garlic

1 cup finely diced tomatoes

½ cup white wine

1 quart vegetable stock

4 cups coarsely chopped or
scallop-cut hearts of palm,
(fresh is preferred, or use
unmarinated if from a can
or jar)

1 teaspoon salt

1 teaspoon ground black
pepper

1 teaspoon cayenne or red-
pepper flakes

2 teaspoons seafood
seasoning (Old Bay
preferred)

1 teaspoon chopped fresh
oregano or thyme

4–6 lemon wedges

In a medium stock pot, heat 2 tablespoons of the oil over medium heat
until it ripples. Add the onions, bell pepper, and garlic and cook for 3 to
5 minutes, or until browned. Add the tomatoes and wine and cook for
4 to 5 minutes, or until reduced.

Add the stock, hearts of palm, salt, black pepper, cayenne or pepper
flakes, and seafood seasoning. Reduce the heat to low. Simmer for
10 minutes. Stir in the oregano or thyme and remove the from heat.

Serve immediately, garnished with lemon wedges and drizzled with the
remaining 2 tablespoons oil, if desired.

Moby's Improvised Chili

Moby, musician, DJ

According to Moby, there are no real measurements here—you just kind of throw a bunch of stuff in a pot and at some point you decide it's done. However, for those of us who like more instructions, I've added some pointers (in parentheses).

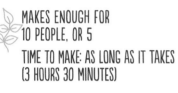

MAKES ENOUGH FOR 10 PEOPLE, OR 5

TIME TO MAKE: AS LONG AS IT TAKES (3 HOURS 30 MINUTES)

Onions, maybe 5? (5 onions, diced)

Garlic cloves, I don't know . . . 10 cloves? (10 cloves garlic, minced)

10 or so? tomatoes (10 plum tomatoes, coarsely chopped)

(4 cups water or vegetable stock)

Frozen corn, a few bags (6 cups frozen corn)

Seitan, a lot (6 cups sliced seitan)

3 cans black beans (15 ounces each)

Lots of chili powder (1 cup chili powder)

1 tube polenta (18 ounces polenta, chopped into 1" cubes)

1 tub tofu (16 ounces extra-firm tofu, drained and cut into 1" cubes)

Cornbread

Fresh salsa

Salt, optional

Coat a large pot with olive oil and heat over medium heat. Add the onion and garlic and cook for 7 to 8 minutes, or until the onion is translucent. Add the tomatoes and water or stock and cook for 15 minutes.

Add the corn, seitan, black beans, chili powder, polenta, and tofu. Cook for about 5 minutes, stirring, so the chili doesn't stick to the bottom of the pot.

Reduce the heat to low, cover the pot, and cook for 3 hours.

Serve with cornbread and fresh salsa. Salt it, if you wish.

Gumbo

Jenné Claiborne, personal chef and creator of the 21-Day Vegan Blueprint

This southern Louisiana dish is famous for its thick and meaty texture and bold flavor. The most delicious gumbos are made in a heavy-bottom pot, so pull out your Dutch oven. Field Roast sausage and a variety of herbs and spices make this vegan version every bit as delicious and satiating as a traditional one. A gluten-free version can be made by replacing the vegan sausage with chickpeas. Serve gumbo with rice (or a side of cornbread).

MAKES 4 TO 6 SERVINGS
TIME TO MAKE: 50 MINUTES

¼ cup grapeseed oil

¼ cup unbleached all-purpose flour

1 large yellow onion, diced

   Sea salt

3 cloves garlic, minced

2 cups chopped celery

1 large green bell pepper, chopped

1 cup frozen or fresh sliced okra

1 can (14 ounces) diced tomatoes

1 vegetable bouillon cube dissolved in 3 cups water, or 3 cups vegetable broth

1 bay leaf

3 cups water (for rice)

1½ cups medium-grain brown rice

2 Field Roast Smoked Apple Sage sausages, sliced

1 teaspoon smoked paprika

1 teaspoon ground black pepper

1 teaspoon dried thyme

1 tablespoon dried sage

1 teaspoon dried rosemary

1 teaspoon fennel seeds

Heat a large Dutch oven or heavy pot over medium heat and add the oil. When it's hot, sprinkle in the flour. Toast the flour in the oil, without stirring, for 3 to 5 minutes, or until it turns golden brown, to make a roux.

Add the onion to the roux, followed by a sprinkle of the salt, and stir. Cook for 2 minutes, or until the onion begins to soften. Add the garlic, celery, and bell pepper and cook for 5 minutes, or until they are soft.

Add the okra, tomatoes, bouillon and water (or vegetable broth), and bay leaf and stir well. Bring the gumbo to a simmer and cook, uncovered, for 25 to 30 minutes.

While the gumbo is cooking, make the brown rice. In a medium saucepan, boil the 3 cups water and add the rice. Add a dash of salt to taste, reduce the heat to a simmer, and cook with the lid ajar for 30 minutes.

Once the gumbo has thickened up, add the sausages, paprika, black pepper, thyme, sage, rosemary, and fennel seeds. Cook for 8 minutes, season to taste, and serve over the rice.

Faki* Soup

Biz Stone (cofounder, Twitter) and **Livia Stone**

Biz Stone and his then-girlfriend Livia McRee came to visit Farm Sanctuary in 2000. They were both interested in animal rights, but neither was a vegan. It took a weekend for that transformation to take place—both of them left as dedicated plant-eaters. Since that time, Biz has been not only a powerful and compelling voice for a humane, sustainable food system but is also an investor in and member of the board of directors of a company called Beyond Meat, which produces meat substitutes that use fewer resources and are less expensive and more humane than animal-based products. Oh, and Biz is a cofounder of Twitter.

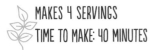

MAKES 4 SERVINGS
TIME TO MAKE: 40 MINUTES

2 cups brown lentils

3 cups vegetable stock, or more as needed

1 tablespoon olive oil

1 medium onion, chopped

3 cloves garlic, coarsely chopped

1 rib celery, chopped

1 can (14.5 ounces) diced tomatoes

1 bay leaf

⅛ cup chopped parsley + 2 tablespoons minced

Salt and ground black pepper

High-quality balsamic vinegar

Add the lentils to a large pot. Cover with the stock and add the oil, onion, garlic, celery, tomatoes, bay leaf, and chopped parsley. Bring to a boil and simmer for 30 minutes, or until the lentils are tender. Add more stock if the soup gets too thick. Season with salt and pepper to taste.

To serve, swirl a little vinegar over the top and garnish with the minced parsley.

Faki is Greek for soup.

Black Beluga Stew with Swiss Chard

Tanya Petrovna, founder of Native Foods Restaurants

Says Tanya: "Swiss chard was a bumper crop this year in my home garden, and my lemon tree was making offerings to me faster than I could accept. Often I start with an item or two, then do a kitchen walk-through and see what's in stock that would inspire a combination to create a delicious dish.

"I always keep a pack of non-common legumes on hand, and I had just bought some Urfa pepper because it sounded cool. Urfa is a purple crushed-flake chile of medium heat from the Urfa region of Turkey. I was having some guys come over to help me build a cat house, and I know a good soup can feed a few hungry friends, hence this recipe."

MAKES 8 TO 10 SERVINGS
TIME TO MAKE: 35 TO 40 MINUTES

1 bunch red Swiss chard, leaves removed from the stems

¼ cup olive oil

2 tablespoons smoked paprika

2 teaspoons cumin seeds

1 onion, chopped

3 shallots, chopped

3 cloves garlic, chopped

4 teaspoons salt

2 cups black Beluga lentils, rinsed

8 cups water

Grated peel and juice of 1 lemon

2 teaspoons Urfa or Aleppo chile flakes

Lemon wedges

Slice the chard stems into ¼" pieces. Slice the leaves in half lengthwise, then slice them crosswise into ¼" ribbons.

In a 4-quart pot, heat the oil over low heat. Add the smoked paprika and cumin seeds and gently stir for 1 minute. Add the chard stems, onion, shallots, garlic, and salt. Cook, stirring occasionally, for 5 to 7 minutes, or until the onions are lightly browned. Add the lentils and water and stir a few times. Bring to a simmer and cook for 20 minutes.

Add the chard leaves, lemon peel and juice, and chile flakes. Stir the soup until the leaves are lightly wilted, about 5 minutes, and serve immediately. Garnish with lemon wedges.

Beyond Meat Moroccan Stew

Caitlin Grady of Beyond Meat

Says Caitlin: "We love a good stew at Beyond Meat, and we like life to be a little spicy. Here's the perfect combo of spice and stew. What better way to amp up a cold winter day?"

MAKES 4 SERVINGS

TIME TO MAKE: 35 MINUTES

1 white onion, diced

2 cloves garlic, minced

1 tablespoon olive oil

2 carrots, diced

2 ripe medium tomatoes, seeded and diced

2½ cups vegetable stock

1 tablespoon ground black pepper

1 teaspoon ground coriander

1 teaspoon ground cumin

1 teaspoon ground turmeric

1 teaspoon ground cinnamon

1 teaspoon cayenne

1 bay leaf

1 teaspoon salt

¾ cup canned or cooked chickpeas

16 ounces Beyond Meat Chicken-Free Strips

In a large skillet over medium heat, cook the onion and garlic in the oil for 5 minutes, or until they are soft. Add the carrots and cook for 5 minutes. Add the tomatoes, stock, black pepper, coriander, cumin, turmeric, cinnamon, cayenne, bay leaf, salt, and chickpeas. Simmer for 20 minutes.

Strain, reserving the liquid. In a blender, puree two-thirds of the cooked vegetables and return to the pot along with the unpureed vegetables and the Beyond Meat strips. Add enough of the reserved liquid to create a thick stew. Simmer for 5 minutes.

APPETIZERS and SIDES

Shiitake and Smoked Tofu Dumplings with Black Vinaigrette

Chad Sarno, vegan chef, instructor, and bestselling author

Says Chad: "Right next to making fresh pasta, homemade dumplings win my heart. The tedious nature of folding each one perfectly is such a great meditation and, with a bit of patience, pays off greatly. Whenever I make dumplings, I create an event out of it, making a few larger trays of them to stock up in my freezer. Once they are folded, place them on a tray to serve or store them in an airtight container or zip-top bag in the freezer to use later on for a quick meal."

MAKES 28 TO 35 DUMPLINGS
TIME TO MAKE: 20 TO 25 MINUTES

Dumplings

- ½ cup water chestnuts
- 15 dried shiitake mushrooms, soaked for 10 minutes in equal parts dry sherry and warm water to soften, stems removed
- 1 block (7–8 ounces) baked or smoked tofu, cubed
- 2 tablespoons maple syrup
- 2 tablespoons toasted sesame oil
- ¼ cup sliced green onions
- 2 cloves garlic, minced
- 2 tablespoons minced fresh ginger
- 1 tablespoon cornstarch
- ½ teaspoon sea salt
- 1 pack vegan round dumpling skins

Black Vinaigrette

- ¼ cup dry sherry or xiao xing wine
- 3 tablespoons tamari
- 3 tablespoons agave nectar
- 2 cloves garlic, minced
- 1 teaspoon finely chopped ginger
- 1½ tablespoons sambal oelek (a type of Asian chile paste)

To make the dumplings: In a food processor, pulse the water chestnuts until they are coarsely chopped. Drain the mushrooms. Chop the softened shiitake mushrooms. Add the shiitakes and tofu to the food processor and pulse until they are minced. Transfer to a mixing bowl and stir in the maple syrup.

Heat the oil in a small skillet over medium-high heat. Add the green onions, garlic, and ginger and cook for 2 to 3 minutes. Remove the pan from the heat. Add the onion mixture to the bowl with the shiitakes and tofu and stir in the cornstarch and salt.

Lightly sprinkle cornstarch over a baking sheet (this will keep the dumplings from sticking to the pan). Have a small cup of water ready and set out the dumpling skins. Place about 1 tablespoon of dumpling filling in the center of each dumpling skin. Using a small bit of water on your fingers, moisten a half edge of the dumpling skins. Pick up the dumpling and fold it into a taco shape. Starting with one end, crimp closed the open edge of the dumpling skin. Place on the baking sheet. Repeat with the remaining dumpling skins and filling.

FRY AND STEAM METHOD: In a large skillet over medium heat, add a small amount of oil or cooking spray. Sear the dumplings until golden on the bottom. Add a generous splash of water to the pan and immediately cover it with a lid for about 2 minutes, to steam the dumplings. Remove from the heat when done.

STEAM-ONLY METHOD: Steam the dumplings for 3 minutes. Make sure they are not stacked on top of each other, to avoid sticking. Remove from the heat when done.

To make the vinaigrette: In a small bowl, whisk together the sherry or wine, tamari, agave, garlic, and ginger. (You can also use this vinaigrette to dress Asian noodle salads.)

Serve the dumplings with the sambal oelek and black vinaigrette.

Hearts of Palm Cakes with Dill Mayo

Ellen Quinlan and
Alan Gould, owners,
Darbster Bistro, West Palm Beach

What's a vegan to do in South Florida, known for its crab cakes? Well, Darbster put its own creative twist on the crab cake and introduced what is now its signature dish: the Palm Cake. Wonderfully seasoned, crispy on the outside, and moist on the inside, it's an appetizer, entrée, or a sandwich. It has become so popular that a local health food store now carries them.

MAKES 8 CAKES
TIME TO MAKE: 1 HOUR 30 MINUTES

Dill Mayo

- 1 cup raw cashews
- 2 dates
- ½ cup water
- 1½ tablespoons apple cider vinegar
- 2 teaspoons lemon juice
- ¼ teaspoon garlic powder
- ½ teaspoon dried dill or 1 teaspoon fresh
- Pinch of salt and ground black pepper
- 2 tablespoons extra-virgin olive oil

Cakes

- ½ medium red onion, chopped
- 1 red bell pepper, chopped
- ½ teaspoon mild chili powder
- ½ teaspoon onion powder
- ½ teaspoon garlic powder
- ½ teaspoon ground black pepper
- ¼ cup Bragg Liquid Aminos
- 1 can (28 ounces) sliced hearts of palm, rinsed
- 2½ cups panko bread crumbs, divided
- ½ cup Vegenaise
- 1 green onion, thinly sliced
- 1–2 teaspoons Earth Balance spread

To make the dill mayo: In a blender, combine the cashews, dates, water, vinegar, lemon juice, garlic powder, dill, salt, pepper, and oil. Puree, adding more water as needed to achieve the desired consistency.

To make the cakes: Coat a medium skillet with oil and heat over medium heat. Add the red onion and bell pepper and cook for 6 to 7 minutes, or until soft. Add the chili powder, onion powder, garlic powder, and black pepper and cook for 1 minute. Add the Liquid Aminos to the pan and quickly stir for about 15 seconds. Remove from the heat and transfer to a bowl. Cover the bowl and transfer it to a refrigerator to chill for at least 30 minutes.

In a food processor, add the hearts of palm. Pulse to a coarse, even consistency, but do not puree them. Transfer to a large mixing bowl and add the chilled veggies, 1½ cups of the panko, the Vegenaise, and green onion and mix well. Form into 8 cakes and roll them in the remaining 1 cup panko.

In a wide skillet, melt the Earth Balance over medium-high heat. Working in 2 batches, fry the cakes for 4 minutes per side.

Serve each cake with a dollop of the dill mayo. There will be some left over.

Buttermilk-Fried Cauliflower with Purple Potato Salad and Tarragon Ranch

Jay Astafa, vegan chef and owner of Jay Astafa Catering

Says Jay: "This is one of my most favorite hors d'oeuvres. I created this for Kristin Lajeunesse's Will Travel for Vegan Food end-of-trip party back in August of 2013. Since then it's been one of my signature hors d'oeuvres that I serve at so many events. The inspiration behind this hors d'oeuvre was travel and southern food. I took a traditional southern fried chicken technique and applied it to cauliflower. The result is amazing, and cauliflower is transformed into something so delicious. This is one of my favorite ways to prepare cauliflower. I'm a big fan of making vegetables the star, and this is exactly what happens with cauliflower with this recipe. "

MAKES 25 SERVINGS
TIME TO MAKE: 1 HOUR 20 MINUTES

Cauliflower

- 2 cups unsweetened soy milk
- 2 tablespoons lemon juice
- 2 tablespoons nutritional yeast
- 1 teaspoon garlic powder
- 1 teaspoon paprika
- 1 teaspoon salt
- 1 teaspoon ground black pepper
- 2 tablespoons chopped fresh thyme
- 1 small head cauliflower, cut into bite-size florets
- Canola oil

Potato Salad

- 1 pound peeled purple potatoes, cut into medium dice
- 1 rib celery, finely diced
- 2 tablespoons vegan mayo
- 1 tablespoon lemon juice
- 1 teaspoon Dijon mustard
- 1 tablespoon dried tarragon
- Salt
- Dash of microgreens per spoon

Flour Mixture

- 2 cups all-purpose flour
- 2 tablespoons garlic powder
- 2 tablespoons onion powder
- 2 tablespoons paprika
- 2 tablespoons salt
- 2 tablespoons ground black pepper
- 2 tablespoons dried oregano
- 2 tablespoons chopped fresh thyme
- 1 tablespoon chopped fresh parsley
- ¼ cup nutritional yeast

Ranch Dressing

- ¼ package (12.5 ounces) silken tofu, drained
- ¾ cup vegan mayo
- ¼ cup soy milk
- 1 tablespoon lemon juice
- 1½ teaspoons chopped fresh tarragon
- ¼ teaspoon garlic powder
- ¼ teaspoon onion powder
- ¼ teaspoon nutritional yeast

To make the cauliflower: In a large mixing bowl, combine the soy milk, lemon juice, nutritional yeast, garlic powder, paprika, salt, black pepper, and thyme. Add the cauliflower to the bowl and let marinate for at least 1 hour. Toss the cauliflower in the marinade every 15 minutes.

(continued on page 192)

To make the potato salad: While the florets are marinating, heat a medium pot of water to boiling. Add the potatoes. Boil for 10 minutes, or until tender. Drain and transfer to a bowl to cool. In a separate bowl, combine the celery, mayo, lemon juice, mustard, tarragon, and salt to taste. Once the potatoes are cool, gently toss with the celery mixture.

To make the flour mixture: In a medium mixing bowl, combine the flour, garlic powder, onion powder, paprika, salt, black pepper, oregano, thyme, parsley, and nutritional yeast.

To make the ranch dressing: In a large mixing bowl, whisk together the tofu, mayo, soy milk, lemon juice, tarragon, garlic powder, onion powder, and nutritional yeast.

Heat the oil to 375°F in a heavy pot or deep fryer. Toss the cauliflower in the flour mixture. Working in batches, fry the cauliflower for 5 to 7 minutes, or until golden and crispy. Drain on a paper towel.

Spoon 1 tablespoon of the potato salad onto a tasting spoon. Top with a piece of cauliflower and drizzle with the ranch dressing. Garnish with microgreens.

Truffled Popcorn

Bonnie-Jill Laflin, NBA scout, ESPN radio host, and entrepreneur

Says Bonnie-Jill: "I'm a fiend for popcorn, and as a sportscaster and sports fanatic, this treat is extra yummy while watching your team on game day! Who doesn't love the smell of fresh popcorn in the air? People spend a lot of money buying premade gourmet popcorn when it's so easy to make at home. Go ahead and indulge a little . . . your secret is safe with me."

MAKES 4 CUPS
TIME TO MAKE: 10 MINUTES

1 package (3 ounces) unsalted natural organic microwave popcorn

2 tablespoons vegan margarine

½ teaspoon white truffle oil

1 tablespoon olive oil

Sea salt

Cook the popcorn according to the package directions, then place in a bowl. In a small saucepan, melt the margarine. Stir in the truffle oil and olive oil. Allow to cool slightly. Pour over the popcorn and toss together. Season with salt to taste.

Korean Fried Cauliflower Wings with Kimchi Aioli

Adam Sobel, chef and owner of The Cinnamon Snail organic vegan food truck

These cauliflower wings get their Korean flavor from a chile paste called gochujang. The heat from the chile paste is balanced by the cool, tangy kimchi aioli, the perfect finish for these lively cauliflower wings. The wings make a pretty badass vegan appetizer or platter for any party, or you can hook up the wings and aioli with some greens (and pickles, of course!) between 2 toasted halves of a crisp French baguette for a legendary sandwich.

MAKES 24 WINGS
TIME TO MAKE: 40 MINUTES

Kimchi Aioli

- ¾ cup Vegenaise
- ⅓ cup vegan kimchi
- ½ teaspoon paprika
- 1 green onion, minced
- 1 tablespoon minced cilantro leaves

Batter

- 2 cups soy milk
- 2 teaspoons umeboshi plum vinegar
- 1 teaspoon crushed red-pepper flakes
- 1½ cups all-purpose flour
- 2 tablespoons arrowroot

Wings

- ⅔ cup canola or safflower oil
- 1 medium head cauliflower
- ½ cup arrowroot

Glaze

- ½ cup gochujang
- 4 teaspoons maple syrup
- 2 tablespoons toasted sesame oil
- 1 tablespoon brown rice vinegar
- 2 tablespoons water

Garnish

- 1 cup baby arugula, optional
- 2 tablespoons finely minced red onion, optional
- 4 teaspoons toasted black sesame seeds, optional

Chef's Tip: Gochujang paste can be found at most Asian markets, but if you can't find it, you can make your own. Just mix together 7 tablespoons mild yellow miso, 2 tablespoons chili powder, and 2 teaspoons fine sugar.

To make the aioli: In a blender, puree the Vegenaise, kimchi, and paprika until completely smooth. Add the green onion and cilantro and pulse a few times to evenly distribute.

To make the batter: In a medium bowl, whisk together the soy milk and vinegar. Add the red-pepper flakes, flour, and arrowroot and whisk thoroughly until well combined.

To make the wings: Heat the oil in a large skillet over medium-high heat. Cut the cauliflower into about 24 drumstick-shaped florets. Make sure the pieces aren't too large, or they may not get fully cooked through. Gently toss the cauliflower pieces in a medium bowl with the arrowroot, until all sides are well coated and dry. Place a large plate or rack covered with a folded paper towel close to your skillet.

Working with 3 to 4 pieces at a time, submerge the cauliflower in the batter, letting the excess drip back into the bowl. Quickly place them into the hot oil. Fry in batches, making sure that the cauliflower pieces aren't touching one another while they cook. Once the cauliflower pieces have turned golden brown on the bottom, after about 3 minutes, flip them and fry for another 2 to 3 minutes. Toss the pieces in the pan and fry any remaining sides that show uncooked batter. Remove the cauliflower pieces and place them on the paper towel to drain.

To glaze and garnish: In a medium bowl, whisk together the gochujang, maple syrup, sesame oil, vinegar, and water. Toss the hot cauliflower wings in the glaze until all sides are coated. Add a scattering of baby arugula to your serving plates (if using), top with the glazed cauliflower wings, and garnish with the minced onion and toasted black sesame seeds, if desired. Place the kimchi aioli in a ramekin and serve it alongside the wings for dipping.

Toasted Pumpkin Seed Dip with Sun-Dried Tomatoes

Matteo Silverman, Sonoma, California–based executive chef of Chalk Hill Cookery

Says Matteo: "This recipe is a subtle take on one of my favorite Mayan dishes called Sikil Pak. It is a savory blend of toasted ground pumpkin seeds mixed with a puree of roasted onion, garlic, and sun-dried tomato. Serve with your favorite chips, crackers, sliced veggies, or tortillas. This is the recipe you want to try if you are looking for something new and simple to prepare."

MAKES 3 CUPS
TIME TO MAKE: 30 MINUTES

- 2 cups pepitas (green pumpkin seeds)
- 1 medium onion, chopped
- 2 cloves garlic, halved
- 3 tablespoons olive oil, divided
- ¼ cup sun-dried tomatoes, rehydrated in water for 15–20 minutes
- ¾ cup water
- ¼ cup lime juice
- ¼ teaspoon sea salt
- 1 jalapeño chile, diced, or red-pepper flakes, optional

Preheat the oven to 375°F.

Place the pepitas on a baking sheet and roast for 5 to 7 minutes, or until they just begin to turn brown and start to pop. Remove from the oven and let cool. Once cooled, grind them in a food processor until they are powderlike. Place in a large bowl.

Place the onion and garlic on a baking pan and drizzle them with 1 tablespoon of the oil. Roast for 10 to 15 minutes, or until browned.

In a blender, combine the roasted onion and garlic, tomatoes, and water. Puree until smooth. Add to the bowl with the ground pepitas, along with the lime juice, salt, and the remaining 2 tablespoons oil and thoroughly combine. For a little heat, add the chile or pepper flakes to taste, if desired.

Smoky Eggplant and Almond Dip

Miyoko Schinner, author of *Artisan Vegan Cheese,* cohost of television's *Vegan Mashup,* and founder of Miyoko's Kitchen

A smoky, nutty alternative to baba ghannouj, this dip is thick and scrumptious. It's perfect as a snack with toasted pita chips or as a sandwich spread.

MAKES 6 TO 8 SERVINGS
TIME TO MAKE: 1 HOUR

1 large eggplant or 5–6 Japanese or Italian eggplants

¾ cup almonds

2 cloves garlic

¼ cup olive oil + extra for garnish

1–2 teaspoons hot Spanish smoked paprika + extra for garnish

1 teaspoon sea salt

Preheat the oven to 375°F.

Roast the eggplant for 40 minutes, or until you can easily pierce the skin with a fork and the skin is wrinkled. Cut the eggplant into 1" chunks.

Spread the almonds on a baking pan and bake for 12 minutes, or until puffed and brown. Put the almonds in a food processor and pulse until ground. Add the eggplant, garlic, ¼ cup oil, 1 to 2 teaspoons paprika, and salt, and puree until relatively smooth. Transfer to a serving bowl and sprinkle with extra paprika and oil.

Broccoli Puree with Crostini and Raw Veggies

Cornelia Guest, fashion icon and entrepreneur

Says Cornelia: "This puree is high in vitamins A and K, fiber filled, and filling. I like my puree pretty chunky and love using it as a side, a dip, or on toast topped with raw veggies. Enjoy!"

MAKES 2 CUPS
TIME TO MAKE: 20 MINUTES

1 pound broccoli, chopped

2 large cloves garlic, minced

2 tablespoons fresh lemon juice

2 tablespoons extra-virgin olive oil

Salt and ground black pepper

10 crostini

Baby carrots

Sliced zucchini

Steam the broccoli for 15 minutes, or until tender. In a food processor, combine the broccoli, garlic, lemon juice, oil, and salt and pepper to taste. Puree until at desired consistency. Serve with the crostini, carrots, and zucchini.

Queso Dip with Chips

Jennifer Engel and
Heather Goldberg,
co-owners of West Hollywood,
California–based Spork Foods
Cooking Classes

This queso is a great party food—
it's rich and has a complex flavor
that everyone from kids to grand-
parents love. When you serve this
dip, make sure it's warm.

MAKES 4 TO 6 SERVINGS
TIME TO MAKE: 20 MINUTES

1¼ cups cashews, soaked in water for 1 hour and drained

2 cups unsweetened almond milk + additional if needed

1 teaspoon vegan margarine

½ white onion, finely diced

3 cloves garlic, roasted and mashed

1 jalapeño chile, seeded and finely diced

¼ cup nutritional yeast flakes

3 tablespoons fresh lime juice

½ teaspoon sea salt + more to taste

½ teaspoon ground black pepper

½ teaspoon ground cumin

1 can (15 ounces) organic black beans, rinsed and drained

1 organic tomato, seeded and diced

½ cup shredded vegan Mexican-style cheese

1 small bag organic corn tortilla chips

In a blender, combine the cashews and almond milk. Puree to make cashew cream.

Heat a large pot over medium heat and add the margarine, onion, garlic, and chile. Cook for 3 minutes, or until the onion is soft. Stir in the cashew cream, nutritional yeast flakes, and lime juice until well blended. Add the salt, black pepper, cumin, beans, and tomato and cook for 5 minutes, stir-ring frequently.

Add the cheese. Cook for 1 minute, or until creamy and smooth. If the sauce is too thick, add an additional ½ cup almond milk. Remove from the heat. Serve warm with the tortilla chips.

Wok-Fried Shaved Brussels Sprouts with Pistachios and Sriracha

Chad Sarno, vegan chef, instructor, and bestselling author

Says Chad; "Years back when I was combing New York menus for a good brunch place, what caught my eye on one in particular was a similar version to this side dish. From the moment I discovered this dish, I have been addicted and fallen in love with these little holiday gems. For many that do not enjoy the world of Brussels, when they are shaved thin and paired with some hot sauce and flash-fried, anyone will fall in love. I promise."

MAKES 4 TO 6 SERVINGS
TIME TO MAKE: 10 MINUTES

2 tablespoons peanut or coconut oil

3 shallots, thinly sliced

4 cups thinly shaved Brussels sprouts (use a knife or mandoline)

½ cup lightly toasted pistachios

½ teaspoon sea salt

½ teaspoon ground black pepper

Sriracha sauce to taste

Over high heat, add the oil and shallots to a wok or skillet and cook, stirring frequently, until the shallots are translucent and slightly browned, 2 to 3 minutes. Reduce the heat to medium-high and add the Brussels sprouts, stirring constantly. Continue to cook until the Brussels sprouts have become a vibrant green, about 3 minutes. Add the pistachios, salt, and pepper. Remove from the heat and drizzle with Sriracha sauce just before serving.

Roasted Asparagus with Preserved Lemon and Crispy Capers

Rich Landau and **Kate Jacoby,** owners and executive chefs of Vedge Restaurant in Philadelphia

Vedge is one of the most reknowned vegan restaurants in the country. Founded in 2011, it uses the locally sourced ingredients aligned to seasons of the Northeast. This recipe is one of our very favorites.

MAKES 4 TO 6 SERVINGS
TIME TO MAKE: 20 MINUTES

2 bunches asparagus, bottom ⅓ trimmed with a peeler to achieve uniform thickness

3 tablespoons olive oil, divided

2 cloves garlic, minced

2 tablespoons finely chopped preserved lemon (no seeds)

½ teaspoon salt

½ teaspoon ground black pepper

¼ cup capers

Preheat the oven to 400°F. In a medium mixing bowl, gently toss the asparagus with 2 tablespoons of the olive oil, the garlic, the preserved lemon, salt, and pepper. Transfer the asparagus to a baking sheet, and roast the asparagus until the skin crinkles lightly, about 6 minutes. Heat the last tablespoon of oil in a sauté pan over medium heat. Add the capers and cook until they sizzle and pop, about 3 to 5 minutes. When the capers start to brown, remove them from the heat. Top the asparagus with the capers and serve.

Twice-Baked Potatoes

Jill Ryther, animal rights activist, attorney, and founder of Expand Animal Rights Now

Says Jill: "This dish is truly a vegan outreach party pleaser. Whenever I'm invited to a potluck that includes nonvegans I always want to bring a dish that everyone will love. I considered how popular twice-baked potatoes always were while I was growing up, and I thought, what an easy and traditional dish to veganize. I often cut each potato into quarters so they're the perfect size for picking up and eating with your hands. They also travel very well and make excellent leftovers."

MAKES 8 SERVINGS
TIME TO MAKE: 1 HOUR 45 MINUTES

4 russet potatoes

3 tablespoons Earth Balance Buttery Spread, divided

¼ sweet onion, diced (¼ cup)

½ red bell pepper, diced (¼ cup)

½ green bell pepper, diced (¼ cup)

1½ cups shredded Daiya Cheddar Style Shreds

6 ounces Tofutti Better Than Sour Cream

Salt and pepper to taste

½ teaspoon garlic powder

1½ ounces Daiya Cheddar Style Block, grated

1 tablespoon chopped chives, optional

Preheat an oven to 400°F. Pierce the potatoes with a fork several times. Transfer them to the oven and bake for 1 hour. Cut them in half lengthwise and let cool for 10 minutes.

While they are baking, melt 2 tablespoons of the vegan butter in a sauté pan over medium heat. Add the onion and cook, stirring frequently, until it just starts to brown, about 6 minutes. Add the bell pepper and cook, stirring frequently, for another 4 to 5 minutes. Remove from the heat and set aside.

Scoop out most of the potato flesh into a mixing bowl. Combine this with the onion-pepper mix, melted Earth Balance from the sauté pan, the grated Daiya, the Better Than Sour Cream, and the salt and pepper, mixing well.

Line a large baking sheet with foil. Place the potato skins scooped-out-side-down onto the baking sheet. In a small pan, melt the remaining 1 tablespoon of Earth Balance and brush it onto the potato skins. Sprinkle salt, pepper, and garlic powder on them. Flip them over and fill with the potato/Daiya/onion-pepper mix. Top each potato with the grated Daiya.

Bake for 15 to 20 minutes.

Garnish each potato with chopped chives, if using.

ENTRÉES

INSPIRED CREATIONS

Roasted Garlic, Sweet Potato, and Raisin Tamales with Peanut Tequila Mole

Jason Wyrick, executive chef of The Vegan Taste and author of *Vegan Tacos*

Says Jason: "I travel the world on culinary adventures, but I always end up coming back to Mexican food. It's playful and rich, always bold, and always lively. This recipe is no exception. With chiles and tequila, how can it not be? These tamales feature the sweet counterpoint of raisins and sweet potato with the heat of ancho chiles and chipotles in adobo against a backdrop of a rich peanut sauce. Add some tequila on top of that and a few aromatic spices, and you've got a tamale that offers up a new adventure with every bite. You can also separate out the mole (pronounced MOH-lay) recipe to use as a sauce in other dishes, to create a rich soup broth, or to use as a salsa on tacos."

MAKES 12 TAMALES
TIME TO MAKE: 1 HOUR 30 MINUTES

Chef's Tip: Make the mole while the tomatoes are steaming.

Filling

20 whole cloves garlic
1 large white sweet potato, diced
1 tablespoon garlic-infused olive oil
Juice of 2 limes
¼ teaspoon salt
¼ cup golden raisins

Masa

2½ cups masa harina
1 teaspoon fine salt
¾ teaspoon baking powder
2¾ cups warm water
3 tablespoons vegan shortening, optional
Corn husks, soaked in warm water for 20 minutes

Mole

1 roma tomato
1 ancho chile
1 tablespoon corn oil
¼ small white onion, diced
1 clove garlic, minced
1 chipotle chile in adobo sauce
¼ cup roasted peanuts
Pinch of ground allspice
Pinch of ground cinnamon
Pinch of ground black pepper
¼ teaspoon salt
¼ teaspoon sugar
1 bay leaf
Juice of ½ lime
2 tablespoons tequila blanco
1 cup vegetable stock
2 tablespoons olive oil

Garnish

Grated peel of 4 large limes
¼ cup finely chopped peanuts

(continued)

Heat a large dry iron skillet over medium heat. Add the garlic from the filling and tomato from the mole to the skillet. Once the cloves start to brown, about 3 to 5 minutes, flip and lightly brown the other sides. Remove them from the skillet, let them cool, and coarsely chop them. Once the tomato blisters on one side, about 5 to 6 minutes, flip it and blister on the other side. Continue until all sides of the tomato are blistered, then remove from the heat and set aside.

To make the filling: In a large skillet over medium heat, cook the sweet potato in the oil, stirring occasionally, until it just starts to brown, about 5 to 7 minutes. Add enough water to come halfway up the sweet potatoes. Then add the lime juice and salt and let the water cook out. Add the chopped roasted garlic to the sweet potatoes and stir in the raisins.

To make the masa: In a stand mixer,* combine the masa harina, salt, and baking powder and give them a quick stir. Add the warm water and shortening, if using. At medium speed on the stand mixer, whip the masa for about 20 minutes. You can tell when your masa is done (if you used the shortening) by placing a small dollop of it in a glass of water. If it floats, the masa is done. If it doesn't, it needs to be whipped longer. If you did not use the optional shortening, skip this step as it will not float.

To fill and roll the tamales: Lay out a large corn husk. Using a wide spatula, spread about 3 to 4 tablespoons of masa on the left side of the corn husk. The masa should be about 4" wide and 5" tall and there should be uncovered space on the corn husk at the bottom and on the right. On top of the far left side of the masa, add about 1½ tablespoons of filling. Starting with the left side, roll up the corn husk to close the tamale. Fold the uncovered part of the corn husk into the tamale as you roll it closed. Repeat with the remainder of the masa, corn husks, and filling. This will go faster if you lay out all your corn husks at once and do each step for all the tamales at the same time. Transfer the tamales to a steamer and steam them for 30 minutes.

To make the mole: While the tamales are steaming, bring a small pot of water to a gentle simmer. In a dry skillet over medium heat, toast the ancho chile for about 10 seconds per side. Add the chile to the water and simmer until soft. Remove the chile from the water and after it is cool enough to handle, pull out the stem and discard.

In a small skillet, heat the 1 tablespoon of corn oil and cook the onion over medium heat until it just starts to brown. Add the clove of minced garlic and cook for 2 minutes. Place in a blender and add the reserved blackened tomato, chipotle in adobo, peanuts, allspice, cinnamon, black pepper, salt, sugar, bay leaf, lime juice, tequila, and stock. Puree until smooth. Place a fine-meshed strainer over a bowl and pour the sauce through the strainer to make it silky smooth.

In a large pan over medium heat, warm the 2 tablespoons of olive oil. Pour the sauce into the pan and gently stir, cooking it for about 5 minutes.

To assemble and garnish the tamales: Once your tamales are done steaming, unwrap them, put 2 on a plate, and top each individual tamale with 3 to 4 tablespoons of the peanut mole. Top each tamale with a sprinkle of lime peel and chopped peanuts.

Both the tamales and the sauce can be made ahead of time and frozen.

If you don't have a stand mixer, you can combine everything in a mixing bowl and forgo whipping the masa. The masa won't be fluffy when you cook the tamales, but they'll still come out quite well.

Japanese-Style Eggplant Stuffed with Dengaku Tofu

Miyoko Schinner, author of *Vegan Artisan Cheese*, cohost of television's *Vegan Mashup*, and founder of Miyoko's Kitchen

Says Miyoko: "To make sure this doesn't get lost in translation, dengaku is a sweet miso sauce that often accompanies grilled eggplant or tofu. I've combined them all here in my spin on traditional Japanese flavors, by stuffing roasted eggplant with a mashed tofu laced with dengaku sauce. It's savory and delicious, and can be served hot or at room temperature, as an appetizer or an entrée with a side dish or brown rice or other grain."

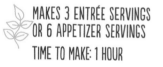

MAKES 3 ENTRÉE SERVINGS OR 6 APPETIZER SERVINGS
TIME TO MAKE: 1 HOUR

3 small eggplants (about 12 ounces each) or 6–8 Japanese or Italian eggplants

1 tablespoon toasted sesame oil

⅔ teaspoon salt

3 tablespoons miso

2 tablespoons maple syrup

1 tablespoon mirin

8 ounces medium or regular-firm tofu (not extra-firm), drained

1 teaspoon black sesame seeds

Preheat the oven to 425°F. Line a baking sheet with parchment paper.

Cut the eggplants in half and use a sharp knife to make hash marks on the cut side. Lightly brush the cut surfaces with the sesame oil and sprinkle with the salt. Place them, cut side down, on the baking sheet and roast for 15 to 25 minutes, depending on the size of the eggplants, until tender. Remove from the oven and let cool enough to be able to handle without burning your hands. Using a spoon, scoop out the flesh, leaving a little on the skins so they don't fall apart. Coarsely chop the eggplant meat.

In a medium bowl, combine the miso, maple syrup, and mirin and stir to make a paste. Crumble the tofu or smash it lightly with a fork. Add the tofu and chopped eggplant to the miso mixture and mix well.

Stuff the eggplant skins with this mixture and sprinkle with the sesame seeds. Bake for 15 to 20 minutes, or until the tops are slightly browned.

Black Garlic and Porcini Pizza

Jason Wyrick, executive chef of The Vegan Taste and author of *Vegan Tacos*

Says Jason: "I created this recipe because I had two things I absolutely had to use: black garlic, which I had never worked with before, and a pizza oven I had just built in my backyard after returning from Italy. Once you have wood-fired pizza, it's hard to go back. Black garlic has a pungent sweetness to it with this overtone of acidity. It was complex and intriguing, so I had to find another ingredient that could be its equal. Porcini was it!

"I love this recipe in particular because it relies on just a few toppings used in moderation to make an incredible pizza. All of this goes on a traditional Napoli-style crust with a San Marzano tomato sauce that could be eaten on its own! Pizza ovens typically reach temperatures of up to 900°F, but that's not feasible with traditional home ovens, so make sure to crank your oven as high as it will go and use a pizza stone to mimic the effect of the firebrick of a wood-fire pizza oven. I promise, you'll end up with some of the best pizza you've ever had."

MAKES 2 PIZZAS
TIME TO MAKE: 3 HOURS 30 MINUTES

Crust

7 tablespoons warm water

½ teaspoon sugar

¼ teaspoon active dry yeast

1 tablespoon olive oil + more for brushing the crust

1 cup Type 00 flour or unbleached all-purpose flour

½ teaspoon salt

Cornmeal

Sauce

1 cup crushed San Marzano tomatoes

2 cloves garlic, minced

1 teaspoon fresh oregano leaves

⅛ teaspoon ground black pepper

¼ teaspoon salt

1 tablespoon olive oil

Toppings

2 bulbs black garlic or roasted garlic

8 slices Teese Vegan Mozzarella

½ cup dried porcini, rehydrated in hot water

To make the crust: In a medium bowl, combine the warm water, sugar, and yeast. Once the yeast creates a foam in the water, add the 1 tablespoon of olive oil to the water, then the flour and salt. Mix until thoroughly combined.

Lightly flour a flat working surface. Divide the dough evenly into two balls. Knead the dough until it no longer sticks to your hands. Brush the dough with a bit of oil, place in a bowl, cover, and let sit in a warm area of your kitchen for 2 hours. Uncover the dough, punch it down, and re-form into a ball. Cover and let it rise 1 hour.

To make the sauce: In a small pot over medium-low heat, simmer the tomatoes, garlic, oregano, pepper, salt, and oil for 10 minutes.

To assemble the pizza and toppings: Remove the individual cloves of black garlic from the garlic bulb. Place a pizza stone in your oven. Preheat the oven as high as it can go. Typically, this is 550°F.

Lightly flour a flat working surface. Gently roll out the dough into a very thin disk, about ⅛" thick. Brush the dough with olive oil. Sprinkle a pizza peel with cornmeal and carefully transfer your dough to the peel. Spread the sauce on top. Place the mozzarella on the pizza. Spread the garlic cloves and rehydrated porcini on the pizza.

Transfer to the pizza stone and bake for 3 to 4 minutes.

Lobster Mushroom Tostada Tower

Joshua Katcher, vegan fashion entrepreneur and founder of the Web site The Discerning Brute

Says Joshua: "The lobster mushroom is one of Earth's strange and incredible inventions. But don't be scared off by the fact that it's actually not a mushroom but a parasitic ascomycete (a parasite-fungus that is hosted by, and consumes, mushrooms). When this delicious fungal parasite takes over the mushroom, it engulfs it and turns it red, giving it a lobsterlike appearance and, strangely, a subtle seafood taste.

"This dish is like fancy-shmancy fish tacos, but vegan and minus the whole devastation of coral reefs and other ocean ecosystems. And unlike seafood, this mushroom will still probably be around in 2048. The crisp layering of toasted tortillas, the smoothness of the hearty kale-potato sauce, and the crispy-edged, pan-seared lobster mushroom sautéed with shallots and garlic all come together quite wonderfully. The texture of sautéed and seared lobster mushroom is tender, slightly chewy, and very satisfying. Lobster mushroom isn't cheap, so save it for a special occasion. This dish is vegan, soy, and gluten free! Mercury free, too!"

MAKES 2 SERVINGS
TIME TO MAKE: 25 MINUTES

- 2 small red potatoes, cut in half
- 1 packed cup fresh green kale
- 1 tablespoon olive oil
- 2 cloves garlic, minced
- 2 large shallots, minced
- 1 large or 2 medium lobster mushrooms, sliced into ½"-thick slices, or 1½ cups of oyster mushrooms
- 2 tablespoons apple cider vinegar
- ¼ cup unsweetened almond milk
- 1 teaspoon salt
- 1 teaspoon ground black pepper
- 1 tablespoon nutritional yeast
- 1 cube unsalted vegetable bouillon
- ¼ cup raw cashews
- ¼ cup water
- 2 small corn tortillas

Steam the potatoes and kale for 10 to 12 minutes.

Meanwhile, heat the oil in a large skillet over medium heat. Add the garlic and shallots and cook for 5 minutes. Add the mushrooms to the skillet and cook for 5 to 6 minutes per side. Add the vinegar to the skillet, stir, and cook for 5 minutes. Remove the skillet from the heat.

In a blender, combine the steamed potatoes and kale, the milk, salt, pepper, nutritional yeast, and bouillon. Puree until smooth. Pour into a large bowl.

Rinse out the blender and add the cashews and water. Puree until smooth.

Cut the tortillas in half. Either toast or fry them. To toast them, heat a pan over medium heat. Add the tortillas and let them sit for 5 minutes per side, or until crisp. To fry them, add ⅛" oil to a pan and bring it to medium-high heat. Add the tortillas and fry for 1 minute per side, or until crispy.

On each plate, place 1 tortilla half, then a layer of kale sauce, followed by lobster mushroom slices. Place another tortilla on top, then another layer of kale sauce, and another layer of lobster mushroom slices. Then make a second "tostada tower." Top each tower with 1 tablespoon of the cashew cream (you will have some left over) and some of the garlic and shallots from the skillet.

Kimchi Mayo–Smothered Red Bean Bread
with Braised Trumpet Mushrooms

Joshua Katcher, vegan fashion entrepreneur and founder of the Web site The Discerning Brute

Says Joshua: "I am obsessed with this bread, and it's so easy to make. This lunch, which I smothered in vegan kimchi-mayo, is filling, healthy, and gluten free. I experimented making some bread with red beans and flax meal, and it came out light, chewy, and excellent. It's packed with protein and omega fatty acids. The type of starch contained in beans gives you the satisfaction of eating starch without the heavy carb load. Serve on a bed of purple kale and top with braised mushrooms, tempeh bacon, and onion."

MAKES 4 SERVINGS
TIME TO MAKE: 1 HOUR 15 MINUTES

Chef's Tip: You can place a bamboo steamer filled with the kale over the mushrooms and tempeh bacon as they cook. As the water and wine boil, the steam they release will steam the kale.

Bean Bread

- 1 can (15 ounces) red beans, rinsed and drained
- 1 unsalted vegan bouillon cube
- ½ cup flax meal
- 2 tablespoons nutritional yeast
- 2 tablespoons apple cider vinegar
- 1 teaspoon salt
- 1 teaspoon ground black pepper

Mayo

- ¼ cup Vegenaise
- ¼ cup spicy kimchi

Mushroom Tempeh Bacon

- ¼ cup water
- ¼ cup white wine
- 1 unsalted vegan bouillon cube
- 2 cloves garlic, minced
- ½ medium onion, diced
- 1 cup sliced trumpet mushrooms
- 4 ounces tempeh bacon, chopped

Kale

- 4 large purple kale leaves

To make the bean bread: Preheat the oven to 425°F. Layer a baking sheet with waxed or parchment paper.

In a medium mixing bowl, mash the beans and bouillon. Stir in the flax meal, nutritional yeast, vinegar, salt, and pepper until you have a smooth dough. Using a fork, spread the dough onto the baking sheet, about 1" thick. Bake for 20 minutes. Lower the temperature to 400°F and bake for 30 to 35 minutes. Remove from the oven.

To make the mayo: Meanwhile, in a small blender or food processor, combine the Vegenaise and kimchi. Puree until smooth.

To make the mushroom tempeh bacon: In a large skillet, bring the water and wine to a boil over high heat, then reduce the heat to medium. Add the bouillon, garlic, onion, mushrooms, and tempeh bacon. Simmer for 10 minutes, or until the liquid cooks out.

To make the kale and assemble the dish: Steam the kale for 10 minutes, or until soft.

To plate this, first slice the bean bread into sandwich bread–size triangles. Place the kale at the bottom of each of 4 plates to make a bed. Place a couple of bean bread triangles on top, then the mayo, then the mushroom tempeh bacon.

French Fries Smothered in Brown Gravy

Lauren Toyota and
John Diemer of the
hot for food blog

The couple behind the hot for food
blog have taken this truly
Canadian dish, called a poutine,
and given it a well-deserved make-
over, because even vegans need
their poutine fix!

MAKES 2 LARGE SERVINGS
TIME TO MAKE: 1 HOUR 30 MINUTES

French Fries

4 russet potatoes, cut into
pieces ½" thick and
3"–4" long

¼ cup sunflower oil (or other
neutral-tasting, high-smoke-
point oil)

1 teaspoon sea salt

½ teaspoon ground black
pepper

½ teaspoon paprika

Gravy

1 tablespoon coconut oil

1½ cups finely chopped button
or cremini mushrooms

1 shallot, minced

1 clove garlic, minced

3 tablespoons vegan butter

⅓ cup all-purpose flour or
brown rice flour

1½ cups vegetable broth

1 tablespoon onion powder

2 tablespoons tamari, soy
sauce, or liquid aminos

2 teaspoons molasses

¾ cup water

Topping

½ block of Daiya Jack-style
vegan cheese, crumbled, or
⅓ cup crumbled vegan
cheese of your choice

To make the fries: Preheat the oven to 425°F. Boil the potatoes for
10 minutes. Drain. On a baking sheet, gently toss them with the oil, salt,
pepper, and paprika and then spread them out evenly. Bake for 55 minutes, tossing every 15 minutes. Once the french fries come out of the
oven, bunch them together on the baking sheet. Reserve.

To make the gravy: In a large saucepan over medium heat, melt the
coconut oil. Cook the mushrooms and shallot for 5 minutes. Add the garlic
and cook for 5 more minutes.

While the mushrooms and shallot are cooking, make a roux. In a separate
small pan over low heat, melt the vegan butter. Gradually add the flour and
stir for 2 to 3 minutes. Remove from the heat so the roux doesn't burn. Add
the vegetable broth to the pan with the mushrooms and stir, scraping the
bottom of the pan. Bring back to a simmer and add the roux. Reduce the
heat to low and whisk until everything is thoroughly incorporated. Whisk in
the onion powder; tamari, soy sauce, or liquid aminos; and molasses. Then
slowly add the water, ¼ cup at a time, whisking at each addition.

To assemble the poutine: Preheat the broiler. Pour the gravy over the
mound of french fries on the baking sheet and top with the crumbled
vegan cheese. Broil for 2 minutes to melt the cheese.

Provençal Stuffed Zucchini

Jennifer Engel and
Heather Goldberg,
co-owners of West Hollywood,
California–based Spork Foods
Cooking Classes

The mixture of white beans, spelt bread, and zucchini makes this dish a meal all by itself. It's perfect for a small family dinner or doubled to feed a crowd.

MAKES 4 TO 6 SERVINGS
TIME TO MAKE: 50 MINUTES

Zucchini

- 4 medium zucchini, sliced in half lengthwise
- 1 teaspoon maple syrup
- 1 teaspoon sherry vinegar or red wine vinegar
- 2 teaspoons extra-virgin olive oil
- ¼ teaspoon sea salt
- ¼ teaspoon ground black pepper

Filling

- 3 slices spelt bread (Rudi's brand preferred)
- 2 teaspoons extra-virgin olive oil
- 1 teaspoon maple syrup
- 1 teaspoon sherry vinegar or red wine vinegar
- 1 tablespoon finely chopped fresh rosemary
- ¼ teaspoon sea salt
- ¼ teaspoon ground black pepper
- 1 can (16 ounces) white beans, rinsed and drained (Eden brand preferred)
- 2 teaspoons neutral-tasting oil, such as safflower oil

To make the zucchini: Preheat the oven to 425°F.

Hollow out and discard the centers of the zucchini halves with a melon baller or spoon. In a large shallow dish, combine the maple syrup, vinegar, oil, salt, and pepper. Divide the sauce between the 8 zucchini shells, spooning it into each shell. Let sit for 10 to 20 minutes.

To make the filling: In a food processor, combine the bread, olive oil, maple syrup, vinegar, rosemary, salt, and pepper. Pulse until it reaches a bread crumb consistency. Transfer to a mixing bowl. Fold in the beans. Place about 3 tablespoons of the bread crumb mixture into each zucchini.

Heat a large ovenproof skillet over medium heat and add the neutral-tasting oil. Add the stuffed zucchini to the skillet, stuffed side up, and cook for 8 to 10 minutes. Place it in the oven, and bake for 10 minutes, or until the filling is golden.

Chef's Tip: If the zucchini are very round, you can shave the bottoms of them flat to make them stable.

Brandy BBQ Chick'n Apple Sausage Sauté

Greg Rekas, head R&D chef of Tofurky

Says Greg: "When I worked in traditional food service, I developed a recipe that featured chicken, apples, brandy, and cream. In order to update this nutritionally and veganize it, I pulled out the cream and used the sweet and smoky notes from the BBQ sauce. While the sauce has a great punch, it still allows the subtly sweet and savory Tofurky sausage to shine through. This recipe gets rave reviews at potlucks and corporate lunches at Tofurky headquarters and, more importantly, at home, when I serve this to my wife!"

MAKES 4 SERVINGS
TIME TO MAKE: 20 MINUTES

Vegan Barbecue Sauce: Many barbecue sauces are not vegan. Avoid those that have "natural flavors" listed in the ingredients as this is usually a red flag for animal products.

3 tablespoons canola oil

4 Tofurky Chick'n Apple Sausages or other Tofurky sausages

1 medium onion, cut into thin strips

1 medium carrot, sliced into thin rounds

1 head bok choy, chopped into bite-size pieces

2 cloves garlic, minced

¼ cup applejack brandy

¼ cup vegetable stock

¼ cup vegan barbecue sauce

Salt and ground black pepper

In a large skillet, heat the oil over medium heat. Add the sausages and brown for a few minutes on each side. Remove them from the skillet.

In the same skillet, cook the onion and carrot for 5 to 6 minutes, stirring occasionally, or until they begin to brown. Add the bok choy and cook for 4 to 6 minutes. Stir in the garlic. Pour the brandy into the skillet and quickly stir the ingredients a few times. Add the vegetable stock and barbecue sauce. Let this simmer for 2 minutes. Add salt and pepper to taste.

Slice the sausages, if desired, and add them back to the pan. Toss everything together and remove from the heat.

Baked Potatoes or Sweet Potatoes Three Ways

Patti Breitman, author and cofounder of Dharma Voices for Animals

You can always keep baked potatoes or baked sweet potatoes in the fridge for a fast meal. Reheat them in the microwave oven and serve them topped with commercial or homemade salsa, vegan sour cream, leftover soup, or any one of these three toppings.

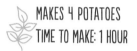

MAKES 4 POTATOES
TIME TO MAKE: 1 HOUR

4 potatoes or 2 large sweet potatoes

One of the toppings below

Preheat the oven to 450°F.

Prick the potatoes with a fork several times and wrap them in foil. Bake for 50 to 60 minutes. If you are baking sweet potatoes, put a layer of foil or a baking sheet underneath them to catch any wayward liquids that might spill out. Add the desired topping (below) and serve.

Pureed Cauliflower Topping

1 head cauliflower

½ cup water, or more as needed

½ teaspoon herbs of your choice—I like a basil-cumin combo or oregano-basil or Herbs de Provence (but all herbs are good!)

Cut the cauliflower into 10 or more chunks. Steam them over boiling water for 10 minutes, or until soft. Transfer to a blender and add the water and herbs. Blend until smooth. Add water as needed to attain a thick sauce.

Miso-Tahini Sauce

3 tablespoons miso

5 tablespoons tahini

½ cup water, or more as needed

In a small bowl, whisk or blend the miso, tahini, and water into a smooth sauce. Add extra water, if needed, to achieve the desired consistency.

Easiest Peanut Sauce

¼ cup peanut butter

¼ cup water, or more as needed

1 tablespoon seasoned rice wine vinegar

1 green onion, chopped, optional

Dash of red-pepper flakes, optional

In a small pot over medium heat, combine the peanut butter, water, vinegar, green onion (if using), and pepper flakes (if using). Heat to a boil, stirring the whole time. Remove from the heat immediately.

Rich Roll's Ultra Meatless Tempeh Loaf

Rich Roll, ultramarathoner and author of *Finding Ultra: Rejecting Middle Age, Becoming One of the World's Fittest Men, and Discovering Myself*

This is a nourishing dish that hits the spot. It's a great example of hearty, healthy, animal-friendly, farm-style food.

MAKES 6 SERVINGS
TIME TO MAKE: 1 HOUR 30 MINUTES

Loaf

- 1 pound tempeh
- ½ bottle (16–18 ounces) great-quality barbecue sauce or teriyaki-style marinade
- ¼ beet, grated
- ½ large carrot, chopped into ⅛" pieces
- 6 green beans, chopped into ⅛" pieces
- ½ cup chopped fresh cilantro
- ¾ teaspoon sea salt
- 1 tablespoon ground cumin
- 1 shallot, sliced
- ½ tablespoon olive oil
- 1 tablespoon arrowroot, optional

Sauce

- 1½ cups dry-packed sun-dried tomatoes
- 1½ cups Brazil nuts
- 1 cup organic cherry tomatoes
- 2 tablespoons olive oil
- ½ small clove garlic
- 2 basil leaves

Soak the tempeh in filtered water for at least 30 minutes. In a separate bowl, soak the sun-dried tomatoes and Brazil nuts for the same amount of time.

To make the loaf: Crumble the presoaked tempeh into a large mixing bowl. You can use a meat pounder to get the consistency really fine, or just use your hands and crumble away. Add the barbecue sauce or marinade, beet, carrot, green beans, cilantro, salt, and cumin and mix until thoroughly combined.

In a medium skillet over medium heat, brown the shallot in the oil for 4 to 5 minutes. Add to the tempeh mixture. Using your hands, mix it all up and form a loaf shape in the center of a large rectangular baking dish or loaf pan. If the mixture feels wet, add the arrowroot, mix again, and reshape.

Preheat the oven to 350°F.

To make the sauce: In a large, dry cast-iron skillet, slightly blacken the cherry tomatoes on high heat. Transfer to a high-speed blender and add the oil, garlic, basil, and the drained sun-dried tomatoes and Brazil nuts. Puree until smooth.

Pour the sauce over the tempeh meat loaf. Cover with foil and bake for 40 minutes.

Tal Ronnen's Agave-Lime Grilled Tofu with Asian Slaw and Mashed Sweet Potatoes

Tal Ronnen, author of *The Conscious Cook* and founder/executive chef of Crossroads Kitchen in Los Angeles

My friend Tal has helped revolutionize modern plant-based eating, working with celebrities like Oprah and Ellen and influential business leaders, getting vegan food on main-street menus. He recently opened Crossroads, one of Los Angeles's best restaurants.

MAKES 4 SERVINGS
TIME TO MAKE: 3 HOURS

Tofu

- 1 pound extra-firm tofu, drained and cut into 8 (¼"-thick) slabs
- ¼ cup light agave nectar
- ½ cup soy sauce
- 3 cloves garlic, smashed
- 2 sprigs fresh thyme
- 1 teaspoon ground black pepper
- Juice of 2 limes
- 1½ tablespoons lightly packed brown sugar

Slaw

- 3 tablespoons rice wine vinegar
- 1 teaspoon light agave nectar
- ½ teaspoon sea salt, or more
- 2 tablespoons freshly squeezed lime juice
- 1 teaspoon soy sauce
- ¼ cup safflower oil
- 1 large carrot, julienned
- ½ daikon radish, julienned
- ½ small head Napa cabbage, shredded
- 1 green onion, julienned
- ½ teaspoon mixed black and white sesame seeds

Sweet Potatoes

- 2 large sweet potatoes, peeled and chopped
- ½ cup finely ground cashews*
- 2 tablespoons all-natural buttery spread
- 1 chipotle chile in adobo sauce, minced
- Sea salt and ground black pepper

*Note: The cashews can be ground to a bread-crumb consistency in a food processor.

(continued)

To make the tofu: Place the tofu in a single layer in a shallow nonreactive dish. In a small bowl, whisk together the agave nectar, soy sauce, garlic, thyme, pepper, lime juice, and sugar. Pour over the tofu, cover the dish, and marinate in the refrigerator for 2 hours.

Preheat the oven to 300°F. Lightly oil a baking sheet.

Using a slotted spoon, remove the tofu from the marinade, reserving the marinade. Arrange it in a single layer on the baking sheet. Bake for 15 minutes.

Meanwhile, pour the marinade into a small saucepan. Cook over medium-high heat for 8 minutes, or until reduced to a syrupy glaze.

Heat an outdoor grill or preheat a grill pan over medium-high heat. Transfer the tofu slabs from the baking sheet to the grill and grill for 3 to 4 minutes, or until grill-marked. Turn the tofu over and generously brush with the glaze. Grill for 3 to 4 additional minutes, or until grill-marked. Remove the tofu to the baking sheet, turning it over so the glazed side is down, and then glaze the top side.

To make the slaw: In a large bowl, whisk together the vinegar, agave nectar, salt, lime juice, and soy sauce. Continue whisking vigorously in one direction as you slowly pour in the oil in a thin stream until emulsified. Add the carrot, radish, cabbage, green onion, and sesame seeds and toss to coat.

To make the sweet potatoes: Cook the sweet potatoes in a pot of boiling water for 20 minutes, or until tender. Drain. In the bowl of a stand mixer fitted with the whisk attachment, place the sweet potatoes, cashews, buttery spread, and chipotle chile. Alternatively, put the ingredients in a large bowl and use a handheld mixer. Whip on medium-high speed until smooth and fluffy. Season with salt and pepper to taste.

To assemble the dish, place one-quarter of the sweet potatoes in a scoop in the middle of a plate. Top with one-quarter of the slaw. Place 2 tofu slices on top of the slaw or angled against the sweet potatoes and slaw. Repeat on 3 more plates with the remaining ingredients.

Pan-Seared Herb Seitan with Cauliflower Puree and Truffled White Wine Sauce

Angel Ramos and **Jorge Pineda,** head chefs of the Candle restaurants in New York City

Whenever I get to New York, I always try to eat at one of Candle's three great plant-based restaurants. I particularly love their seitan dishes, especially this one.

MAKES 4 TO 6 SERVINGS
TIME TO MAKE: 2 HOURS

Seitan

4–6 cloves garlic, minced

1 tablespoon + ¾ cup olive oil

½ teaspoon ground black pepper

½ teaspoon sea salt

1 teaspoon chopped fresh thyme

1 teaspoon chopped fresh rosemary

1 teaspoon chopped fresh oregano

1½ pounds seitan,* cut into 4–6 cutlets

Cauliflower Puree

1 large head cauliflower, stem and tough stalks trimmed, florets coarsely chopped

2 tablespoons olive oil

1 large white onion, chopped

Pinch of sea salt

Pinch of ground black pepper

Sauce

2 tablespoons olive oil

¼ cup minced shallots

2 cups diced cremini mushrooms

1 teaspoon sea salt

¼ teaspoon ground black pepper

1 tablespoon unbleached all-purpose flour

½ cup white wine

2 cups vegetable stock or water

1 teaspoon chopped fresh flat-leaf parsley + additional for garnish

1 tablespoon truffle oil, white preferred

Lemon slices, for garnish

You may wish to use premade seitan cutlets like those made by Gardein.

To make the seitan: In a large bowl, mix together the garlic, 1 tablespoon of the oil, the pepper, salt, thyme, rosemary, and oregano. Rub the seitan cutlets in the mixture and let sit for 1½ hours.

In a medium, heavy-bottom skillet, heat the remaining ¾ cup oil over medium-high heat. Add the seitan (only a couple of pieces at a time) and sear for 3 minutes on each side, or until golden brown and crispy. Place on a paper towel to soak up any excess oil. Repeat with the remaining cutlets.

To make the cauliflower puree: Bring a large pot of salted water to a boil. Add the cauliflower, reduce the heat to a simmer, cover the pot, and cook for 20 to 25 minutes, or until soft. Place the mixture in a blender and puree.

Heat the oil in a small saucepan over medium-high heat. Add the onion and cook for 5 to 7 minutes, or until soft and lightly browned.

Add the onion, salt, and pepper to the cauliflower in the blender and blend to the desired consistency.

To make the sauce: In a medium skillet, heat the oil over medium heat. Add the shallots, mushrooms, salt, and pepper and cook for 5 to 7 minutes, or until soft and translucent. Add the flour and cook for 2 minutes, stirring constantly, to make a roux.

Add the wine to deglaze the pan and stir well to incorporate the flour. Add stock or water and 1 teaspoon of the parsley and cook over medium heat for 10 minutes, or until the sauce becomes slightly glossy. Remove from the heat and stir in the truffle oil.

To serve, spoon ½ cup cauliflower puree onto each individual plate. Place 1 to 2 seitan cutlets (depending on the size) on top of the puree and cover with sauce. Garnish with chopped parsley and lemon slices and serve immediately.

Wild Mushroom and Spinach Roulade

Owner and executive chef **Jeff Sanford** and chef and creative director **Sadhana Berkow** of the Ravens' Restaurant at the Stanford Inn, Mendocino, California

Ravens' is a vegan restaurant located between the Pacific Ocean and the North Coast's forests, which are noted not only for redwoods and firs but also for wild mushrooms. These porcinis, matsutakes, hedgehogs, chanterelles, and more. Chefs have stuffed them into tofu, beggar's purses, sauces, cannelloni, and salads. Every year Mendocino County's Mushroom Festival motivates them to do something new. In 2013, inspired by an ice-cream roll, they created a Wild Mushroom Roulade. The best part? Almost any mushroom or combination of mushrooms will work and the dish remains outstanding.

MAKES 4 TO 6 SERVINGS
TIME TO MAKE: 3 HOURS

Chef's Tip: Serve with black rice and choice of steamed green beans, roasted Brussels sprouts, roasted cauliflower, or other seasonal vegetable. The port wine reduction pairs well with all of these, so garnish them with a drizzle of the reduction.

Fresh Mushroom Filling

- 2 tablespoons olive oil
- 2 yellow or white onions, sliced in thin half-circles
- 4 shallots, sliced in thin half-circles
- 4 cups wild mushrooms (like chanterelles or hedgehogs), finely chopped
- ½ teaspoon salt
- 2 tablespoons dried or chopped fresh thyme
- 1 bunch chives, minced
- 1 tablespoon ground white pepper
- 1 teaspoon ground green peppercorns
- ¼ cup dry white wine
- 1 tablespoon mirin
- 2 teaspoons balsamic vinegar, golden preferred
- 1 teaspoon ume plum vinegar
- 8 cups chopped spinach

Dried Mushroom Filling

- 2 cups dried porcini mushrooms (porcini have the best flavor for this dish, but you may also substitute shiitakes or matsutakes)
- 1 cup white wine
- 1 cup vegetable stock
- 2 tablespoons minced garlic
- 1 teaspoon salt

Roll

- 10 sheets phyllo dough
- Olive oil spray
- Paprika

Port Wine Reduction

- 1 bottle inexpensive organic port wine
- Maple syrup, optional

(continued)

To make the fresh mushroom filling: In a large skillet over medium heat, heat the oil and cook the onions and shallots for 5 minutes. Add the mushrooms and cook for 3 minutes. Add the salt, thyme, chives, white pepper, and peppercorns and cook for 5 minutes, or until the mixture is browned.

In a separate bowl, whisk together the wine, mirin, balsamic vinegar, and plum vinegar. Add to the skillet and quickly stir until the liquid mostly evaporates. Add the chopped spinach, stir a couple of times, and remove from the heat. The residual heat in the pan will cook the spinach.

To make the dried mushroom filling: In a large skillet, combine the dried mushrooms, wine, stock, garlic, and salt. Simmer for 15 to 20 minutes, until the mushrooms are soft and all of the liquid has cooked out of the pan. Let cool.

Chop the rehydrated mushrooms into small pieces. Add to the fresh mushroom filling and mix well.

To make the roll: Carefully lay a single sheet of phyllo dough on a clean surface. Lightly spray it with oil, then lightly sprinkle it with paprika. Lay a second sheet of phyllo on top of the first, spray it with oil, and sprinkle with paprika. Repeat this for the next 2 sheets. Add a fifth sheet, but do not spray it. Cover three-quarters of that sheet with half of the mushroom filling, spreading it about ¼" thick. Lightly spray the exposed part of the phyllo sheet with oil. This will help seal the roll. Roll the mushroom mixture and phyllo from one long end to the other long end, forming a very tight roll. Refrigerate for 1 to 2 hours to firm it up.

Repeat with the remaining phyllo sheets and mushroom filling.

Preheat the oven to 350°F. Lightly oil a baking sheet.

Cut the rolls into 1" rounds. (Note: You can wrap the rolls in plastic wrap and freeze them before slicing them. They will last about 2 months frozen.) Transfer the rounds to the baking sheet. Bake for 15 minutes.

To make the port wine reduction: Place the port wine in a saucepan and bring to a simmer, cooking it until it is reduced by half. If the port is too sour, add the maple syrup to taste at the end of the cooking process.

To serve, place 3 filled phyllo medallions on a plate and drizzle with the port wine reduction.

Eggplant Cannelloni

Owner and executive chef **Jeff Sanford** and chef and creative director **Sadhana Berkow** of the Ravens' Restaurant at the Stanford Inn, Mendocino, California

According to the chefs at Ravens' Restaurant, this dish began as a napoleon: layers of zucchini, eggplant, and herbed tofu ricotta. Looking to create a more interesting dish, they dropped the zucchini and kept the eggplant, thinly slicing and grilling it. They then rolled and filled each slice with herbed hemp-seed ricotta rather than tofu, preferring a "whole food" approach—an outstanding change. Served with their house marinara sauce and enhanced with dried apricots, this is an easy main course.

MAKES 4 TO 6 SERVINGS
TIME TO MAKE: 45 TO 60 MINUTES

Marinara Sauce

- ½ white onion, diced
- 1 tablespoon olive oil
- 5–6 cloves garlic, minced
- 3 organic unsulfured dried apricots, diced
- 1 teaspoon dried basil
- 1 teaspoon dried oregano
- 1 teaspoon dried parsley
- 1 teaspoon salt
- ⅛ teaspoon ground black pepper
- 6–8 large fresh tomatoes, chopped, or 1 can (28 ounces) crushed tomatoes

Hemp Ricotta

- 2 cups hemp seeds
- ½ cup vegetable stock
- ½ cup filtered water
- Juice of 1 lemon
- ½ tablespoon golden balsamic vinegar or white balsamic vinegar
- 1 teaspoon ume plum vinegar or additional golden or white balsamic vinegar
- ½–1 teaspoon mellow miso paste, white preferred
- 1 teaspoon salt
- 2 tablespoons olive oil
- ½ teaspoon ground white pepper
- 1 tablespoon dried or chopped fresh basil
- 1 tablespoon chopped fresh chives
- 1 tablespoon chopped fresh thyme
- 1 tablespoon dried or chopped fresh oregano or marjoram
- 2 tablespoons nutritional yeast

Eggplant and Garnish

- 1 globe eggplant, peeled and thinly sliced with a knife or mandoline*
- High-heat organic spray oil
- Salt
- ¼ cup thinly sliced fresh basil

*Use your mandoline safety guard or hand guard to keep fingers and body parts away from the blade. For extra protection, consider using cut-resistant safety gloves.

(continued)

To make the marinara sauce: In a saucepan over medium heat, cook the onion in the oil for 3 minutes, or until softened. Add the garlic and cook, stirring constantly, for 1 to 2 minutes. Add the apricots, basil, oregano, parsley, salt, and pepper and cook for 30 seconds. Add the tomatoes and stir well to combine. Reduce the heat to low and simmer for 10 minutes.

Blend the sauce with an immersion blender, or allow it to cool and use a standard blender. The consistency should be slightly chunky.

To make the hemp ricotta: In a blender, combine the hemp seeds, stock, water, lemon juice, vinegars, miso paste, salt, oil, white pepper, basil, chives, thyme, oregano or marjoram, and nutritional yeast. Puree until smooth.

To make the eggplant: Preheat the grill or oven to 450°F.

Spray the eggplant slices with the cooking oil and dust with the salt. Grill or broil the eggplant slices until they are soft but not crispy. Remove the eggplant slices from the grill or oven and let them cool to the point where you can safely handle them. Leave your oven set at 450°F to bake the assembled eggplant. If you have not done so, preheat the oven to 450°F now.

To assemble, place 1 to 2 tablespoons of the hemp ricotta on each slice of eggplant and roll it closed. Transfer the eggplant rolls to a baking dish. Bake for 10 minutes.

Put 4 to 6 eggplant rolls on each plate, and pour ¼ cup of the marinara over the rolls. Garnish with the basil.

Risotto Veganese

Caryn Hartglass (host of the radio show *It's All About Food* and the podcast *Ask a Vegan*) and vegan chef **Gary De Mattei**

Say Caryn and Gary: "Risotto Veganese is our vegan version of the braised rice dish from northern Italy, an adaptation of Risotto alla Milanese. The distinctive ingredient in both the classic version and ours is good-quality saffron from Spain. Spanish saffron will set you back around $20 an ounce in a specialty food store. It may be a little bit less at an outdoor market in Barcelona, but who's got time to go to Spain when you're running a nonprofit organization?"

MAKES 6 SERVINGS
TIME TO MAKE: 30 MINUTES

5–6 cups vegetable stock
1 teaspoon saffron threads
¼ cup extra-virgin olive oil
1 medium onion, cut into ¼" pieces

2 cups Arborio rice
½ cup white wine
4 tablespoons vegan butter

In a stock pot over medium-high heat, heat the vegetable stock until steaming and add the saffron, stirring to infuse. Reduce the heat to medium-low to keep the stock warm.

In a 12" to 14" skillet, heat the oil over medium heat. Add the onion and cook for 8 to 10 minutes, or until softened and translucent but not browned. Add the rice and stir for 3 to 4 minutes, or until toasted and opaque.

Add the wine to the rice and stir until the rice has absorbed almost all the wine. Ladle into the rice ½ cup of the saffron-infused stock and continue cooking and stirring the rice until the stock has been mostly absorbed. Continue this process, adding ½ cup of stock, stirring until it is mostly absorbed, then adding another ½ cup of stock, stirring, and so on until the rice is tender and creamy. The finished texture of the rice should be al dente, not mushy. Once this point is achieved, stir in the vegan butter and remove the risotto from the heat.

Aloo Mattar—Potatoes and Green Peas in a Curry Tomato Sauce

Darshana Thacker, vegan chef featured in *Forks Over Knives*

This recipe was prepared at a wonderful dinner I had not long ago in Los Angeles with John Joseph, the lead singer for the Cro Mags; Brian Wendel, the producer of *Forks Over Knives*; and Darshana Thacker, a well-known vegan chef. I asked her about it, and here's what Darshana said: "When I was growing up in India, eating out in restaurants or having food catered was uncommon. In my family, my mother, sister, and visiting aunts did virtually all the cooking. While I was impressed with my relatives' handiwork, I was content being an occasional observer. Today, however, I've become passionately interested in making my own meals—and especially enjoy replicating the delicious flavors of my childhood foods. Aloo Mattar is a traditional Indian dish of potato and peas in a flavorful tomato-based curry. This particular version is my mother's. The mix of spices my mom uses gives the dish a unique and delicious flavor."

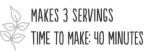

MAKES 3 SERVINGS
TIME TO MAKE: 40 MINUTES

Chef's Tip: Serve this with cooked brown rice.

Tomato Sauce

- ¼ teaspoon black mustard seeds
- 1–2 green cardamom pods
- 4 whole cloves
- 1 1" cinnamon stick
- ¼ teaspoon cumin seeds
- Pinch of asafetida,* optional
- 5–6 medium tomatoes, cubed
- ¾ cup water
- Cayenne, to taste
- 1 teaspoon ground cumin
- 1½ teaspoons ground coriander
- Salt to taste

Potatoes and Peas

- 2–3 cups water
- 3 small russet potatoes, unpeeled
- 1 cup green peas, fresh or frozen, rinsed
- 2 teaspoons minced fresh cilantro, optional

To make the sauce: In a large, dry skillet over medium heat, toast the mustard seeds, cardamom pods, cloves, and cinnamon stick for 1 to 2 minutes, stirring once the mustard seeds start to pop. Add the cumin seeds and asafetida, if using, and toast for 1 minute. Add the tomatoes and cook for 3 to 4 minutes, or until they soften. Add the ¾ cup water and cook for 2 to 3 minutes. Add the cayenne, cumin, coriander, and salt. Stir together and cook for 10 to 15 minutes.

To make the potatoes and peas: Meanwhile, in a small pot, bring the 2 to 3 cups of water to a boil, add the potatoes, and cook for 10 to 15 minutes, or until they are soft. Drain and let cool. Peel the potatoes and cut them into 1" cubes.

To assemble: Stir the potatoes and green peas into the sauce and cook for 7 to 10 minutes. Remove from the heat, remove the cinnamon stick and cardamom pods, and sprinkle the cilantro on top, if using.

Asafetida is a spice derived from the resin extracted from a plant root. It has a pungent aroma that is very strong when raw but works as a flavor enhancer when cooked. It gives a unique flavor to most Indian dishes. Also called hing, it is available in most Indian grocery stores.

Jambalaya

Jenné Claiborne, personal chef
and creator of the 21-Day Vegan
Blueprint

Jambalaya is a delicious, filling,
and fairly easy dish to make and
enjoy year-round. This vegan version uses chickpeas, shiitake mushrooms, and tempeh to replicate the
meatiness of nonvegan jambalaya.
Don't let the number of ingredients
intimidate you. This gluten-free
recipe comes together easily.

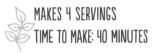

MAKES 4 SERVINGS
TIME TO MAKE: 40 MINUTES

3 tablespoons grapeseed oil

1 medium yellow onion, diced

2 cloves garlic, minced

3 ribs celery, chopped

1 green bell pepper, chopped

1 can (14 ounces) diced
tomatoes

1 can (14 ounces) chickpeas,
rinsed and drained

1 package (8 ounces) tempeh,
cut into bite-size pieces

2 cups fresh sliced shiitake
mushrooms (stems
removed)

2 cups vegetable broth,
or 1 vegetable bouillon cube
dissolved in 2 cups water

3 bay leaves

1 cup cooked brown rice

1 tablespoon Cajun seasoning

1 teaspoon vegan
Worcestershire sauce

1 teaspoon hot sauce + more
if needed

Salt and ground black
pepper

In a large pot, heat the oil over medium heat. Add the onion, garlic, and
celery. Cook for 5 minutes, or until the onion is translucent. Add the bell
pepper, tomatoes, chickpeas, tempeh, and mushrooms. Stir well and cook
for 5 minutes.

Stir in the vegetable broth and bay leaves. Bring to a simmer and cook for
10 minutes. Add the rice, Cajun seasoning, Worcestershire sauce, and
1 teaspoon of hot sauce. Stir well and simmer for 10 minutes. Season to
taste with salt and pepper and more hot sauce, if desired.

Gardein Bolognese

Jason Stefanko, executive chef of Gardein

Says Jason: "When I get home after working a long day as a chef, I sometimes want something easy, traditional, and comforting. Friday night, a bottle of wine, some of my grandfather's old records playing in the background, and this hearty comforting pasta make for a perfect end to the week."

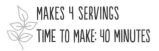

MAKES 4 SERVINGS

TIME TO MAKE: 40 MINUTES

2 tablespoons olive oil

1 tablespoon vegan butter

1 large carrot, chopped

1 rib celery, chopped

4 large shallots, diced

2 cloves garlic, minced

½ cup chardonnay

1½ cups marinara sauce

1 can (28 ounces) whole San Marzano tomatoes, drained

1 teaspoon fine sea salt

¼ teaspoon coarse black pepper

¾ teaspoon red-pepper flakes

½ package Gardein Ultimate Beefless Ground

1 pound rigatoni pasta

¼ cup chopped fresh basil, optional

1 tablespoon chopped Italian parsley

2 tablespoons Parmela Parmesan Style Aged Nut Cheese

In a large saucepan, heat the oil and vegan butter over medium heat. Add the carrot, celery, shallots, and garlic and cook for 5 minutes, or until the shallots are translucent. Add the wine and cook for 5 minutes, or until it is reduced by half.

Add the marinara sauce, tomatoes, salt, pepper, and pepper flakes. Cover the pan and cook on low for 25 to 30 minutes, or until the tomatoes soften. Using a wooden spoon, break the tomatoes into ½" to 1" pieces.

While the sauce is cooking, place the Ultimate Beefless Ground in a skillet and cook for 6 to 8 minutes, or until browned. Add it to the sauce.

Cook the rigatoni according to package directions.

Toss the pasta with the sauce. If extra flavor is desired, add the basil. Garnish with the parsley and vegan cheese.

Osso Vita

Caryn Hartglass (host of the radio show *It's All about Food* and the podcast *Ask a Vegan*) and vegan chef **Gary De Mattei**

Say Caryn and Gary: "We love taking old favorite recipes and making them vegan. One recipe that Gary's wanted to re-create, vegan style, is the Italian classic Osso Buco (translated from Italian, it literally means 'bone hole') the dish he loved so much at Harry's Bar in Venice. Here is the recipe, salty and chewy, right down to the 'bone.' Our secret ingredient for this chewy, tasty 'bone' is parsley root. Serve with Risotto Veganese on page 237 and braised veggies of your choice."

MAKES 6 SERVINGS
TIME TO MAKE: 3 HOURS 30 MINUTES

Seitan Roast

- 1 gallon water
- 2 cups vital wheat gluten flour
- ¼ cup millet flour
- ¼ cup nutritional yeast
- 2 teaspoons sea salt
- 2 teaspoons granulated onion
- 2 teaspoons dried ground rosemary
- 2 teaspoons dried ground herbes de Provence
- 2 teaspoons ground fennel seeds
- 1 teaspoon smoky paprika (if you like it hot, use hot paprika)
- ½ teaspoon ground black pepper
- 1 cup vegetable stock
- ½ cup olive oil
- 2 tablespoons molasses
- 2 tablespoons Bragg Liquid Aminos
- 1 tablespoon brown sugar
- 1 "bone" an 8"- to 10" white root vegetable, cut to the length of the roast with about ½" revealed on both sides until wrapped and tied*

Braised Seitan Chops

- ¼ cup vegan butter or olive oil or a mixture
- 1½ cups finely chopped onions
- ½ cup finely chopped celery
- ½ cup finely chopped carrots
- 1 tablespoon finely chopped garlic
- 1 cup dry white wine
- ½ teaspoon dried basil
- ½ teaspoon dried thyme
- 3 cups drained whole tomatoes (save the juice for another use)
- 6 sprigs parsley
- 2 bay leaves
- ¾ cup vegetable stock
- ½ cup olive oil, divided
- 1 cup flour
- Salt and ground black pepper

Gremolata

- 1 tablespoon grated lemon peel
- 2 cloves garlic, minced
- 3 tablespoons finely chopped parsley

We used a parsley root, which is very tough and holds up well to the boiling and the braising. If unavailable, use a parsnip or a daikon radish. A peeled stalk of sugarcane might even work, but we haven't tried it yet. If you do, tell us how you like the results.

(continued)

To make the seitan roast: In a very large pot, bring the water to a simmer.

Meanwhile, in a large bowl, whisk together the flours, nutritional yeast, salt, granulated onion, rosemary, herbes de Provence, fennel, paprika, and pepper. In a separate bowl, whisk together the stock, oil, molasses, Liquid Aminos, and brown sugar. Add to the flour-spice mixture. Knead for 5 minutes, until you have a wet dough and are able to form it. It should feel very spongy but not sticky.

Form into an 8"- to 10"-round roast-type loaf and insert the root vegetable down the middle.

Place the roast on one double-thick piece of 24" X 16" cheesecloth and roll it up like a rolled roast (not too tightly). Tie each end with a piece of kitchen string, then tie a string in the middle, and then tie the middle of either side. You should have 5 ties, evenly spaced, and it should look like a traditional tied roast.

Place the roast in the pot with the simmering water, cover, and simmer for 1 hour 15 minutes. Take the roast out of the liquid and remove the cheesecloth. Slice the roast into six 1"-thick chops. You will use these to make the braised seitan chops.

To make the braised seitan chops: Use a Dutch oven or an ovenproof/stove-top-proof baking dish with a tight-fitting lid large enough to hold 6 seitan chops (each about 4" in diameter) in a single layer.

Over medium heat, melt the butter or oil in the Dutch oven or ovenproof dish. Add the onions, celery, carrots, and garlic and cook until soft. Add the white wine, basil, thyme, tomatoes, parsley sprigs, bay leaves, and stock. Bring the braising mixture to a boil. Reduce the heat and simmer uncovered.

Preheat the oven to 350°F.

Brush the seitan chops with about 2 tablespoons of the olive oil. Dredge them in the flour, seasoned with a little salt and pepper to taste. Dust off any residual flour and set the chops on a plate.

Heat a large heavy skillet. Add the remaining 6 tablespoons olive oil and heat until a haze forms on the oil. Brown the chops on both sides, adding more olive oil if needed.

Add the chops to the simmering braising mixture (make sure the chops are coated but not drowning in the mixture). Cover and place in the oven. Bake for 1 hour 30 minutes.

To make the gremolata: In a small bowl, combine the lemon peel, garlic, and parsley. Dress the roast with gremolata to taste. Keep the rest refrigerated in a sealed jar for later use in other recipes.

Serve the chops on a bed of the braising mixture sprinkled with a little of the gremolata.

Ellen's Red Beans and Rice

Roberto Martin in conjunction with **Ellen DeGeneres,** actress, talk show host, and philanthropist; and **Portia De Rossi,** actress and philanthropist

Ellen and Portia have been supporters of Farm Sanctuary for many years. They are compelling voices against factory farming and are committed to compassionate vegan living. They came up with this recipe with their chef Roberto, and it appeared in his wonderful book, *Vegan Cooking for Carnivores.*

MAKES 6 SERVINGS
TIME TO MAKE: 30 MINUTES

2 cups brown or white basmati rice

7 cups water

2 cans (15 ounces each) organic kidney beans, rinsed and drained

2 tablespoons Better Than Bouillon Vegetable Base

2 Field Roast Smoked Apple Sage sausages or other vegan sausage of your choice

2 Field Roast Italian sausages or Tofurky sausages or other vegan sausages of your choice

1 tablespoon grapeseed or safflower oil

1 large white onion, diced

6 ribs (6") celery, diced

4 cloves garlic, minced

1 teaspoon chili powder

1 teaspoon dried thyme

1 red bell pepper, finely chopped

Salt and ground black pepper

½ cup thinly sliced green onions

Rinse the rice thoroughly. Add the rice and 3 cups of the water to a pot and bring it to a boil. Cover, reduce the heat to low, and cook for 20 minutes. Remove from the heat and keep covered until ready to serve.

Meanwhile, in a blender, combine three-quarters of the beans with the remaining 4 cups water and the vegetable base. Puree until smooth. Stir the remaining beans into the mixture, but do not puree them.

Cut the sausages in quarters lengthwise, then cut them crosswise into ⅛" pieces.

Heat a 4- to 5-quart stock pot over high heat, add the oil, and wait until it shimmers. Add the onion and celery and cook, stirring slowly, for 10 minutes, or until they are translucent. Add the garlic and cook for 2 minutes. Add the sausages, chili powder, thyme, bean mixture, and bell pepper. Bring to a simmer and cook for 10 to 15 minutes, stirring frequently.

Season with salt and pepper to taste. Serve the red bean mixture over the rice and garnish with the green onions.

Cuban-Gone-Conscious Black Beans and Quinoa

Angela Carrasco and **Sam Polk** of Los Angeles's Groceryships, the "scholarship" for vegan foods

Sam is a former high-powered Wall Street executive who traded in his suit and tie after watching *Forks Over Knives*, changed to a plant-based diet, and moved to Los Angeles. There he founded Groceryships, a health program for low-income families struggling with obesity. Angela Carrasco is the director of programming and marketing for Groceryships and also its lead health coach. This particular dish is derived from one her grandmother used to make: Moros y Cristianos, black beans and rice cooked together.

MAKES 3 TO 4 SERVINGS
TIME TO MAKE: 25 MINUTES

3 cups water

1½ cups quinoa

¾ teaspoon pink Himalayan sea salt

1 teaspoon ground cumin

1 teaspoon dried oregano

¼ teaspoon cayenne, optional

½ medium bell pepper (any color), chopped

1 small red onion or 2 shallots, diced

1 cup corn kernels

1 can (15 ounces) black beans, rinsed and drained

½ cup chopped fresh cilantro

2 tablespoons apple cider vinegar

If preparing this on the stove top, bring the water to a boil. Add the quinoa, salt, cumin, oregano, and cayenne, if using, and stir. Cover, reduce the heat to low, and cook for 18 minutes.

If preparing this in a rice cooker, add the water, quinoa, salt, cumin, oregano, and cayenne, if using, and stir. Cook until the rice cooker indicates that the quinoa is done.

While the quinoa is cooking, heat a medium skillet to medium-high heat. Add the bell pepper and onion or shallots and cook for 8 minutes, or until the pepper is soft and the onion or shallots are lightly browned. Remove from the heat.

Once the quinoa is done cooking, stir in the bell pepper mixture, corn, beans, cilantro, and vinegar.

Greens and Chickpea Curry Bowl

Christy Morgan, chef, vegan fitness trainer, and author of *Blissful Bites*

The makings of a good bowl will have three main food groups: a grain, a vegetable, and a protein. Sometimes the protein and vegetables are all mixed together like in this dish. Sometimes they are separated in their own little compartments. Either way, they all come together to make a delicious meal.

MAKES 2 SERVINGS
TIME TO MAKE: 15 MINUTES

1 cup filtered water

1 sweet potato, cut into 1" cubes (1 cup)

Pinch of sea salt

1 cup bite-size broccoli florets

2 collard leaves, finely chopped

1 cup coconut milk

½ cup cooked chickpeas, rinsed and drained

3 tablespoons tomato paste

1–2 tablespoons curry powder

1 tablespoon lime juice

1 tablespoon tamari

Dash of ground cinnamon

Dash of cayenne

Salt

Place the water, sweet potato, and salt in a large saucepan and bring to a boil over medium-high heat. Reduce the heat to low, cover, and simmer for 3 minutes. Add the broccoli, collard leaves, milk, chickpeas, tomato paste, curry, lime juice, tamari, cinnamon, and cayenne. Bring to a boil over medium-high heat, then cover, reduce the heat, and simmer for 5 to 8 minutes. Season with salt to taste.

Sesame Soba Noodles with Collard Greens and Tempeh Croutons

Nava Atlas, cookbook author and founder of vegkitchen.com

Says Nava: "I'm a complete noodle fanatic, but a bowl of pasta with tomato sauce doesn't quite do the trick for me. For me, an ideal noodle dish is one in which veggies have at least equal billing. This Asian-flavored dish of soba noodles and calcium-rich collard greens is flavored with a triple dose of sesame (another great source of calcium): tahini, seeds, and oil. Another bonus—soba noodles made purely of buckwheat are gluten free. If that's not of concern to you, other long noodles—udon or even whole wheat spaghetti—can be substituted."

MAKES 4 SERVINGS
TIME TO MAKE: 20 TO 25 MINUTES

Sauce

- ⅓ cup tahini
- ¼ cup lime juice
- 2 tablespoons reduced-sodium natural soy sauce or tamari, or more if needed
- 2 tablespoons natural granulated sugar (cane, coconut, or date) or agave nectar

Croutons

- 2 teaspoons dark sesame oil
- 1 tablespoon reduced-sodium natural soy sauce or tamari
- 1 package (8 ounces) tempeh, any variety, cut into ½" pieces

Noodles

- 1 package (8 ounces) soba (buckwheat) noodles
- 10–12 collard green leaves
- 1 tablespoon dark sesame oil
- 1 large red or yellow onion, cut in half and thinly sliced
- ¼ small head green cabbage, cut into long, narrow shreds
- 1 medium red bell pepper, cut into long, narrow strips
- ½ cup chopped fresh cilantro, basil, or Thai basil leaves, or more as desired
- 1 tablespoon black or tan sesame seeds

  Red-pepper flakes or Sriracha sauce

(continued)

To make the sauce: In a small bowl, combine the tahini, lime juice, soy sauce or tamari, and sugar or agave nectar.

To make the croutons: In a large or wide-bottomed skillet, heat the oil and soy sauce or tamari over medium heat. Add the tempeh and stir to coat. Increase the heat to medium-high and cook the tempeh until most sides are golden brown. Remove the tempeh croutons to a plate.

To make the noodles: Cook the noodles according to package directions. When they're al dente, remove from the heat and drain.

Meanwhile, cut the stems from the collard leaves with kitchen shears or a sharp knife. Stack 6 or so halves of leaves at a time. Roll the leaves up tightly from one of the narrow ends, almost like a cigar shape, then thinly slice them. Let them unroll to create ribbons of collard greens. Give them a good rinse in a colander.

In the same skillet used to make the croutons, heat the oil. Add the onion and cook over medium heat until softened and golden. Add the collard ribbons, cover, and cook for 7 to 8 minutes, or until they wilt down a bit. Add the cabbage and bell pepper. Increase the heat and cook for 3 minutes, or just until the veggies are on the other side of raw. Remove the skillet from the heat.

Add the cooked noodles to the pan and use a large fork to mix the noodles thoroughly with the veggies. Pour the sauce over the mixture. Add the cilantro or basil and sesame seeds. Scatter the croutons on top. Season with the pepper flakes or Sriracha to taste. This can be served warm or at room temperature.

Oh Fun Rice Noodle Stir-Fry

Sharon Gannon, author and cofounder of the Jivamukti Yoga Method

The fun part of this dish is the noodles. They are broad, fat, slippery, and chewy! Also, since this dish is loosely based on Beef Chow Fun, a popular meat dish in Chinese restaurants, the real fun is that this dish is cruelty free!

MAKES 4 SERVINGS
TIME TO MAKE: 20 MINUTES

8 cups water

7 ounces ho fun flat dried rice noodles (sometimes called shahe fen noodles) or other fettuccine-size flat rice noodles

3 tablespoons toasted sesame oil

1 carrot (8"), sliced diagonally into thin pieces

4 dried shiitake mushrooms (2" diameter), rehydrated in hot water

3 ounces baked tofu, cut into 1" x ¼" pieces

2 cups loosely packed thinly sliced white cabbage

¼ red bell pepper, sliced into 1"-long strips

2 ribs celery (8" each), sliced diagonally into thin pieces

1 teaspoon Chinese five-spice powder mixed with ½ cup water

1 cup fresh mung bean sprouts

2 cups loosely packed fresh spinach

1 tablespoon soy sauce + additional to taste

Hot sesame oil

Salt and ground black pepper

Bring the water to a boil. Boil the noodles for 2 minutes, then drain. Do not overcook them.

Bring a wok or large skillet to high heat, then add the toasted sesame oil. Add the carrot, mushrooms, and tofu and cook for 3 minutes. Add the cabbage, bell pepper, and celery and cook for 2 minutes. Pour in the five-spice powder and water. Immediately add the noodles, bean sprouts, spinach, and 1 tablespoon soy sauce. Cook until the spinach starts to wilt. Remove the pan from the heat.

After plating the noodles, add the hot sesame oil, additional soy sauce, if desired, and salt and pepper to taste.

Spicy Peanut Curry Sea Palm

Owner and executive chef **Jeff Sanford** and chef and creative director **Sadhana Berkow** of the Ravens' Restaurant at the Stanford Inn, Mendocino, California

Say the chefs at Ravens' Restaurant: "Years ago the owners of Mendocino Sea Vegetable Company gave us dried sea palm and said, 'See what you can do with this.' We created our signature dish, Sea Palm Strudel. Sea palm, an incredibly nutritious brown seaweed, is harvested on our coast, which is unpolluted. Here, the rivers are short, and there are no cities or major agricultural operations along their banks. Since then, we have continually worked with sea palm to exploit its delicate taste and fettuccine-like texture. Our Spicy Peanut Curry Sea Palm uses sea palm as a noodle with an East Indian flair. This is a satisfying and filling entrée.

"This is a multipart dish but worth it. Start the sea palm the day before and make the sauce and braise the vegetables the same day you plan on serving it. It's a versatile dish, so you can use any combination of raw vegetables you like, and you can even use regular pasta in place of the sea palm. The real star of the dish is the spicy curry peanut sauce."

MAKES 3 SERVINGS
TIME TO MAKE: 7 HOURS

Sea Palm Noodles

- 3 ounces dried sea palm (about 2 cups), soaked in water for at least 6 hours, then drained, or pasta or wakame, soaked for 5 minutes
- 2 cups water
- ¼ cup tamari
- 2 tablespoons grated fresh ginger
- 3 tablespoons minced garlic
- ¼ teaspoon red-pepper flakes, optional
- 1 teaspoon toasted sesame oil
- 2 tablespoons brown rice syrup
- 2 tablespoons brown rice vinegar

Vegetables

- ½ cup vegetable broth
- 1 teaspoon tamari
- ¼ cup coarsely chopped yellow onions
- ½ cup broccoli florets or broccolini
- ½ cup cauliflower florets
- 1 red bell pepper, thinly sliced
- 1 yellow bell pepper, thinly sliced

- 1 cup chopped yellow squash (¼" pieces)
- 1 baby eggplant, cut into bite-size chunks
- 2 cups sliced bok choy

Sauce

- ½ cup organic creamy peanut butter
- ½ tablespoon ground coriander
- 1 teaspoon ground cumin
- ½ tablespoon ground turmeric
- Grated peel of 1 lime
- Juice of 1 lime
- ⅛ teaspoon red-pepper flakes
- ½ jalapeño chile, seeded
- ⅛ cup agave nectar
- ½ tablespoon minced fresh ginger
- 1 clove garlic
- ⅛ cup minced red onions
- ½ can (14 ounces) organic coconut milk
- Salt and ground black pepper

- 5 cups cooked brown rice
- Roasted peanuts
- Lime wedges

(continued)

To make the sea palm noodles: In a large saucepan, cover the sea palm (or pasta or wakame) with the water, tamari, ginger, garlic, pepper flakes, sesame oil, rice syrup, and vinegar. Bring to a simmer and cook for 20 to 30 minutes, or until the sea palm is tender like a cooked noodle. Do not overcook, or the sea palm will be too soft.

To make the vegetables: Heat a wok over medium-high heat and add the broth and tamari. Quickly add, in order, the onions, broccoli or broccolini, cauliflower, bell peppers, squash, eggplant, and bok choy, stirring and tossing them as they're added. Keep tossing and cook for 4 to 5 minutes, but no more. The vegetables should remain firm. Remove from the heat.

To make the sauce: In a blender, combine the peanut butter, coriander, cumin, turmeric, lime peel and juice, pepper flakes, chile, agave nectar, ginger, garlic, onions, and milk. Puree until smooth, adding extra water as needed to create a creamy texture. Season with salt and pepper to taste.

To plate, place a serving of brown rice at the bottom of a pasta bowl. Top with ½ cup of the sea palm noodles. Drizzle with the sauce and top with ½ cup of the vegetables. Lightly drizzle more sauce on top. Garnish with a sprinkling of roasted peanuts and lime wedges.

Dan Dan Linguine

Robin Robertson, cookbook author and cofounder of Vegan Heritage Press

This version of Dan Dan Mian, or spicy Szechuan noodles, uses linguine instead of Chinese noodles, but feel free to use any type of noodle or pasta you prefer. For a heartier dish, add 8 ounces of diced baked tofu and/or 2 cups of steamed broccoli florets or other cooked vegetable.

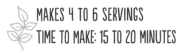

MAKES 4 TO 6 SERVINGS
TIME TO MAKE: 15 TO 20 MINUTES

12 ounces linguine

1 tablespoon toasted sesame oil

1 tablespoon grapeseed oil

1 small red bell pepper, chopped

1 cup chopped shiitake mushroom caps

4 green onions, minced

3 cloves garlic, minced

2 teaspoons grated fresh ginger

⅓ cup creamy peanut butter

1 teaspoon sugar

¼ cup soy sauce

1 tablespoon rice wine vinegar

½ teaspoon red-pepper flakes

1 cup vegetable broth or hot water + additional as needed

2 tablespoons crushed roasted peanuts

Boil the linguine in salted water until just tender. Drain, then return the linguine to the pot. Add the sesame oil and toss to coat.

Meanwhile, heat the grapeseed oil in a large skillet over medium heat. Add the bell pepper, mushrooms, green onions, garlic, and ginger and cook, stirring, for 2 to 3 minutes.

In a small bowl, stir the peanut butter, sugar, soy sauce, vinegar, pepper flakes, and broth or water until the mixture is smooth. Stir the mixture into the skillet with the vegetables. Add more broth or water, if needed, to make a smooth sauce. Remove from the heat and keep warm.

Add the sauce to the hot noodles and toss to coat. Divide the mixture among bowls and sprinkle with the peanuts. Serve hot.

Maitake Mushroom and Artichoke Heart Gluten-Free Lasagna with Vegan Lemon Ricotta

Chloe Jo Davis, founder of the Web site GirlieGirlArmy

Says Chloe: "Let's just say if you've never made lasagna before, you can make this one. I'm promising you this isn't as hard as it sounds. You'll want to wind up with a layer of Daiya on top so it can burn a little or brown when it cooks. Because, let's be honest, nothing is yummier than slightly crispy vegan cheese. Enjoy."

MAKES A 10" X 10" LASAGNA
TIME TO MAKE: 1 HOUR

Lasagna

- 12 ounces lasagna pasta (we use Tinkyada gluten-free kosher brand)
- 1 tablespoon olive oil
- ½ teaspoon salt
- 3 cups chopped maitake mushrooms or mushrooms of your choice
- 2 portobello mushrooms, chopped into bite-size pieces
- 4 cups chopped broccoli rabe (in bite-size pieces)
- 8 cups coarsely chopped spinach
- 2 cups coarsely chopped artichoke hearts (use marinated and grilled artichoke hearts for a fancier lasagna)
- 3 cups pasta sauce
- 2 cups Daiya shredded vegan mozzarella cheese
- 2 cups thinly sliced fresh basil

Ricotta

- 2 packages (12 ounces each) silken tofu, drained
- 5 tablespoons lemon juice
- 2 tablespoons dried oregano
- 2 tablespoons dried basil
- 2 tablespoons garlic powder
- 2 cups nutritional yeast

To make the lasagna: Preheat the oven to 450°F.

Cook the pasta until it is barely al dente, then drain.

In a large dry skillet over medium heat, add the oil and salt and then cook the mushrooms, broccoli rabe, spinach, and artichoke hearts for 10 minutes, or until they are soft. Mix them together well.

To make the ricotta: In a food processor, combine the tofu, lemon juice, oregano, basil, garlic powder, and nutritional yeast. Puree until smooth.

To assemble: Spread a thin layer of the pasta sauce in a large baking dish. Layer 5 or 6 lasagna noodles on top of the sauce. Add a layer of ricotta, then a layer of the veggies, then basil, then a layer of vegan cheese. Add another layer of sauce, then noodles, then ricotta, then veggies, then the remaining basil, and finish up with a layer of vegan cheese.

Bake for 30 minutes. Let cool for at least 5 minutes before cutting and serving the lasagna.

DESSERTS

Hazelnut Truffles

Chloe Coscarelli, cookbook author and winner of television's *Cupcake Wars,* and **Ann Marie Monteiro,** a graduate of the Natural Gourmet Institute for Health and Culinary Arts

Says Chloe: "There is nothing more indulgent than a chocolate truffle. Well, actually, there is something more indulgent—a hazelnut truffle. These are the perfect after-dinner dessert with a great cup of coffee. I also keep them in the fridge and pop them in my mouth when I need a sweet fix!"

MAKES 34 TRUFFLES
TIME TO MAKE: 1 HOUR 45 MINUTES

½ cup canned coconut milk, mixed well before measuring

Pinch of salt

2 tablespoons Frangelico hazelnut liqueur

3½ cups semisweet vegan chocolate chips, divided

1¼ cups finely chopped hazelnuts

In a small saucepan, heat the coconut milk over medium-low heat until it just begins to boil. Reduce the heat to low and add the salt, liqueur, and 1½ cups of the chocolate chips. Let the chocolate melt, whisking frequently, until smooth. Remove from the heat and transfer to a 9" x 5" loaf pan. Let cool and refrigerate until firm and set.

Using a small scoop or melon baller, scoop the set chocolate onto a parchment-lined tray and freeze for 20 to 25 minutes. Remove from the freezer and shape into balls using the palms of your hands. Freeze for 15 minutes, or until firm.

Melt the remaining 2 cups chocolate chips in a double boiler or microwave oven. Remove the tray of chocolate balls from the freezer. Place the hazelnuts in a bowl. Dip each ball into the melted chocolate and remove it using 2 forks. Roll the balls immediately in the hazelnuts until completely coated. Refrigerate the truffles until serving.

Sweet & Sara Peanut Butter Chocolate Rice Crispy Squares

Sara Sohn, founder of the vegan marshmallow manufacturer Sweet & Sara

Sara adds a warning to this recipe: "These are addictive! To make them extra addictive, use the optional mini marshmallows."

MAKES 16 SQUARES
TIME TO MAKE: 40 MINUTES

¼ cup vegan margarine

1 container (6 ounces) Sweet & Sara vanilla marshmallows

¼ cup tapioca, rice, or corn syrup

4 cups rice cereal

Sweet & Sara mini marshmallows, optional

1 cup semisweet vegan chocolate chips

¼ cup peanut butter

Melt the margarine in a medium pot over low heat. Add the marshmallows and cook, stirring, for 5 to 6 minutes, or until they are completely melted. Remove from the heat.

In a small pot over medium heat, warm the syrup until it starts to bubble, then immediately stir it into the marshmallow mixture. Stir in the rice cereal and mini marshmallows, if using, until the cereal is well coated. Spread the mixture into an 8" x 8" pan and press down until the mixture is level.

Melt the chocolate chips in a double boiler, then stir in the peanut butter. Pour over the marshmallow-cereal mixture. Transfer to the refrigerator and let chill for 20 minutes, or until firm. Cut into 16 squares and enjoy!

Salted Caramel Chocolate Bliss Bites

Deb Gleason, certified holistic nutritionist and vegan lifestyle coach

Says Deb: "This recipe woke me up at the creative ambrosia hour of 4 a.m., pleading with me to get out of bed and write it down. This nocturnal burst of inspiration led me to create a healthy snack with a taste comparable to the Turtle Chocolates I grew up with. These delicious little bites never last long, so be sure to make a double batch."

MAKES 15 TO 20 BITES
TIME TO MAKE: 20 TO 25 MINUTES

¾ cup pecans

½ cup unsweetened shredded coconut

20 large soft Medjool dates, pitted

2 teaspoons vanilla extract

½ teaspoon sea salt

½ cup hemp seeds (Hemp Hearts brand preferred)

½ cup dairy-free chocolate chips

Preheat the oven to 350°F. Line 2 baking sheets with parchment paper.

Place the pecans on 1 baking sheet and toast them in the oven for 8 to 10 minutes, or until you begin to smell them (be careful not to allow them to burn). Remove from the oven and place in a bowl to cool.

Place the coconut on the second baking sheet and toast in the oven for 3 to 5 minutes. Keep a close eye on it. When the color starts to change and you can smell sweet, toasted coconut, it's ready to be removed from the oven.

Place the toasted pecans in a blender or food processor. Blend or process until they are ground into small pieces. Place ½ cup of the ground pecans in a large bowl and ¼ cup in a small bowl.

In a blender or food processor, combine the dates, vanilla, and salt. Blend or process until you have date paste (smooth and creamy looking). You may need to stop the blender a few times during this process to stir the ingredients. Remove the date paste, spooning it into the large bowl with the pecans. Also add the hemp seeds and toasted coconut and mix everything together with your hands until well combined.

Roll a small amount of the mixture into a small ball in your hands. Then roll the ball in the small bowl of pecans to coat. Continue until you have a plate full of bliss bites.

Warm the chocolate chips in a small saucepan over low heat until just melted, stirring often to avoid burning the chocolate. Dip the bliss bites into the melted chocolate, covering half of each one with chocolate. Place them on a plate lined with parchment paper. Cool in the refrigerator and enjoy.

These can be stored in the refrigerator for up to a week or in the freezer for several months.

Alicia Silverstone's Coffee-Infused Brownies

Alicia Silverstone, actress and vegan activist

Longtime vegan advocate and Farm Sanctuary supporter, Alicia has helped many people switch from eating animals to eating plants. Her kind and welcoming approach has served our cause well. She is also a font of excellent advice and mouthwatering recipes, including this one, which I love to serve to vegans and nonvegans alike—none of the latter ever know it's vegan.

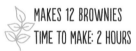

MAKES 12 BROWNIES
TIME TO MAKE: 2 HOURS

Brownies

- ½ cup walnuts
- ¾ cup whole wheat pastry flour
- ¾ cup brown rice flour
- ½ cup unsweetened cocoa powder
- 1 teaspoon baking powder
- 1½ teaspoons baking soda
- 1 teaspoon salt
- 1½ cups maple sugar
- ¾ cup nondairy milk
- ¾ cup brewed decaf coffee
- ½ cup canola oil

Glaze

- 1½ cups grain-sweetened vegan chocolate or carob chips
- ½ cup Earth Balance buttery spread

Preheat the oven to 325°F. Oil an 8" x 8" or 9" x 9" square baking dish.

To make the brownies: Place the walnuts on a baking sheet and bake for 10 minutes, stirring once, or until they are lightly browned and fragrant. Transfer to a bowl and let cool.

In a large bowl, sift together the pastry flour, brown rice flour, cocoa powder, baking powder, baking soda, and salt. Stir in the sugar. In a medium bowl, combine the milk, coffee, and oil. Add to the dry ingredients, stirring until well combined. Stir in the walnuts until they are evenly distributed in the batter.

Pour the batter into the baking dish and bake for 25 to 30 minutes. Insert a toothpick into the center of the brownies. If it comes out clean, the brownies are done. If it does not, return the brownies to the oven for another 5 minutes and repeat until they are done. Transfer the baking dish to a wire rack and let the brownies cool completely.

To make the glaze: After the brownies have cooled, in a double boiler, melt the chocolate or carob chips and Earth Balance, gently stirring until thoroughly incorporated. If you do not have a double boiler, you can place a stainless steel bowl over a pot of gently boiling water. Once the glaze is ready, pour it over the brownies.

Transfer the baking dish to the refrigerator and allow to cool for 1 hour, or until the glaze has completely set.

Cut the brownies into 12 squares and serve.

Chocolate Spice Cake

Gita Devi, owner of The Ginger Cat Bed & Breakfast, a few miles north of the Watkins Glen Farm Sanctuary

Says Gita: "Two things are guaranteed when people arrive at The Ginger Cat B&B: There are friendly cats, and there will be a piece of this cake waiting for you. It's based on a World War II recipe and is vegan from the get-go. I've modified it by adding spices and different liquids. Using cinnamon and powdered ginger make it very warming, perfect for winter. So does a pinch of hot cayenne pepper. Feel free to experiment. I often use leftover cold coffee, orange juice, nondairy creamer—whatever is in the fridge. It never fails. And in the summer, serve with a spoonful of vegan ice cream and strawberries!"

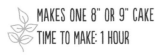

MAKES ONE 8" OR 9" CAKE
TIME TO MAKE: 1 HOUR

1½ cups unbleached all-purpose flour

1 cup unbleached sugar

¼ cup cocoa powder

½ teaspoon salt

1 teaspoon baking soda

1 teaspoon ground cinnamon

½ teaspoon ground ginger

¼ teaspoon cayenne, optional

1 tablespoon vinegar

⅓ cup canola oil

1 teaspoon pure vanilla extract

1 cup cold liquid (use water or nondairy milk for a neutral flavor, or coffee or orange juice for an interesting twist)

Preheat the oven to 350°F.

In an 8" x 8" or 9" x 9" square baking pan, combine the flour, sugar, cocoa powder, salt, baking soda, cinnamon, ginger, and cayenne, if using. Mix well. Scoop out 3 holes. Put the vinegar in 1, the oil in 1, and the vanilla in 1. Pour the cold liquid over it all and mix thoroughly with a fork until everything is blended together.

Bake for 35 to 40 minutes, or until a wooden pick inserted in the cake comes out clean. Cool thoroughly before cutting into pieces and serving.

Lemon Cupcakes

Madelyn Pryor, chef and national culinary instructor for The Vegan Taste

Says Madelyn: "Lemon desserts are a family favorite for generations. When I became vegan, I lamented losing the ability to make my mom's infamous Lemon Pound Cake. I did not lament long. Instead, I transformed that lush lemon dessert into cupcakes! These are the ultimate expression of spring to me. If you want, top them with a few sprinkles of turbinado sugar once they are frosted. The turbinado sugar acts like edible glitter and gives a little crunch to the soft cupcake."

MAKES 12 CUPCAKES
TIME TO MAKE: 1 HOUR 35 MINUTES

Cupcakes

- ½ cup vegan butter or your favorite substitute
- ¾ cup granulated sugar
- 1⅓ cups nondairy milk
- 3 tablespoons fresh lemon juice
- 2 tablespoons grated fresh lemon peel
- 1 teaspoon lemon extract
- 1 teaspoon vanilla extract
- 1½ cups all-purpose flour
- ¼ cup cornstarch
- 1 teaspoon baking powder
- ½ teaspoon baking soda
- ¼ teaspoon salt

Frosting

- ¼ cup vegan butter or your favorite substitute
- ¼ cup vegan shortening
- Small pinch of salt
- 2 tablespoons fresh lemon juice
- 1 teaspoon lemon extract
- 1 tablespoon grated fresh lemon peel
- 1 package (16 ounces) confectioners' sugar

To make the cupcakes: Preheat the oven to 350°F. Line a 12-cup muffin pan with paper liners.

In a large bowl, beat the butter and sugar, using a mixer, until light and fluffy. Add the milk, lemon juice, lemon peel, lemon extract, and vanilla. Mix until thoroughly combined.

In a medium bowl, combine the flour, cornstarch, baking powder, baking soda, and salt. Slowly add to the wet ingredients until just combined. Immediately pour into the lined muffin pan. Bake for 12 to 15 minutes, or until light golden brown. Cool the cupcakes completely. I usually wait at least 1 hour.

To make the frosting: In a medium bowl, using a mixer, beat together the butter, shortening, and salt until light. Add the lemon juice, extract, and peel. Use a slightly lower speed on your mixer to prevent splatter. Add the sugar a little bit at a time, blending as you go, until you get a nice, slightly stiff icing.

Frost the cupcakes with either a butter knife or a pastry bag. Use a fun tip with the pastry bag for a great design, if desired.

Cran-Apple Caramel Pie

JL Fields, author of *Vegan Pressure Cooking* and coauthor of *Vegan for Her*

If eating dessert is your thing but baking isn't, this recipe is for you! Start with 2 premade refrigerated vegan piecrusts and add fresh fruit, a decadent vegan caramel sauce, and just a few other ingredients, and be prepared to feel like a genuine baker!

MAKES ONE 9" PIE
TIME TO MAKE: 1 HOUR 10 MINUTES

Cran-Apple Filling

- 4 cups apple slices (from about 6 peeled, cored apples)
- 2 cups fresh or frozen cranberries
- ½ cup chopped pecans
- ½ cup granulated sugar, loosely packed
- ¼ cup brown sugar, loosely packed
- ¾ cup all-purpose flour
- 2 tablespoons potato flour
- 1 teaspoon ground cinnamon
- ½ teaspoon ground nutmeg
- 2 refrigerated or frozen (flat) 9" vegan piecrusts (if frozen, fully thawed)
- ¼ cup Vegan Caramel Sauce, divided

Vegan Caramel Sauce, optional (you can substitute a store-bought sauce)

- ¼ cup coconut cream
- ¼ cup packed dark brown sugar or turbinado sugar
- Pinch of salt
- ¼ teaspoon vanilla extract, optional
- 1 teaspoon bourbon, optional
- ¼ teaspoon ground cinnamon, optional
- Pinch of chipotle or ancho chile powder, optional

To make the filling: In a large bowl, mix the apples, cranberries, and pecans. Add the sugars and mix well. In a small bowl, combine the flours, cinnamon, and nutmeg. Fold the flour mixture into the apple mixture.

Preheat the oven to 400°F.

To make the sauce (if doing): In a small pot over medium-low heat, warm the coconut cream. Whisk in the brown or turbinado sugar, salt, and any (or all!) of the vanilla, bourbon, cinnamon, and chile powder, as desired. Cook for 20 to 25 minutes, stirring constantly. If the mixture starts to boil over, lift the pot off the heat, let it cool for a few seconds, then return it to the heat and keep stirring. If it keeps boiling over, reduce the heat slightly. The sauce will be done when it has thickened and become slightly viscous but is still pourable.

To assemble the pie: Press 1 piecrust into an ungreased 9" pie plate (glass works best), molding the dough to the bottom and sides of the plate. Pour the filling into the crust.

Drizzle 2 teaspoons of the caramel sauce over the fruit. Place the second piecrust over the fruit filling, pinching the bottom and top crusts together.

Bake for 45 to 50 minutes, or until the crust is golden brown.

Remove the pie from the oven and drizzle 2 tablespoons of caramel sauce over it. Serve warm.

Raw (Almost) Pumpkin Pie

Michael Falso, executive chef of The Springs in Los Angeles

You may naturally think pumpkin when making a pumpkin pie, but butternut squash is a pumpkin analog that works wonders, as well. With a maple cashew crust spiked with vanilla and a filling redolent of cinnamon and nutmeg, it's no wonder that author and pumpkin pie aficionado Michael Falso says he prefers this version to the traditional pumpkin pie he grew up eating. Make this well ahead of time before serving to give the pie a chance to set.

MAKES ONE 9" PIE
TIME TO MAKE: 2½ TO 3½ HOURS

Shortbread Crust

2 cups raw cashews

½ cup shredded coconut

1 teaspoon Himalayan salt

½ teaspoon Ceylon cinnamon

2 tablespoons maple powder

2 tablespoons maple syrup

1 teaspoon vanilla extract

Filling

1½ cups cashews, soaked in warm water for 1 hour

½ cup maple syrup

½ cup fresh carrot juice

½ cup butternut squash, peeled and chopped

1 teaspoon vanilla extract

2 teaspoons Ceylon cinnamon

2 teaspoons freshly grated nutmeg

1 teaspoon Himalayan salt

½ cup melted coconut oil

1½ teaspoons sunflower lecithin,* optional

*Using the sunflower lecithin will help bind the filling together but is not absolutely necessary.

To make the crust: Place the cashews in a high speed blender. Blend, starting at the lowest speed and slowly progressing to the highest speed, until the cashews resemble flour. Immediately stop the blender, or else your cashews will turn into cashew butter. Transfer the cashew flour to a bowl and set it aside. Repeat this process with the shredded coconut until it turns into coconut flour, then transfer it to the same bowl as the cashew flour.

Add the salt, cinnamon, and maple powder to the bowl and whisk until everything is evenly combined. Add the maple syrup and vanilla extract and combine everything by hand, squeezing the mixture together into a "dough" once all the ingredients are evenly combined.

Press the dough evenly into a 9-inch tart pan with a removable bottom. You can use the crust as is, or if you prefer a more bready crust, dehydrate it in the tart pan at 118°F for 2 hours. If you do not have a dehydrator, bake it in the oven at 200°F for 10 minutes.

To make the filling: Rinse the soaked cashews and strain them. In a high speed blender, puree the cashews, maple syrup, carrot juice, butternut squash, vanilla, cinnamon, nutmeg, and salt. Continue pureeing the mixture until it is completely smooth and slightly warm.

With the blender still running, slowly pour in the coconut oil and keep blending until it is thoroughly incorporated. At this point, with the blender still running, add the optional sunflower lecithin, if using, blending until it is also thoroughly incorporated.

To finish the pie: Pour the mixture into the tart pan until the mixture comes to the rim of the crust. Tap the tart pan gently but firmly on a countertop so the mixture can settle. Place the pie in the freezer to set for 1 to 2 hours. Once it is completely frozen, transfer it to a refrigerator to thaw before serving. Slide sides of the tart pan off the pie and serve.

Mint Chocolate Ganache Tart

Owner and executive chef **Jeff Sanford** and chef and creative director **Sadhana Berkow** of the Ravens' Restaurant at the Stanford Inn, Mendocino, California

Say the chefs at Ravens' Restaurant: "We put our Chocolate Ganache Tart onto the menu more than 14 years ago. We tweak it continuously to ensure that we remain excited by this, our most popular dessert. The crust has changed many times—from somewhat of a chocolate piecrust, to a chocolate walnut crust, and, in this iteration, a gluten-free chocolate, almond, and hazelnut crust. The almonds are from nearby, and we have recently started growing our own hazelnuts. We added mint 2 years ago and haven't looked back. A refreshing and satisfying dessert that diners often leave saying, 'I can't believe it's vegan!'"

MAKES 9 TO 12 SERVINGS
TIME TO MAKE: 2 HOURS 40 MINUTES

Crust

1¼ cups almonds

1¼ cups hazelnuts

¼ cup cane sugar

1½ tablespoons cacao powder

¾ teaspoon salt

6 tablespoons coconut oil, softened

½ tablespoon vanilla extract

Water, as needed

Filling

½ box (12 ounces) silken tofu (Wildwood SprouTofu preferred), drained

½ cup water

½ tablespoon vanilla extract

1 teaspoon mint extract, or ½ bunch fresh mint

½ cup unbleached cane sugar

Scant pinch of salt

½ cup semisweet vegan chocolate chips

To make the crust: Preheat the oven to 350°F.

In a food processor, combine the almonds and hazelnuts. Grind the nuts to a very fine consistency. Add the sugar, cacao powder, and salt and pulse the ingredients. Pour the mixture into a large bowl. Add the oil and vanilla and toss, adding water until the mixture sticks together.

Press the mixture into a 12" x 12" baking dish and bake for 10 minutes, or until brown. Let cool before pouring the filling on top.

To make the filling: Place the tofu, water, vanilla, mint, sugar, and salt into a medium saucepan. Mash the tofu lightly into smaller pieces with a potato masher or whisk. Bring the mixture to a boil. Reduce the heat and let simmer for 15 to 20 minutes, or until the liquid reduces and the tofu turns light brown. Turn off the heat, add the chocolate chips, and stir until melted.

Place the mixture in a high-speed blender and blend until smooth. Pour into the cooled crust. Refrigerate for at least 2 hours, or until well chilled. Slice and serve cold.

Any remaining filling can be refrigerated. It will stiffen when cool, but can be melted down over low heat or in a double boiler and poured into a prebaked tart shell.

Berrylicious Fruit Tart

Chef AJ, chef and author of
Unprocessed

Says Chef AJ: "I made this in an Iron Chef completion where I had three surprise ingredients and only 20 minutes, and won! If persimmons are out of season, use 1 pound of strawberries. If they aren't sweet enough, add a few dates to sweeten."

MAKES ONE 10" TART
TIME TO MAKE: 20 MINUTES

Crust

- 1 cup gluten-free oats
- 1 cup unsweetened shredded coconut + 2 tablespoons for garnish
- 1 cup raw walnuts
- 12 ounces pitted dates + more if needed (about 1½ cups)
- 2 tablespoons lime juice
- Grated peel of 2 limes

Sauce

- 8 ounces hulled strawberries
- 8 ounces Fuyu persimmons (about 2 persimmons or ½ cup)
- ¼ cup chia seeds

Filling

- 2 pounds fresh mixed berries (blackberries, blueberries, raspberries), about 4–5 cups

To make the crust: Combine the oats, 1 cup coconut, and nuts in a food processor fitted with the "S" blade. Process into a flour. Add the dates until the mixture clumps and you can form a ball, adding more dates, if necessary. Add the lime juice and peel. If the mixture becomes too wet, knead in a few more oats and more coconut by hand.

Press the dough into a 10" fluted tart pan.

To make the sauce: Combine the strawberries and persimmons in the food processor and puree. Add the chia seeds and blend again.

To make the filling: Place the mixed berries in a large bowl. Pour the strawberry-persimmon sauce over the berries and stir gently. Pour the filling mixture over the dough. Sprinkle with shredded coconut.

Peanut Butter Date Cookies

Madelyn Pryor, chef and national culinary instructor for The Vegan Taste

Says Madelyn: "My husband loves peanut butter cookies. Once I discovered this, I worked diligently to perfect my vegan peanut butter cookie recipe. Adding dates and walnuts makes these cookies chunky, hearty, and perfect for lunch boxes, picnics, or the holidays. Really, they are perfect whenever."

MAKES ABOUT 4 DOZEN
TIME TO MAKE: 45 MINUTES

- ¾ cup vegan butter
- ¾ cup peanut butter
- ¾ cup granulated sugar
- ½ cup firmly packed brown sugar
- ½ cup nondairy milk
- 2 tablespoons real maple syrup
- 2 teaspoons vanilla extract
- 1 teaspoon almond extract
- 2¼ cups all-purpose flour
- 1 teaspoon baking powder
- 1 teaspoon baking soda
- ½ teaspoon salt
- ¾ cup chopped walnuts
- 1½ cups sliced or chopped dates, loosely packed

Preheat the oven to 325°F. Line 2 baking sheets with parchment paper or use silicone baking sheets for easy removal.

In a large bowl, using a mixer, cream together the butter, peanut butter, granulated sugar, and brown sugar until light and fluffy. Add the milk, maple syrup, vanilla, and almond extract. Beat together until well combined.

Using a clean bowl, stir together the flour, baking powder, baking soda, salt, walnuts, and dates. Slowly add to the wet ingredients, until just combined.

Drop rounded teaspoons of the dough 2" apart onto the baking sheets and bake for 15 minutes. Cool and remove from the sheets.

Peanut Butter Date Cookies (top, left) and Cornmeal Blueberry Cookies (bottom, right).

Cornmeal Blueberry Cookies

Madelyn Pryor, chef and national culinary instructor for The Vegan Taste

Says Madelyn: "These unexpected little cookies never fail to delight when I make a batch. The cornmeal lends the cookies a slightly crunchy texture while the blueberries, once baked, burst in your mouth. I always use fresh blueberries with this recipe (instead of dried) and fold them in gently because otherwise, you will have bright blue cookies!"

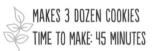

MAKES 3 DOZEN COOKIES
TIME TO MAKE: 45 MINUTES

1 cup vegan butter

1 cup granulated sugar

½ cup nondairy milk combined with 2 tablespoons cornstarch

1 teaspoon almond extract

1 teaspoon lemon extract

1¾ cups all-purpose flour

1 cup yellow cornmeal

1 teaspoon baking soda

1 teaspoon baking powder

½ teaspoon salt

1 cup dried blueberries

Preheat the oven to 350°F. Line 2 baking sheets with parchment paper or use a silicone baking sheet for easy removal.

In a large bowl, using a mixer, cream together the vegan butter and sugar until light and fluffy. Add the milk-cornstarch mixture and almond and lemon extracts.

In a medium bowl, stir together the flour, cornmeal, baking soda, baking powder, and salt. Gently toss in the blueberries. Fold into the wet ingredients until combined.

Drop tablespoons of the dough 2" apart onto the baking sheets and bake for 10 to 12 minutes. Cool for at least 5 minutes before removing from the sheets.

Sweet & Sara S'mores Cookies

Sara Sohn, founder of the vegan marshmallow manufacturer Sweet & Sara

Says Sara: "I'm Korean, and in every Korean household marshmallow chocolate pies are a staple, so when I became a vegan 22 years ago, saying good-bye to these guys was tough. This inspired the creation of our famous Sweet & Sara S'mores and this s'mores recipe, a homemade version of the chocolate pies I so dearly loved as a kid and so dearly missed as an adult."

Note: Instead of making the graham crackers, you can use 16 store-bought vegan graham crackers.

MAKES 16 COOKIES
TIME TO MAKE: 40 MINUTES

1¾ cups all-purpose flour

1¼ cups whole wheat flour

1 teaspoon baking soda

⅛ teaspoon salt

8 ounces vegan margarine

¾ cup sugar

1¼ tablespoons molasses

20 ounces vegan chocolate

3 containers (6 ounces each) Sweet & Sara vanilla marshmallows

Preheat the oven to 350°F.

In a medium bowl, whisk together the flours, baking soda, and salt. In a large bowl, place the margarine, sugar, and molasses. Using a mixer on medium speed, beat until light and fluffy, scraping down the sides of the bowl. Add the flour mixture and mix until well incorporated.

Lightly flour a flat working surface. Roll out the dough until it is ⅛" thick. Cut it into squares using a 3"-diameter cookie cutter. Use a spatula to transfer each disc of dough to an ungreased baking sheet, spacing them about 1" apart. Bake for 15 minutes, or until golden brown, rotating the pan halfway through. Let cool completely.

Melt the chocolate in a double boiler. Drizzle half of the melted chocolate over the graham crackers. Place 4 marshmallows on top of each graham cracker. Pour the remaining half of the chocolate over the marshmallows. Chill the s'mores for 10 minutes before serving.

Pumpkin Pie Crème Brûlée

Chloe Coscarelli, cookbook author and winner of television's *Cupcake Wars,* and **Ann Marie Monteiro,** a graduate of the Natural Gourmet Institute for Health and Culinary Arts

Says Chloe: "I know what you are thinking: Why change pumpkin pie at all? Well, believe me, this is pumpkin pie's fancy cousin, and you won't be disappointed. This is easy to make and absolutely delicious!"

MAKES 6 SERVINGS
TIME TO MAKE: 4 HOURS 30 MINUTES

¼ cup soy, almond, or rice milk

¼ cup cornstarch or arrowroot

1 can (13.5 ounces) coconut milk

¾ cup sugar, divided

⅛ teaspoon salt

1 teaspoon pure vanilla extract

1 teaspoon pumpkin pie spice

1 cup canned pumpkin puree

In a small bowl, thoroughly mix the milk and cornstarch or arrowroot with a whisk or fork.

In a medium saucepan, whisk together the coconut milk, ½ cup of the sugar, the salt, vanilla, pumpkin pie spice, and pumpkin puree. Heat over medium-high heat just until boiling. Reduce the heat to medium and slowly drizzle the cornstarch mixture into the saucepan, whisking continuously. Cook, whisking frequently, for 1 to 2 minutes, or until the mixture becomes very thick in texture, like pudding.

Divide the custard evenly among 6 (5"-diameter) crème brûlée dishes or ramekins. Smooth the tops. Let cool for 10 minutes, then chill in the refrigerator for 3 hours or overnight.

Remove the custards from the refrigerator 1 hour before torching, so that they come to room temperature.

Sprinkle about 2 teaspoons sugar onto each custard, then give it a little shake so that the sugar spreads evenly. Hold a torch about 2" to 3" from the sugar and melt the sugar until it bubbles and turns slightly golden. Be sure to move your torch back and forth continuously so that the sugar does not burn in one spot. Once there is no more visible dry sugar, let the crème brûlée sit for 3 to 5 minutes, then serve immediately.

For an extra-thick crackly top, add 2 more teaspoons sugar and repeat the torching process.

Vanilla Bean Coconut Rice Pudding

Jennifer Engel and **Heather Goldberg,** co-owners of West Hollywood, California–based Spork Foods Cooking Classes

This dessert is quick to whip up. It makes the kitchen smell amazing, and you can serve it warm or cold, so it's great for any night of the week.

MAKES 4 TO 6 SERVINGS
TIME TO MAKE: 30 MINUTES

2 cups water

1 cup short-grain organic Arborio rice

½ vanilla bean, split lengthwise

2 cinnamon sticks

2 slices (1" long each) lemon peel

¼ teaspoon ground cloves

14 ounces (1½ cans) organic coconut milk

½ cup organic evaporated cane sugar

Dash of sea salt

¼ cup raisins or currants, optional

2 tablespoons cinnamon sugar

In a large pot, bring the water to a simmer. Add the rice and stir gently. Add the vanilla bean, cinnamon sticks, lemon peel, and cloves. Cook at a simmer over low heat for 12 to 15 minutes, or until the rice is tender and the liquid is almost absorbed.

Stir in the milk, cane sugar, salt, and raisins or currants, if using. Cook for 8 to 10 minutes, stirring frequently.

Remove from the heat and place in small glasses or cups. Top with the cinnamon sugar. Serve warm or chilled.

Kona Coconut Tapioca

Tanya Petrovna, founder of Native Foods Restaurants

Says Tanya: "When vegan high school biology teacher Jason Tate asked me to do a cooking demo for his Physiology of Digestion class, I made this recipe times four to give sample sizes to all the students. The students loved it. Jason offers his students and their friends, family, and everyone at Indio High School (Indio, California) a chance each year to take part in a 30-day vegan challenge. Check out his blog *It's Groovy Being Vegan*."

MAKES 6 TO 8 SERVINGS
TIME TO MAKE: 40 MINUTES

½ cup medium tapioca pearls

1½ cups water

2 cups unsweetened coconut cream

1 cup nondairy milk

5 tablespoons organic sugar

1 tablespoon Tahitian or Madagascar vanilla extract

1 tablespoon coconut flavoring (not imitation)

¼ teaspoon salt

Fresh fruit, such as mangoes or strawberries

In a medium saucepan, place the tapioca pearls and the water and let sit for 30 minutes. Stir in the coconut cream, milk, sugar, vanilla, coconut flavoring, and salt. Bring to a simmer, then reduce the heat to medium-low and cook, stirring continuously, for 3 minutes.

Remove from the heat and pour it into a serving dish or portion into individual dishes. Garnish with the fresh fruit.

Pumpkin Bread Pudding with Brandy Nog Crème Anglaise

Miyoko Schinner, author of *Artisan Vegan Cheese*, cohost of television's *Vegan Mashup*, and founder of Miyoko's Kitchen

Says Miyoko: "If you love the warmth and spice of pumpkin pie but don't want to bother with the fuss of a crust or are looking for a lower-fat alternative, this bread pudding will tickle your heart. Served with the crème anglaise, this might just replace that pie at holiday time. To make this, you'll want slightly stale or lightly toasted bread so that it soaks up the custard. You can use any kind of bread you like, but I recommend something on the lighter side—this is not a dessert that beckons for a heavy rye or hearty whole grain bread."

MAKES 6 TO 8 SERVINGS
TIME TO MAKE: 50 MINUTES

Bread Pudding

- 6 cups cubed light-textured stale bread, crust trimmed
- 1 pound pureed pumpkin (1 can is fine)
- 8 ounces medium-firm tofu, drained and mashed
- ¾ cup soy or almond milk
- 1 cup maple syrup
- 2 tablespoons cornstarch or arrowroot
- 2 teaspoons ground cinnamon
- ½ teaspoon grated fresh nutmeg
- 1 teaspoon grated fresh ginger
- ½ teaspoon sea salt
- ½ cup raisins (soak in rum for an hour if you want a little extra punch!)

Brandy Nog

- ¾ cup water
- Scant ½ cup raw cashews
- ¾ cup maple syrup
- 2¼–2½ tablespoons brandy
- 1½ vanilla beans, split, or 1 teaspoon vanilla extract
- ¼ + ⅛ teaspoon grated fresh nutmeg
- Pinch of salt

To make the bread pudding: Preheat the oven to 350°F. Prepare a 13" x 9" baking dish by lightly oiling it or coating it with cooking spray. If your bread is fresh, not stale, toast the cubes in the oven for 10 to 15 minutes to dry it out.

In a blender or food processor, combine the pumpkin, tofu, milk, maple syrup, cornstarch or arrowroot, cinnamon, nutmeg, ginger, and salt. Puree until smooth.

Fill the baking dish with the bread cubes. Pour the pumpkin mixture and the raisins over the bread and mix well with a spoon. Cover with aluminum foil and bake for 40 minutes, or until the custard has set.

To make the brandy nog: In a blender or food processor, combine the water and cashews. Puree until smooth. Pour into a saucepan and add the maple syrup, brandy, vanilla beans or vanilla, nutmeg, and salt. Bring to a gentle simmer over low heat while stirring frequently with a wooden spoon. As it heats, it will thicken. The sauce is ready when it is thick enough to coat the back of the spoon.

Top the bread pudding with the brandy nog.

Chipotle Chocolate Pudding

Matthew Kenney, restaurateur
and award-winning chef and author

This smoky take on a classic raw
avocado chocolate pudding is sure
to make your tongue dance. It's
creamy with a dark allure, lively
but not overly sweet, and can be
made in just a few minutes. Now
that's perfection.

MAKES 2 SERVINGS
TIME TO MAKE: 10 MINUTES

1 avocado, pitted

½ cup hazelnut milk

¼ cup maple syrup

1 teaspoon vanilla extract

¼ teaspoon chipotle powder

Pinch of ground cinnamon

Pinch of salt

¼ cup raw cacao powder

Chopped hazelnuts for
garnish

Cacao nibs for garnish

In a blender, puree the avocado, hazelnut milk, maple syrup, vanilla, chipotle powder, cinnamon, and salt. Add the cacao powder and blend until
fully incorporated. Pour into 2 chilled wine glasses, sprinkle with a pinch
of the chopped hazelnuts and cacao nibs, and serve.

Cowgirl Up! Chunky Monkey Ice "Cream"

Kayle Martin of the Web site Cowgirls and Collard Greens

Says Kayle: "While craving ice cream late one evening, I got the idea to try and re-create my pre-vegan favorite ice cream flavor (Ben & Jerry's Chunky Monkey). I had no idea where to start, but I knew I needed bananas, chocolate, and walnuts. I whipped up this recipe in a few minutes and was amazed at how much it tasted like and resembled my old favorite. Put on your cowgirl (or cowboy) hat and serve this up to your friends and family. It's a favorite amongst both kids and adults!"

MAKES 2 SERVINGS
TIME TO MAKE: 1 HOUR

2 organic bananas, peeled and frozen

1 teaspoon vanilla extract or raw vanilla bean powder

¼ cup vegan chocolate chips (or chop up your favorite vegan dark chocolate bar)

¼ cup finely chopped walnuts

In a high-powered blender, combine the frozen bananas and vanilla. Puree until creamy (this may take several minutes). Transfer the mixture to a medium bowl.

Slowly stir in the chocolate chips and walnuts. Place the mixture in the freezer for 45 minutes to 1 hour, or until hardened. Serve in your favorite bowl or, if you're sassy like me, your favorite chilled cocktail glass.

Chocolate Peanut Butter Popcorn

Joshua Katcher, vegan fashion entrepreneur and founder of the Web site The Discerning Brute

Says Joshua: "I came home from dinner with a hankering for something sweet, chocolatey, crunchy, and just a little bit salty, so I experimented with tossing together a big batch of Chocolate Peanut Butter Popcorn to share with my friends. It needed to be fast and easy and really yummy. It turned out so satisfying, I think it might become a staple snack in my apartment. Don't forget to put some aside in a bag to take to work the next day, because otherwise you will eat it all. I promise."

MAKES 8 TO 9 CUPS
TIME TO MAKE: 10 MINUTES

½ cup organic popcorn kernels

2 tablespoons Earth Balance spread

2 tablespoons Peanut Butter & Co.'s Dark Chocolate Dreams*

¼ cup almond milk

2 tablespoons sugar

Pop the popcorn, preferably using an air popper. Transfer the popcorn to a mixing bowl.

In a small saucepan, melt the Earth Balance over medium-low heat. Stir in the peanut butter, almond milk, and sugar. Continue stirring until the mixture begins to bubble and is silky smooth. Once the sauce is silky smooth, immediately pour it over the popcorn and toss together.

*If you are unable to get Dark Chocolate Dreams, use plain peanut butter and add 1 tablespoon cocoa powder and 1 extra tablespoon sweetener or ¼ cup vegan chocolate chips.

ACKNOWLEDGMENTS

I am indebted to so many people who helped me write this book, but I want to start by thanking my parents, Gene and Kay Baur, for their abiding love and support; and my life partner, Suzanne Pender, with whom I am blessed to share this journey.

I also want to thank Farm Sanctuary's board of directors and our executive leadership, Hank Lynch, Leila Melody, and Drew Alexis, for their encouragement and counsel. Thanks go to our dedicated staff, including Sylvia Moskovitz, Susie Coston, Bruce Friedrich, Luke Hess, Michelle King, Samantha Pachirat, Sarah Lux, Amanda Fortino, Martin Linney, Meredith Turner, and Wendy Matthews, for their valuable input and contributions. I am deeply grateful to the countless volunteers, interns, and supporters of Farm Sanctuary who inspire me every day and without whom this vital work would not be possible.

A particular thanks goes to Dorr Begnal, John Talbot, James Costa, John Archibald, Lyn Devon, Sean McVity, Robin Ishmael, The Melrose Family, Chris and Sharon Platt, Satish Karandikar,

Brad and Sunny Goldberg, Tracey and Jon Stewart, Kathy Freston, Terrin Card, Stacey and Dennis Barsema, Todd Denlinger, Denise Goodman, Hope Ferdowsian, Nik Kulkarni, Marlene Titus, David Golden, Cynthia Dodson, Dr. Roger White, Marilyn Crawford, The Michele & Agnese Cestone Foundation, Paul Harvey Jr., Dina Kinnan, Audrey Burnand, Allene Lapides, Emily Deschanel, Kevin Nealon, Ellen DeGeneres and Portia de Rossi, Diane Warren, Sally Juday, Bill Maher, and Bruce and Deborah Wagman.

Another big thank you to John Bartlett, Bob Comis, and Jon Camp, whose heartening stories serve as positive examples for others.

I am fortunate for the friendship and guidance of colleagues like Jim Mason, Zoe Weil, Ari Nessel, Jane Velez-Mitchell, Neal Bernard,

Paul Shapiro, Josh Balk, Josh Tetrick, Sharon Gannon, David Life, Wayne Pacelle, Michael Markarian, Aaron Gross, Steve Gross, Seth Tibbott, Tal Ronnen, Ethan Brown, Jason Stefanko, Joyce Tischler, Kim Stallwood, Peter Singer, Tom Regan, Melanie Joy, Leilani Munter, John and Ocean Robbins, Nathan Runkle, Erica Meier, Michael Greger, Brian Wendel, Martin Rowe, Mia MacDonald, Will Potter, Ken Shapiro, Timothy Pachirat, Nick Cooney, Nancy Perry, Karen Dawn, David Wolfson, Marisa Miller Wolfson, Jonathan Balcombe, Marc Bekoff, Jane Goodall, Jeffrey Masson, Matthew Scully, Sebastiano Cossia Castiglioni, Jane Patterson, Jeff and Sabrina Nelson, John Pierre, Scott Jurek, Rich Roll, Matt Frazier, Brendan Brazier, Rip Esselstyn, T. Colin Campbell, Antonia Demas, Michelle Simon, John Merryfield, Livia and Biz Stone, Kim Kaspari, John Joseph, Nick Bromley, Miranda Spencer, Jasmin Singer, Mariann Sullivan, Stewart and Terry David, Phillip Lymbery, and Joyce D'Silva. Friends like these and so many others remind me of the generosity, idealism, and compassion of which human beings are capable.

For their excellent photographs, thanks to Derek Goodwin, Connie Pugh, and Jo-Anne McArthur.

I want to thank my wonderfully supportive agent, Yfat Reiss Gendell, and all the terrific people at my publisher, Rodale, including Jess Fromm, Christina Gaugler, Marilyn Hauptly, Aly Mostel, Evan Klonsky, and especially my editor, Ursula Cary, whom I still hope to turn into a vegan someday.

A hearty thank you to everyone who contributed recipes and especially to our food editor, Chef Jason Wyrick, who did an amazing job organizing and editing the recipe section.

Finally, I am very grateful to Gene Stone, without whom this book would never have happened. He is an accomplished writer, a good friend, and a cherished colleague working to create a happier, more compassionate world.

PHOTO CREDITS

INDEX

Boldface page numbers indicate photographs. <u>Underscored</u> references indicate boxed text.

ABOUT THE AUTHORS

Gene Baur

Gene Baur is the president and cofounder of Farm Sanctuary and has been hailed as "the conscience of the food movement" by *Time* magazine. For more than 25 years, he has worked to stop the abuses of factory farming and promoted compassionate vegan living. A pioneer in the field of undercover investigations, Gene has visited hundreds of farms, stockyards, and slaughterhouses to document the deplorable conditions, and he has rescued thousands of farm animals. His pictures and videos have aired nationally and internationally, educating millions, and his work has been covered by the *New York Times, Los Angeles Times, Washington Post, Wall Street Journal*, ABC, NBC, CBS, Fox, CNN, and NPR. He has a master's degree in agricultural economics from Cornell University, and his first book, *Farm Sanctuary: Changing Hearts and Minds About Animals and Food*, was a national bestseller. He is a longtime vegan, a marathon runner, and an Ironman triathlete. He lives outside Washington, DC.

Gene Stone

A graduate of Stanford and Harvard, Gene Stone is a former Peace Corps volunteer, journalist, and book, magazine, and newspaper editor for such publications as the *Los Angeles Times* and *Esquire* and for Simon & Schuster as well. He has also ghostwritten 30 books for a diverse lot of people, including theoretical physicist Stephen Hawking, Atari and Chuck E. Cheese's founder Nolan Bushnell, and TOMS shoes founder Blake Mycoskie. Gene has written many titles under his own name as well, including *The Secrets of People Who Never Get Sick*, which has been translated into more than 27 languages. Gene has also written many books on his primary interests: animal rights and plant-based nutrition, including the number one *New York Times* bestseller *Forks Over Knives* and, as a cowriter with Rip Esselstyn, the best-selling *The Engine 2 Diet* and *My Beef with Meat*. Gene's newest book is *The Awareness*, a novel about the day all mammals gain humanlike consciousness.